Small Town Teacher

SMALL TOWN TEACHER

Gertrude H. McPherson

Harvard University Press, Cambridge, Massachusetts   1972

To Karen and Chris
and to the memory
of my father,
John Kirtland Wright

CONTENTS

Figures

PREFACE

This book is about teachers, elementary school teachers in a small rural New England school. And so it is also about a school, the Adams Elementary School, its two hundred pupils and their parents, the administrators, and the villagers.* But the focus is on the teachers. I decided to study these teachers, partly because I was one of them and also because, as I shared the experiences of teaching with them, I began to share their defeatism and their cynicism. I wanted to understand why, in a school so far removed from the complexities of the big city, so little touched by racial and ethnic strife, so traditional and slow-moving, teaching should be viewed by teachers as frustrating and painful, its results so meager. Adams was not the ghetto; the teachers did not fear for their physical safety; the school was no "Blackboard Jungle." But my earlier starry-eyed picture of the elementary teacher as opening children's eyes, introducing them to the world, sharing with them the excitement of a good book or the challenge of an arithmetic problem began to seem little more than a dream in a situation where one was continually having to rethink one's expectations for oneself in the face of the recalcitrance of the pupils, the wishes of anxious parents, the demands of administrators and fellow teachers. And we failed so often; there were too many children whom we seemed to damage rather than to teach, and too many others whom at best we left untouched, those for whom the school did nothing.

*All names of people and places have been changed.

As the years passed, I became a "better" teacher, but this process scared me. To become better, that is, more competent and more acceptable, meant also to become in some ways less sensitive, less imaginative, less innovative, less flexible. As a sociologist it became clear to me that the teacher's role was shaping me and my colleagues. We became what it required, some slipping more easily into the garment, others more awkwardly, but everyone having to fit. I decided to investigate this role, in part for myself. Through objective scrutiny I might recapture some of my own sense of independence. But I also did the study for them, my colleagues and other teachers. Implications might emerge from it for improvement of the teacher's lot, higher morale, and thus a "happier" school, happier pupils, and better education. Now, a number of years later, the study seems to me to have been of some value. Personally it enabled me to carry on for four more years as a less-frustrated elementary teacher. More significantly, the hypotheses, data, and conclusions may contribute not merely to a greater understanding of the problems of teachers, thus suggesting directions for change, but they may also increase understanding of the dimensions of role-expectations and role-conflict.

The intense concern about the public education system in our country has naturally been focused primarily on what happens to the children who go through it. Much has been written exposing the deadening, even brutalizing effects of our schools on children and young people. And this, of course, must be the center of concern for all of us. However, this study does not focus directly on this subject which has been so well and eloquently treated by others. The emphasis is on the teacher — what the system does to her, what the role-pressures are, and why she so often fails to fulfill the high goals we set for her and which she sets for herself. This to me seems one necessary kind of inquiry if we are to understand why the impact of the schools on children has been so unsatisfactory. It is not enough either to castigate the teachers for incompetence, stupidity, and even cruelty, or to absolve them of all responsibility, blaming the administrators, the parents, or the system. We must try to understand what happens to teachers, what they are trying to do, what elements dominate their self-image, what pressures they respond to that drastically affect the ways in which they teach and work with children. This is but one strand in a complex pattern, but one worth probing if we are to make any sense of the problem.

From college teacher and sociologist, I became in the late fifties an elementary school teacher (my earliest job aspiration) thanks to the teacher shortage plaguing American schools. No longer did one have to be certified through the regular teachers' college channels, a requirement that had deterred me from elementary school teaching for years. Special programs were instituted in many states to recruit into teaching individuals who had not taken the full teachers' college course. Through a special program I was able with slight formal preparation to become certified as an elementary school teacher and I taught for ten years in the Adams Elementary School — fourth grade for one year, fifth and sixth grades for nine. An alien in the town and in the school, trained as historian and sociologist, my work experience only in college teaching, I found myself looked upon at first by the other teachers with some suspicion, hostility, and amusement. After the difficult first year when my inexperience, lack of formal training, and personal inability to act as a firm disciplinarian had made the whole experience painful, I began to settle into the job and discovered that I was thinking of myself as a teacher and responding to the tensions and pleasures of the position much as my colleagues did. Also, my colleagues began to treat me as one of them.

I undertook this study in my sixth year of teaching and a sociology dissertation was the product of that one year's intensive research. I engaged in concealed participant observation for that year, methodically recording everything that I could learn about the teachers at school. My concealment was effective; my colleagues did not know they were being studied and a dissertation written, resulting in this book on the Adams teachers and the Adams School.

Little seems to have changed in Adams since the study. What is described and analyzed still seems fundamentally true, although details differ. The school has been regionalized and enlarged; there is more administrative hierarchy and bureaucracy; there are more teachers. The basic conditions of the teacher's role seem unchanged, the tensions and frustrations no less. Innovations in teaching come and go; some of these touch Adams. The teachers do try new things, although restraints on innovation are the same now as ten years ago. More innovations will come as outsiders move into the school and older teachers leave. With professionalization or greater administrative control the teachers at Adams may experience some relief from their tensions and frustrations. However, such changes may bring new problems. Those of the 1960s may then seem to have been minor and manageable. To the teachers they were of major importance. I believe that the factors that produce anxiety, anger, and a sense of helplessness among teachers are so basic that they remain constant despite superficial external changes.

More than a simple acknowledgment must go to Robert K. Merton without whose encouragement this study would not have been attempted and without whose own theoretical contributions and critical analysis of the manuscript it could never have been concluded. It was from his conceptual categories and on the basis of his illuminating and penetrating insights that I began the study of the elementary school teacher. I am also much indebted to Peter M. Blau who directed my attention to unpublished dissertations at the University of Chicago that have been important for this study, and to Rose Coser and Edward J. Abramson whose provocative ideas and suggestions were invaluable to me in clarifying my own thinking about the teacher's relationship with pupil and parent.

My debt to members of my family has been great: to my mother, Katharine M. Wright, for editorial assistance; to my father, John K. Wright, for his assistance in the conceptual formulation of the teacher's expectations for the pupil; and to James L. McPherson, who gave me far more than encouragement and support. His editorial revisions, stylistic emendations, and his own sociological background and insight have been a part of this study since its inception.

Deep, though unfortunately inexpressible, appreciation must go to the Adams teachers whose dedication and devotion to their often thankless jobs made my teaching years with them stimulating, often inspiring, and even worthwhile.

Small Town Teacher

INTRODUCTION

In this book I describe a group of teachers in the Adams Elementary School during the course of one school year. It is of some importance to discuss the methods I used to obtain the data for this case study and the soundness as well as the pitfalls of these methods.

The types of research methods to be employed in a particular inquiry are dictated by the subject to be studied, the resources available to the researcher, his own predilections and talents, and often by fortuitous circumstances. In this particular study, the circumstances under which the research was undertaken, that I had been an elementary teacher for five years and that I was committed to teaching and wished to remain as a teacher after finishing the research, made it imperative for me not to do anything that would separate me from my job, make me a stranger in the school, turn me from fellow worker to investigator. Therefore, concealed participant observation seemed the only feasible method to use, and I now believe the only meaningful one for my research purposes. Only by involving myself in the ongoing interactions and events could I probe the internal as well as the external significance of the ways in which the teachers handled all the pressures that they imposed on themselves and that were imposed on them. While built into this study are both the advantages and disadvantages inherent in any use of concealed participant observation,[1] I am convinced that any value this study has derives in great part from its method.

I carried on intensive, concealed observation of the teachers and the school for a full school year, 180 school days, in the Adams Elementary School. After the study was completed I continued teaching in the same school. The only other data, beyond the intensive observations of one year and the more casual observations for nine, were some information derived from short interviews that I conducted with each of the elementary teachers.

Intensive, concealed observation meant for me reliance on memory. I could take no notes on the job; I carried no concealed tape recorder. I had a job to do, a job which insulated me for much of each day from the other teachers. But I attempted to remember every conversation involving teachers, with one another, with me, with pupils, parents, or principal, and as many incidents of each school day as I could. And at home I wrote it all down in as complete detail as possible. A spy yes, and not one especially trained for espionage. My poor memory and my forgetfulness were problems. Luckily for the research, I improved with practice, and luckily also I had a husband who knew how to ask the right questions to make me recall forgotten incidents and events that often turned out to be significant.

How now that the notecards have been melted down, first into a dissertation and then into a book, can I avoid the ethical implications of my spying? There are some ready rationalizations. I am on the griddle as much as my colleagues, but then I gave my consent; they did not. The implications of this study are sufficiently important to justify the snooping that was involved. Maybe. I did not snoop for personal gossip, only for that information relating to the job, the role, and so what is revealed is no reflection on any individual as a person. It is a portrait of the pressures implicit in the role a person plays. True, but ineptitude, incompetence, or callousness in role-performance does reflect on the person, even if it should not. Can one fall back on anonymity, a scrambled set of characters and conversations, personal identifying characteristics changed, even completely invented, and a false name for town and school? One hopes so, but there is the nagging sense of doubt. I want to help not hurt, to offer insights that might show the way to a better lot for teachers. I have only respect and admiration for these teachers after working with them for ten years, and I can only ask that the reader not impute blame for those actions that result from circumstances, not look for villains where there are none, not forget that an elementary teacher's job is more often painful, frustrating, exhausting, and demoralizing than it is exciting, stimulating, and satisfying, and yet many teachers go on year after year doing their best for small reward.

Most-of my observation was of unplanned undirected situations, dependent on where I was and what I was doing at any particular moment. However, occasionally I would attempt to direct conversation or to set up situations in order to observe certain kinds of interaction. I did this infrequently because I found that my own identification with my job tended to take precedence over my new role of observer. Detachment came afterward, away from the situation, when I realized how my own absorption in being a teacher had made me forget to listen, made me neglect to involve myself in potentially significant conversations. I was also sometimes too emotionally involved myself with colleagues, parents, or pupils to record accurately what happened.[2] In addition, I was unable to find out much about aspects of teaching in which I was not personally engaged. The high school was almost entirely out of bounds, and even the world of the elementary teacher was only partially open to me. My contact with the teachers of grades one through four was limited to conversations before and after school hours and at noontime. The fact that I smoked made my frequent visits to the teachers' room acceptable and made available to me much otherwise unrecordable conversation. However, informal group barriers did prevent me from observing in detail the attitudes, opinions, and contacts among these teachers. I found it useful that in earlier years I had become friends with the kindergarten teacher, Mrs. Garten, and the fourth grade teacher, Mrs. Gregory, so I could talk to them informally and easily about many aspects of the job without arousing their suspicions about my nosiness.

I was not self-conscious with my colleagues. My behavior on the job was only slightly different from what it had been before I started observing them and myself. My own "teacher" responses to situations provided part of the data, particularly since I found that they tended to parallel those of my colleagues. Perhaps I tended to listen more often to gossip and to ask more questions than I had previously. As my fifth grade colleague, Mrs. Crane, once said to me when I asked a prying question, "But you have never been interested in gossip. Why do you ask?" I am convinced that what I recorded was true and honest expression, not put on for the benefit of an observer, and that I received as clear a picture of the teacher in her daily teaching life as was possible through use of this method.

The formal interviews were conducted at a later time only to give me information about the teacher's formal education, her father's occupation and her previous teaching experience — information not readily obtainable through random conversation. I also wished to discover whether the opinions expressed about pupils, parents, and administrators in a formal interview significantly differed from those offered in casual conversation. For the most part, I found little discrepancy. Certain reticences, not noticeable in daily conversation, appeared in the interview, but no unexpected or contradictory opinions were expressed. Since I was by this time an accepted group member and posed no threat as an interviewer, the answers were congruent with my other data. Although my colleagues knew that I was studying teaching and therefore was interviewing for this purpose, they expressd no interest in what I did with the interview data or in any conclusions I might draw. They hesitated in answering my questions only because they thought they might be "incompetent" ("I don't know enough"). None of my colleagues ever knew that I studied them and myself, and I suspect few of them would have cared if they had known.

It is extremely difficult for a participant observer to evaluate his own significance in what happens. I know that I was able to do this research as an accepted unthreatening group member both because I had taught for a number of years and because I was adaptable. Although the older teachers assumed well into my second year that I would not remain a teacher at Adams, that I was odd and different, they began to accept me as I outlasted others. My colleagues talked to me, told me their troubles, joked with me. They became my friends, and more and more my responses to teaching matched theirs. I had some power among the elementary teachers; what I said was listened to; I was asked for help and advice; what I did was often imitated. I even felt it possible to be my "real" self and talk of my own interests. The others listened to me with tolerance and did not seem to reject me because of my differences from themselves. Looking back I see that I was in portant in cementing certain informal ties throughout the teachers' group and that to an extent I provided a link between the different groups of teachers.

I find it hard to look upon any job I hold with distance and detachment. Although my background was different, I shared with my colleagues similar emotional responses to parents, similar anxieties over conflicts of expectations, and similar reactions to administrative confusion. I did not have to put on appropriate attitudes; I had them.

Any case study conducted by one observer can be critically appraised as emotionally biased, perceptually limited, too personal, subjective, and ungeneralizable. This is certainly true of this study. The Adams School is not every other school, even every other small rural New England school. It is in some ways unique, with its own oddities of structure, personnel, and history. The data I have collected are limited by my perspective, my involvement, my own blinders. To some extent, the lack of statistical significance may be compensated for by the sheer quantity of data collected. The unusual, the idiosyncratic, the contradictory item stands out baldly in the more repetitive material, making it easily distinguishable and thus subject to evaluation.[3]

One restriction on the scope of this study is crucial and deliberate. I am looking at the teacher from her own point of view. I am concerned with the teacher's expectations for herself, for pupils, for parents, for the administration, and with her response to the ways in which she defines the expectations of others toward her. I do not deal, for example, with the "real" expectations that parents have of teachers, unless these have been directly stated to the teacher. I have made no attempt to interview parents, administrators, or children. So I have investigated the *perceived* conflicts, the way in which the teacher handles the expectations she perceives from outside and also the expectations she holds for herself.[4] She may suffer from false perception, but it is to this that she responds, not to some objectively verifiable situation out there. This is an analysis of the role of teacher from the point of view of the teacher. This study thus differs from the works which, while purporting to investigate role-requirements teachers define for themselves, actually represent the authors' delineation of ideal roles. It also differs in some degree from more recent works (many of which are opening up exciting new avenues for the study of role-conflict) that detail the role-expectations of teachers, administrators, parents, and pupils for themselves and for one another, and their potential and real contradictions.[5] This study is deliberately limited to an in-depth analysis of one perspective.

Observations not only do not speak for themselves, but they are only meaningfully arrangeable within a conceptual framework. Many works have offered invaluable insights, suggested directions of inquiry, indicated possible parallels, and these are cited throughout as they become relevant. The most important guides for the underlying frame of reference have been Willard Waller, Robert K. Merton, and Neal Gross and his associates. Willard Waller's classic work, *The Sociology of Teaching*, published forty years ago has been my most valuable source. He anticipated what I often thought my own ingenious ideas, and his insights into the roots of the enmity between teacher and parent, the double teacher stereotype, and the problems of professionalism have not been invalidated in the ensuing years.

Robert K. Merton who coined the term *role-set* has supplied the crucial concept and framework for this study.[6] The parallel research by Neal Gross[7] has provided conceptual refinements that have been useful throughout. The details of the conceptual scheme will be revealed as particular topics are discussed and will be far more meaningful in than out of context. However, in the interests of clarity a few definitions and distinctions will be made here.

The term *role-set* although short is hardly euphonious. However, it is too useful to abandon merely in the interests of avoiding jargon, itself a most praiseworthy goal. By role-set, Merton refers to "that complement of role relationships which persons have by virtue of occupying a particular social status."[8] The status under scrutiny is that of teacher, and her role-set comprehends the relationships she has with numerous role-partners, their expectations of her, her expectations of them and of herself. The role-set is no unified, smoothly functioning guide for performance, but rather a cluster of changing, often conflicting pressures to which she must try to adapt. It is on these conflicting pressures, their causes, and the ways in which the teacher handles them or attempts to handle them that I focus.

Any close investigation of a particular role-set reveals quickly that one cannot assume consensus, cannot assume that the expectations of the different role-partners are congruent with one another or with those of the status-occupant.[9] How much congruence exists, how much conflict and disagreement there is must be determined for each aspect of the teacher's performance. The tensions and anxieties of the Adams teachers derived far more from internal conflict within the teacher's role-set than from conflict among the expectations of the different statuses they occupied.[10] Conflict arises because role-expectations do not necessarily translate directly into behavior. Role-expectations are normative; they say what behavior should be. These must be distinguished from role-anticipations, what we predict will be, and role-behavior, what the person actually does in the status. These are not the same and their variations must be probed. As a teacher my role-expectation for the pupil is that he should do his homework; my role-anticipation is that this is not going to happen; and the role-behavior of the pupil may fit either picture. It is also necessary to distinguish two types of role-expectations that teachers have, both of which are normative, one of which is "idealistic," the other "realistic." What a teacher expects depends on her past experiences and on her assessment of present reality. So the "idealistic expectations," what one would hope to find if one could have anything one wanted, and the "realistic expectations," what one will settle for in the world as it is, do not always coincide. The realistic role-expectations emerge over time, through continual change and redefinition, as a compromise between the idealistic expectations that have grown up on the basis of reading, moral training, utopianism, or nostalgia, and the actual behavior encountered so frequently as to be regularly anticipated. Role-expectations cannot ever be seen as static.[11] What a teacher expects of pupils in September is different from what she expects in June, and I am not talking here about anticipations. Her expectations are still normative, what ought to be, but her perception of what ought to be has been scaled down somewhat to more realistic proportions. The process of role-learning, the modification of expectations through contact with reality, the adaptation of personality to status and status to personality, the pressure from conflicting expectations, all these contribute to a fluid and changing pattern.[12]

One factor which influences the shifting between idealistic and realistic expectations is the operation of stereotypes.[13] These are rigid anticipations,[14] what one predicts about a person as an occupant of a position, narrowly and often fallaciously defined. In part, learning to play a role involves learning to build reality from the stereotype, which may be more or less fixed depending on the length of time it has existed and the extent to which it has become popularly recognized in talk, cartoons, fiction, and motion pictures. The negative stereotype of the elementary school teacher[15] has importantly influenced the ways teachers act, the relation between teachers and the community, the process of recruitment into teaching, and the expectations to which teachers must respond. The fixity of this stereotype tends to reinforce the holding of idealistic expectations even while day-to-day role-playing pushes one toward more realistic expectations. So I found the Adams teachers returning each September to idealistic expectations that had been abandoned by them the previous June.

One additional conceptual distinction is important. The teacher's role-set revolves around the dominant relationship between teacher and pupil (a relationship similar to that between doctor and patient or employer and employee). It is different in kind from the role-set in which no one relationship is dominant over other relationships (for example, the role-set of school superintendent). For the teacher, the tie between her position and that of the pupil is central. Although she is related in various ways to other positions, these relationships could disappear without destroying the primary link, while if there were no pupil, there would be no teacher's role-set. Naturally, one does not exhaust an analysis of the teacher's role-set by discussing only this primary link,[16] but this relationship is the core.

The most important expectations to which the teacher must respond from other members of her role-set and the most important expectations she has of these other members revolve around the teacher's relationship with the pupil. These expectations may be congruent or incongruent with each other and with those of the teacher herself. Even expectations for a teacher's behavior that seem to relate directly to her rather than to how she treats the pupil, for example, expectations that have been frequently reported as to how a teacher should behave in the community, represent the conviction that the teacher must be a model for pupils as well as a teacher of them. Similarly, the expectations that a teacher holds of the principal, that he give her guidance and direction, that he function as a buffer between her and the parents, primarily reflect her need for freedom from parental interference in handling the pupil, more than they reflect any clear perception as to the ideal relationship between a superior and a subordinate in a formal organization.

The usefulness of this study as a contribution to an understanding of teachers, their problems, and their behavior can only be measured in terms of some answer to the question of usefulness for what. In a decade that has seen publication of significant provocative personal accounts of teachers' experiences in the classroom — Kozol, Herndon, Kohl, and so forth — this study could be seen as another example of reportage about one school and one teacher's experience. If it is only reportage, it describes a situation that is less startling, less devastating, less disturbing than the others. This is not an exposé of a ghetto school; this is not the story of a sensitive, creative teacher battling the bureaucracy and the dead hand of white middle-class rigidity that systematically denies meaningful education to the deprived, the dispossessed, and the intellectually alive. But this is not what this study purports to be. Nor does it claim to be a scientifically validated analysis of the dimensions of the teacher's role throughout American society. No attempt has been made to generalize the experience of the Adams School teacher to all other teachers, even to all other rural school teachers in small New England elementary schools. Participant observation of one school, of one group of teachers, cannot in itself supply the data for all schools, all teachers. But the research is not thereby invalidated through being neither sheer reportage nor universally generalizable. On one level, it is reportage in that it is specific, and its usefulness must rest (as ultimately all sociological research must) on the perceptiveness, sensitivity, and honesty of the investigator. All the tools for increasing accuracy, for extending observation, for reducing investigator bias cannot make up for blunted perception or ensure that the observations are accurate, reported fairly, assessed and weighted scientifically.

No one could check out my conclusions by starting with my boxes of note cards, reports of recollected conversations and events. What went onto note cards was my memory of the day's events, classified by topic and by focus, added to when my memory was jogged by my husband's questions. How much was forgotten, how much was misquoted, how much of the significance lay in the tone of voice that the note card no longer reveals — all this is lost in the past. But could one trace the transition from note cards to conclusions? Could another observer build from the notes the same picture of the teacher, the pressures on her, the responses she made, the ways she felt, that I have built? Again, no, although it might be a fascinating exercise in sociological methodology for someone to attempt to replicate the conclusions of a study of this sort by working with the raw data before reading the refined results. However, there is a necessary limitation to such an enterprise. The significance of any conversation or series of conversations lies in part in the meaning it has for the participants. External pressures are handled in different ways depending on how they are perceived, evaluated, and articulated with the internal self-image and expectations. This is not a study of teachers from the outside, but one of teachers from the inside, and its usefulness to a large extent must rest on how clearly I have been able to express and reveal the internal workings of these processes, not just their external forms. In this sense, complete participant observation was the only possible method with which to do this particular study. Other kinds of research are certainly called for on the basis of the data, but they would not be substitutes for this. This kind of research requires an inside observer, one who experiences the same demands, expectations, and pressures as the respondents and can thus make sense out of behavior and comment from within.

This study has a double focus. First, that which spurred me to do it and that which now makes it worth publishing is my concern as a teacher with the strength of the forces which make it impossible for all but the most unusual teacher in the public schools to "teach," to do other than show children how to fail, to do other than to push the children into the accepted mold and damage in more or less serious ways the ones who do not fit: the geniuses, the dolts, the imaginative, the alive ones. As teachers we see the schools teaching competition, orderliness, failure, routine.

We see ourselves, with varying degrees of self-awareness, contribute to building these into the children we teach. We suffer frustration, tension, discouragement. We do harm of greater or lesser degree. The teachers at Adams probably did less harm than those who teach in many of our large city schools. The teachers at Adams probably did no more harm than teachers before them had done. Most children do go through the elementary school, do make it to high school, do emerge into American society, but what they emerge as is rarely the kind of person envisaged so emptily in schools of education and so persuasively in writings by Fromm, Goodman, or Laing, as the ideal product of education, a person creative, self-aware, critical, alive. I did this study because I wanted to know what happens and why, why teachers are so dissatisfied with themselves, so discontented, and so ineffectual. My questions and my tentative answers, in terms of pressures both from within the self-image of the teachers and from without in the perception of and response to the expectations of parents, administrators, and pupils, antedated the actual year of study. At this point, the second focus became important. I adopted and refined for my own purposes a frame of reference, a conceptual scheme, within which my random and casual observations over five years as a teacher at Adams began to hold together, to be meaningful, and the data I collected during the year of intense observation were organized and arranged in reference to this scheme. And so, from an interest in teachers and teaching, I moved out to consider the more general usefulness and applicability of the role-set concept. In this work, the two are intrinsically connected, the observational data examined within this particular framework. The usefulness of this work then must lie not just in what it may tell us about the teacher and her problems, but also in the applicability of this conceptual scheme to an ongoing process of pressures and responses.

The role-set model and kindred role models have been used in provocative and interesting ways in recent years. Observational and experimental investigations have been made into conflicting expectations as well as into the relationship between expectations and behavior.[17] Our understanding of the teacher's role is being greatly increased as a result of these studies.

This particular study has used the role-set model to attempt what has rarely been attempted (for obvious reasons) in probes into role-conflict, to get inside, to see the conflict and the absence of consensus from the point of view of the participants experiencing the conflict. It is now a truism among sociologists that we cannot assume that role conflict exists merely because we observe and record seemingly contradictory pressures, nor can we understand behavior merely by looking at its external manifestations. However, in much research we are forced to use indirect measures of internal states: interviews, questionnaires, attitude scales, extrapolation from external actions. This study of course is similarly limited. I, as observer, can only be inside my own head, not that of any other teacher. My reading of another teacher is a translation from my reading of me and is likely to be biased by my differences in background, experience, and orientation. The limits are, therefore, still there. However, no matter how incomplete and partial my results, I have been able to detail the kind of process that goes on. This kind of data, therefore, can be a basis for more external and indirect investigations of role-set pressures. It can alert us to some of the sources of strain and to the relative success of devices developed both to reduce pressure and to lower frustration.

The investigator who wanted to check out my conclusions by working from the raw data would not only have the problem of trying to understand the significance of a snippet of conversation on a card without knowing its context, but he would also immediately be trapped into accepting the conceptual framework in terms of which I arranged and organized the data as I collected them. The concepts and orientations changed and were refined as I collected more data and the data were then grouped and recorded in terms of the concepts. The interpenetration of parts would probably make it impossible as well as meaningless to try to separate out the "raw data" and see if they could be read another way.

Many interesting methodological questions emerge in connection with this kind of approach. Gestalts appear. One finds on looking back at one's notes that random observations of diverse sorts begin to be grouped in the note boxes without any memory on the part of the observer as to when the pattern began to reveal itself. If earlier notes were then reclassified to fit the new gestalt, it would be almost impossible at a later date to trace the emergence of the pattern, the nature of the insight which led

one to see observations as grouped, no longer as random. Merely
dating notes does not solve this problem, since the sense of
gestalt comes gradually and probably is operative long before one
goes back and reshuffles the data. At some point in my research I
became aware of the use of the open classroom door by Adams
teachers as a device for maximizing their own success and as a
sanction against other teachers. Once I had a phrase with which
to verbalize this insight, I filed all observations relating to it
together. But when this insight first began to emerge I cannot tell.
Obviously it operated at some level before I verbalized it, since I
have many recorded observations of the phenomenon antedating
the point where I put a label on it. Once I put on the label, I was
able to make sense out of much other data that before this I had
not thought of as fitting together.

Presumably another observer could go through the recorded
data and discover other gestalts that would serve the same
function of organizing and illuminating. What he would write
would be a different book. The book that I have written is
necessarily removed from the original experiences: first cut down
by my obvious inability to record everything; then cut down by
the terms and concepts that began to be significant to me, so that
what was observed and recorded exemplified certain aspects and
not others; and then cut down by grouping and arranging and by
the quality of insight I could bring to the data long after the
events. The book is doubly an artifact, a construct, a refinement,
one always hopes to pure gold, of the ore of observation, that
only dimly reflects the actual density of the experience of
teaching in the Adams School. That this is a limitation is true;
that it is its only justification for being written is also true. To
experience the Adams School as a teacher, one would have to be
an Adams teacher. This book is not masquerading as experience.
It claims to be no more than a picture of the Adams teacher from
inside as revealed through a particular conceptual framework.

So I would ask that this be read as not quite reportage and not
quite formal sociological research, but as something in between.
It is an effort to inform reportage with a sociological point of
view that can thus extend my own experiences beyond the Adams
School toward a clearer understanding of role-conflicts and their
effects on teachers in our world today.

1 ADAMS: HILL AND HOLLOW, TOWN AND SCHOOL

THE TOWN

Adams is a small rural community in New England. The abandonment of rail service in the 1940s and the bypassing of Adams by all major highways has enabled the town to retain its isolation and charm despite its proximity to some major urban centers. It is a beautiful little town, with homes scattered along winding roads in hills and valleys, two rivers, and no industry. A large summer population provides an economic base to support many of the local residents through the long, icy winters.

The year round population of about 2500 people has remained reasonably stable for a hundred years despite frequent dire warnings of burgeoning population growth that will overcrowd the schools and destroy the peace, quiet, and prosperity of the town. Thanks to rigid zoning laws and local power vested in those who wish to keep it unchanged, Adams remains an uncrowded retreat, marred by no billboards or ostentatious store signs. The story is told and vouched for by local residents that when one of the service stations hung up colorful banners a lady from the Hill protested the vulgarity. Receiving no cooperation from the local manager, she called up her "good friend," the president of the company, and the banners disappeared the next day.

Adams is an education-oriented town, with the public school and three private schools (an elementary school serving grades three through eight, a boys' prep school, and a girls' arts high school). Adams is a rural but not primarily a farming community since, aside from many hills, much of the land is reserved by a private corporation for park and recreational use. It is a rich town controlled politically and socially by a group of wealthy old families and former urbanites, who, through strict town planning and acreage restrictions, hold back the forces of change and preserve the "old atmosphere."

Adams is also a divided town. The Hill and the Hollow have little in common. The mile up the Hill from the Hollow is the longest mile in town. People from each area know little of each other, but each has fixed and usually negative ideas about the other. To the Hollow resident, the Hill is snobbish, patronizing, and rich. To the Hill resident, the Hollow is out of sight except for shopping. A rural slum along the river is beginning to impinge on the more visible parts of town. The Hill is embarrassed by the transient and unemployed living there in run-down, unpainted shacks and by the old car junkyard at one of the prettiest spots.

In the Hollow, the shopping area is neat, trim, and colonial. All of the Adams shops with the exception of a small drug store and a separate post office on the Hill are in the Hollow, as are the public school, the fire house, the Town Hall, the Legion Hall, a fancy book store, a branch of the library, and an art gallery. The main town library is on the Hill but few Hollow residents visit it, preferring to use the small branch in the Hollow — a segregated facility.

The Hill is tied to the outer world: many of its residents work in the city and weekend in Adams, travel extensively, or winter in the Bahamas. Few Hill residents have recognizable jobs in town, except for nonpaying volunteer work or elective work on boards and commissions. The Hill also has three exclusive private schools whose faculties live on the Hill rather than in the Hollow (thus being regarded by Hollow residents along with a scattering of artists and writers on the Hill as "upper-class" despite their lack of wealth). When I was planning to move into town, one of the Hill parents told me not to live in the Hollow with the riffraff, and one of the teachers told me not to live on the Hill with the snobs.

Hollow residents are locals: shopkeepers, public school teachers, small business and professional people, unskilled workers on roads, farms, and in the schools, and transients down from the north for the winter, unemployed or temporarily employed, who move their large families from town to town as collection agencies track them down. Many Hollow residents have never traveled farther than neighboring Waterwich; urban America is unknown to them.

Adams is a rich town, but it is also a split town. Many of its residents are poor and children from the Hill and Hollow, while meeting at school or as scouts, soon begin to ignore one another and to divide into cliques distinguished by social class or residence.

There are some Jewish families, no Negroes, and a smattering of foreign-born in town: a few Germans (grocery and restaurant), a few Irish (domestic and grocery), a few Italians (grocery, shoe repair, trash removal), and a few exotics of the artistic type.

Adams is a Church Town. On the Hill are a large and beautiful Congregational church and an equally impressive Episcopalian church. And in the Hollow are a smaller, less wealthy Congregational church, along with an unpretentious Swedish Evangelical church and a popular Catholic church.

Politics is prevailingly Republican (five to one). Since state law requires minority representation on local boards and committees, informal arrangements have developed that tend to allow the few Democrats from the Hill to push through nominations that preserve Hill solidarity. The Republicans of the Hollow follow the lead of Hill Republicans, resisting "federal control," taxes, and "too much" social welfare.

The town, in many ways, has remained static. Old families, both Hill and Hollow, have been there for generations, and the complex interrelations are startling to the outsider. Class lines are often crossed. Families have both advanced and debased branches. For example, a leading Hill resident had a brother who lived with his many relatives in one of the worst Hollow shacks.

Many young people, especially from the Hill families, leave the town. After attending private school and college, many never come back, except for special occasions such as a fancy wedding on the Hill. Although some of the poorer families are transient, occupying the shacks only from month to month, on the whole the population of the Hollow is stable. Most of the Hollow residents remain in town, respectable, traditional, conservative, the backbone of the rural lower-middle class. Things change slowly in Adams; often they seem not to change at all.

Class and location match rather well. The Hill is considered upper class by the Hollow through money, occupation, land, education, and way of life. The Hollow is split between the middle class, the good, respectable, hardworking folk, and the lower class, those hanging on tenuously to any job, on welfare, or just getting by.

I found Adams a strangely anachronistic town: no movies, no liquor store, no large shopping center; split by local feuds and bitter antagonisms, each section internally cemented through tradition and nostalgia for the past. The few efforts, usually by young transplanted urbanites, to change the town, as in the attempt to build a new school, ran up against the combined opposition of the Hill (where lived many old people without children or families with children in private schools) and the Hollow: "Things were all right when I went there." Both groups considered one a newcomer if one had not lived his whole life in Adams. Adams is really two towns. For those on the Hill it is a cultural oasis with book clubs, a fancy book store, an Art Association, classical music programs at the Church, and private school balls. For those in the Hollow it is the traditional American small town with Church suppers, a firemen's carnival, and an American Legion parade on Veterans' Day. Only such a town could resist so strongly the establishment of a school for emotionally disturbed pre-teen-age girls because we might be overrun with the "dangerously insane," and too many outsiders would be let in. Only such a town could find the suggestion that the school should hire a part-time psychiatrist radical and socialistic.

THE SCHOOL AND ITS TEACHERS

It was in the Adams Elementary School in the Hollow, along the river, that I taught. The elementary and high schools for all the children of Adams were combined in a joint plant on spacious grounds. About 15 percent of the pupils walked to and from the school; the rest were transported by school bus. All children remained at the school for the noon hour, eating in the cafeteria and playing on the playground. In earlier years, when the children were free to wander about the village at noon hour, relations between the school and shopkeepers were tense and strained. At the time of the study, the problem existed only during high school examination week, when the high school students raced around town in their free periods.[1]

Although it was part of the same plant as the high school, sharing administration, the cafeteria, the gymnasium, and buses, the Adams Elementary School of approximately two hundred pupils was treated as a separate administrative unit with its own faculty meetings, equipment, schedule, and rules. The school building was an old two-story structure (once a twelve grade school for the whole town) with a new addition of two modern classrooms, the cafeteria, and the teachers' room. The elementary school was connected to the more modern high school plant by an outdoor covered archway. It was in the high school building that the principal had his office, and in the high school gymnasium that the fourth, fifth, and sixth graders had physical education. Although the elementary building was old, it was not run down. The rooms were bright and sunny; each one had a sink, a counter, plenty of cupboard and bulletin board space; the desks were portable; and there was rarely any drastic overcrowding of pupils. The budget seemed to be ample for most supplies the teachers requested, although they often complained about cutbacks, particularly on art supplies, scientific equipment, and textbooks.

During my years at Adams, there were nine classroom teachers in the elementary school, one each for kindergarten through grade four, two in grade five, and two in grade six. The elementary teachers at Adams comprised two distinct groups, the Old Guard and the "new" teachers, with two teachers not clearly in either group. Being Old Guard was only in part a matter of age, membership being more dependent on years of experience, training (normal school), background, and point of view. The Old Guard consisted of Mrs. Gregory, the fourth grade teacher, Mrs. Crane, a fifth grade teacher, and Mrs. Preston, a sixth grade teacher. The Old Guard earlier had included Mrs. Cornhouse, who had taught first grade until her retirement, and Miss Benson, a third grade teacher who had gone to work in neighboring Waterwich a couple of years before this study.

Mrs. Gregory was a local resident who grew up in a nearby town and attended the local teachers' college (then a two-year normal school). She taught school at Adams for many years, left teaching to raise a family, and returned about ten years before the study. Her husband was a member of a local family, worked for years in a factory in another town, and then became a custodian at Adams. Mrs. Crane, in her early fifties, grew up in a town some miles away, but after marrying an Adams resident, an electrician, she moved to Adams where she taught for a number of years before leaving to raise her children. She had attended the teachers' college at about the same time as Mrs. Gregory. Mrs. Preston, for years a sixth grade teacher and the elementary principal, was a local Adams girl. She, too, was in her fifties, had grown children and was married to a local resident, a carpenter. Her teaching background and training resembled that of Mrs. Gregory and Mrs. Crane although she had taught for a few years in another town. Mrs. Cornhouse was also a local girl, married to the milkman, with similar background in normal school and the Adams School. Miss Benson's background differed from the others only in that she was single and that she had taught continuously for over thirty years. These Old Guard teachers were alike in origin, all being native to the state, in training, attendance at the local normal school, and in all having had fathers in blue-collar occupations and husbands in blue-collar or service occupations. When I asked them about their early job aspirations, they all stated that they had wanted to teach or do some other service work, such as being a nurse or a missionary.

Peripheral to the Old Guard were Mrs. Garten, the kindergarten teacher, and Mr. Scranton, the other sixth grade teacher. Mrs. Garten resembled the Old Guard teachers in that she was a local resident married to a mailman, also a local resident. However, she was younger than the members of the Old Guard, in her mid-forties with a son in the elementary school, and she had left the state for special kindergarten training. She, too, had taught for a number of years, all of them in Adams. Mr. Scranton, who came to teach at Adams the year of the study after having been a primary teacher in a neighboring town for a few years, was in his late thirties with a wife and four small children. He had grown up in Adams, was taught in school by some of the members of the Old Guard, and had attended the local teachers' college.

Mrs. Garten could exchange reminiscences with the Old Guard about the past and the people in town, although her out-of-state training, her age, and her association with a somewhat younger crowd did not allow her to be more than peripherally one of them. Mr. Scranton because he was new was also considered to be something of an outsider, and besides, being a man, he was considered to be in some way alienated from the values and attitudes of the Old Guard teachers.

Some of the "new" teachers, those who entered teaching from liberal arts college backgrounds supplemented by the "Special Training Program" at the local teachers' college, seemed strange as well as new. Mrs. Calhoun, third grade teacher at Adams, was the wife of a service station manager in a nearby town with one teen-age daughter. She had been a personal secretary for many years before becoming a teacher. Mrs. Merrick, second grade teacher, and I were the only teachers from out of the state. Mrs. Merrick, although an experienced music teacher, was in her first year of classroom teaching. She came from Nebraska where she had attended a small, religiously oriented midwest college. She lived in a nearby town where her husband worked in a store and where her own children went to school. I was a fifth grade teacher at Adams the year of the study. My background was probably the most remote from the others, since I had been a college teacher before coming to Adams, had a writer for a husband, and many snoopy sociological interests.

The other "new" but not strange teacher was Miss Tuttle, aged twenty-one and "new" because this was her first year of teaching. In other respects, she resembled the Old Guard, being a local resident, daughter of a farmer, graduate of the local teachers' college, and engaged to be married to a local boy who worked on a farm.[2] But Miss Tuttle was not considered genuinely Old Guard by the others despite her proper training because she had not the years of experience, because the teachers' college had changed since the sacred good old days, and because she failed to share many of their old-time assumptions about teaching and schools.

I refer to the teacher as "she" throughout this book. This is undoubtedly unfair to Mr. Scranton, but since he was the only male teacher in the elementary school it is certainly easier to use the female pronoun. It also serves to point up the dominant stereotype of the elementary teacher as a woman.[3] Any male teacher in an elementary school is always at a disadvantage. The other teachers assume that he must be odd to teach there, that he is in some way not a real man. At Adams, the elementary teachers' response to authority, to parents, and to children is understandable as much in terms of their sex as in terms of their role.

While I refer to the teachers by their last names throughout the book, the teachers themselves addressed one another by their first names. The mode of address by others was sometimes important in determining the particular relationships the teachers had with other members of their role-set. For example, the principal addressed the Old Guard teachers formally by their last names, but called the new teachers by their first names.

The administrators in the school included: Mr. Mongoose, new superintendent of schools, who had succeeded Mr. Frank Murdstick: "the last straw of the old-time administrators. It isn't found any more anywhere"; Mr. Hanson, principal of both the high school and the elementary school and, therefore, considered by all the teachers to be the "boss"; and a state-employed "Elementary Supervisor," Mrs. Milton, who worked for five towns of which Adams was one.

Other school personnel with whom the elementary teacher had important contacts were Mr. Trumpet, who had been music teacher for five years at the time of the study, and Mrs. Charles, the art teacher, who was newly appointed.

FORMAL STRUCTURE

Most of the formal aspects of the social structure in the Adams School will be described as the teacher's role-set is investigated. However, certain formal conditions of the job of teacher at Adams should be indicated here. Each elementary teacher had a classroom, a desk, and the same group of children from September to June. The first four grades and the kindergarten were located on the first floor, the fifth and sixth grades occupied the four rooms on the upper floor. All the pupils except for the kindergarteners ate lunch at staggered intervals with their homeroom teachers in the cafeteria, and they all played on the properly designated primary or intermediate sections of the playground at recess time and noon hour. A large part of the grounds was reserved for the high school pupils whose noon hour overlapped briefly with that of the fifth and sixth grades.

Each elementary teacher was officially required to be on duty in her classroom from eight-thirty in the morning to three-thirty in the afternoon, except when supervising the pupils at play, at lunch, or while waiting for the bus. The school day ran from nine to three, and the classroom teacher was in full charge during this period.

A teacher's job included more than classroom instruction. She also had to take care of household management (frequently delegated to "reliable" pupils), which included dusting, washing boards, arranging furniture, decorating the room, and cleaning the sink. She herself was responsible for collecting lunch money, keeping a careful attendance register, and helping pupils with boots and zippers. Her educational duties included in addition to teaching, grading papers, preserving discipline, administering all standardized and other tests, making out report cards, and conferring with parents. She selected her textbooks with the help of Mrs. Milton, the supervisor, planned her instruction in accordance with *The Curriculum Guide,* kept daily plans in a plan book, attended inservice and faculty meetings regularly, conducted parent-teacher conferences in fall and spring. Her time was regulated by the formal schedule of opening exercises, recess, lunch, and dismissal. In addition, Mrs. Milton recommended time allotments for subjects, an hour for reading, twenty minutes for spelling, as well as the appropriate times of day to teach them. Reading was a morning subject; science and social studies were afternoon subjects according to the rationale that reading was more important and therefore should be taught while the pupils were alert. The fifth and sixth grade teachers, operating on a departmental schedule where they each taught one subject, were more limited to defined and scheduled forty-minute periods for each group of children.

Within these general guide lines, each teacher was free to arrange her day, determining the order of instruction, the apportionment of oral and written lessons, the number of tests, and the degree of individual freedom or coercion.

Isolation from her peers, in fact from all other adults, was the primary characteristic of the teacher's job during the working day. But while isolated from the adult world, she was continually visible to and continually observed by her subordinates, the pupils.[4] The prospective teacher in training school is not very well prepared for this isolation since she trains with future teachers under a master teacher or attends classes with her fellow students. It is not until she is doing her final practice teaching or is at last on the job that she confronts this situation. At Adams, the isolation was imposed by the nature of the work and the classroom arrangement, not by law, as in some schools where visiting in the halls is explicitly forbidden: "It doesn't look well."

A teacher's position is defined primarily in relation to her responsibility to teach the pupils, to bring about a systematic change in them. For the most part, her duties are her pupils' rights, the pupils' duties are her rights, and her expectations focus on her behavior toward the pupils and the pupils' behavior toward her. The relationship is reciprocal but not symmetrical, since while the teacher's position is chosen, a status achieved through her training, defined by specified performance standards and financially compensated, the pupil's position is largely involuntary with no payment or occupational criteria. For the child six through sixteen, going to school is not a voluntary activity. So underneath all the formal limitations the teacher is in a position of power and pupils in this respect resemble patients in a hospital or prisoners in a jail.[5] The system exists to do something for them and to them, but they do not choose their place in this system. In a formal sense they are acted upon rather than acting (although as we shall see, this is only partially true in reality), and in this same formal sense any adult in the school is defined as having authority over them. Any teacher can give an order to, reprimand, or discipline any child. The pupil is largely powerless in a system which Waller called a "despotism in a state of perilous equilibrium."[6]

However, the teacher's power is never unlimited. At Adams, as elsewhere, it was hedged in both by formal and informal restrictions. The teacher herself was at the base of the formal authority structure of the school. She had no subordinates. All the teachers, an undifferentiated mass at the bottom, equal to one another in status, with no possibility for mobility as long as they remained teachers, in theory possessed wide power over the pupils, the involuntary participants. But, even without many legal and formal specifications of the rights of pupils, the teacher's position was not necessarily enviable. Since the pupils were not voluntary participants, there was no certainty that the orders given by the teacher to the pupils would be recognized as legitimate and willingly obeyed.[7] There is, after all, one significant difference between the position of teacher and that of jailer. The jailer must keep the prisoner confined, and, through threats and various punishments, docile and obedient. A teacher must do this and more; she is expected to teach, to bring about change. The Adams teacher was also limited in her power by the pressures from other members of her role-set: parents, adminstrators, outsiders. State law, which defined her complex responsibilities to the pupils, also limited her, although I found that few teachers had any clear notion as to what the law was. The Adams teacher knew that she must allow time for physical education and outdoor play, that she must teach about the evils of alcohol, tobacco, and drugs, and that she must be on supervisory duty at all times. She had no right to use corporal punishment or to keep pupils after school if in so doing they were not able to ride the bus, since the law made transportation a legal right. The only officially designated restriction on her dealings with parents was that she should never reveal IQ scores, although there were many other traditional limitations. Finally, she was expected to follow the specified curriculum that was composed by the elementary teachers themselves with Mrs. Milton's guidance. In most cases this curriculum followed that recommended by the State Department of Education. Other general rules that she had to follow related primarily to attendance records, handling of standardized tests, and other forms rather than specifically to her treatment of the pupil.

The formal requirements and limitations provide but a skeleton frame within which the Adams teacher operated. To understand her satisfactions and frustrations, her successes and her failures, we must examine her role-set, the ramifications of which extended far beyond any formal guidelines.

2 THE TEACHER'S SELF-IMAGE

"What do I want to do as a teacher? I want to bring out their potentialities. I want to help the transition from child to adult."

For a person to play any role over time requires more than simple imitation of others, more than automatic responses to external expectations and demands, more than "play-acting."[1] As the role is learned and played, it becomes to some degree part of the person, and the person acts in accordance with the internalized definitions and meanings. To understand the Adams teacher's role-set requires an understanding of what being a teacher meant to her, what her self-image was.

The teacher's picture of herself was composed of clear and fuzzy, self-conscious and unexamined expectations as to what she should be, her obligations, and her rights. These varied expectations clustered around a few central themes. Some expectations she shared with teachers everywhere; some she shared with all other Adams teachers; some were associated directly with her position in the Adams School. Her self-image changed in response to changing situations, becoming more or less consistent over time. As parents, children, and administrators made new demands upon the teacher, her expectations for herself changed and shifted, while at the same time she interpreted these demands in terms of her immediate self-image.

The core of the teacher's self-image was its moral obligation. To teach was to serve; it was not just to make a living. Any Adams teacher would accept to some degree the social stereotype of teachers as "loyal, non-aggressive, martyred public servants."[2] She had done her job well as a teacher only if the pupil had learned. Whatever the raw material, bright, stupid, willing, intransigent, charming, or dull, she had to bring about change in it. So she succeeded when teaching "brings results," when children "grow and mature and use their minds." Even the slow learners could bring her some satisfaction "if there is a little progress; if they finally accomplish something."

This moral obligation was, however, implicitly qualified by the Adams teacher. The change produced in one pupil should not be out of line with that produced in other members of the class.[3] Each pupil had to be judged in relation to the other pupils, and a pupil who stood too far ahead posed as great a problem to the teacher as the one who stood too far behind. Thus the Adams teacher might find herself in conflict with the parent who demanded more progress for the child who was, in the teacher's eyes, "proceeding at the normal rate."

Her picture of herself as performing a moral duty did not blind her to evidence that she had little prestige and power in school and community. Recognizing this low esteem, she had to struggle for dignity and self-respect. She had to be able to overcome her often despairing conviction that "we're just baby sitters for the parents." To some degree, she managed this by delegating the dirty work, the housekeeping aspects of teaching, down the ladder to the janitor or kitchen help:[4] "It's certainly not my job to clean the counter." Failing that, she attempted to integrate the necessary dirty work into her picture of the role itself. She insisted that she must deal with the "whole child." Thus she professed to believe that, although the high school teachers who dealt only with the intellectual development of the pupil might have higher status or prestige, they did less important work, work that was less total in its impact.

Internal contradictions in the self-image of the Adams teacher revealed the tension between high moral justifications and low status. Some of the demands she made upon herself were idealistic and socially sanctioned, but probably unattainable; others were pragmatic, realistic, and limited. Many comments by the teachers revealed this tension: "I know I should not be sarcastic. One should not use sarcasm with children, but in this case I just couldn't resist." Mrs. Gregory was not really apologizing for her failure to live up to her expectations for herself; she was justifying a more pragmatic expectation, that in some situations one must be sarcastic, one must settle for the lesser goal. This tension was self-generated. Both the ideal and the pragmatic expectations were internalized. To some degree, throughout the course of each school year the pragmatic took precedence over the ideal expectations. But there seemed to be no long-run victory. The older, more experienced teachers were as disturbed by role-contradictions as were the newer teachers. Each year I determined that I would be calm, understanding, helpful, never mean or angry. And each year this image was eroded away in favor of such prescriptions as: "With these children, on a day like this, I *should* get angry or they will walk all over me." To some degree one would reduce the internal tensions by blaming someone else: "I could carry out my ideal role if others, such as the parents, had not made it impossible for me."

The four major strands of the Adams teacher's self-image were as disciplinarian, as director of learning, as industrious worker, and as one deserving just and equitable treatment.

TEACHER AS DISCIPLINARIAN

The most clearly observable aspect of a teacher was her success or failure as a preserver of discipline.[5]

"Successful teachers do not have problems."[6]

"To have to send a child to the principal is to 'admit that you can't control the kids.'"[7]

So it was in the area of discipline that the standards of role-performance were clearest and that the attempts at social control by older over younger and newer teachers were most evident. Mrs. Preston criticized me for the noisy way in which my class went through the halls on the way to lunch. A downstairs teacher sweetly asked an upstairs teacher, "What were you doing upstairs today, playing games? We heard terrible noises." More frequently, criticism was indirect. Mrs. Crane remarked to Mrs. Preston that Miss Tuttle must be "having trouble today, poor thing," because her voice was so dreadfully loud. Counterattack sometimes proved the most effective defense. Mrs. Crane said to me, "You must have been having fun this morning, it was so noisy," to which I responded, "What were you doing this afternoon, cleaning house?" A temporary cessation of hostilities.

To be observed put heavy pressure on the teacher to conform to the standards of order and decorum accepted in the Adams school. Not to be observed, however, would have made it impossible for the teacher to emphasize the significance of her role and to reduce negative stereotypes about teaching. While a teacher might resist observation, at the same time she believed that it was necessary if she was to achieve "dramatic realization."[8]

In the effort to let others observe that which was ordinarily hidden, the Adams teachers developed an "open door" policy, a nonverbal series of cues that were never discussed but were tacitly understood by all. A teacher kept her classroom door open during the teaching day to show her control over her class. A good disciplinarian's door stood open; a poor one's door was frequently shut. Unless a teacher punctiliously told the teacher across the hall that she was going to have art (an allowably noisy subject) or do dramatics "which might disturb you," her closed door meant that her class was too noisy and she was afraid of being overheard. However, a good disciplinarian, once her own success had been duly acknowledged by others, could close her door to signal criticism of a less successful neighbor. Mrs. Preston manipulated her classroom door throughout the year to show Mr. Scranton when he was failing in this important role-requirement.

This observability had its limits. The door stood open, but the boundary had to be maintained. It was wrong to enter another teacher's room while she was teaching. A teacher who went into another classroom apologized profusely for intruding and presented a valid excuse. A teacher could not legitimately deny access to the administration, but even here she expected "fair" limits on observation. Justice demanded that there be no "snooping," that there should be fair warning of a visit and "constructive criticism," not nitpicking.

Some teachers stood out as role-models for the group, their accomplishments and merits discussed reverently even after they had left teaching. Mrs. Hotelling, the quiet, shy commercial teacher in the high school, was unanimously revered for her ability to obtain respect and obedience from her pupils without ever raising her voice or yielding any of her self-possession. One historic figure, who years before had taught many of the present Adams teachers, was cited as a model of toughness and temper,

able, despite her small size, to cow the roughest high school boys
with her vituperative tongue and hints of physical violence. Her
ability to instill fear was considered a virtue. But her failure to
preserve her dignity during her performance made her to some
degree less admirable. The qualities most admired and sought
after were self-respect, dignity, and the ability to preserve order
without brutality or anger. The teacher recognized that such a
goal was ordinarily unattainable. Her final criterion was
pragmatic. Whatever worked was good. If patience and dignity
did not produce order in the classroom, then patience and dignity
had to go. Any method, even anger and vituperation, that could
bring respect and obedience was preferable to being "too nice,"
that is, weak: "We should let them know we mean what we say;
they mustn't get away with it." In particular, the male teacher
had to "act like a man so they will take him serious." Mrs. Crane
succinctly summed up the dominant attitude, "You lose respect
for someone if the children have no respect for him."

To be absent-minded, to overlook noise and confusion, was a
handicap to a teacher: "She just sits there as calm as anything. I
wish I could be like that, but of course. . . . " What seemed praise
here was really criticism. As Mrs. Gregory said to Mrs. Calhoun
in sweet insincerity one morning, "It was so noisy in your room
that I thought you weren't there."

Only a rare and unusual teacher could achieve order through
quiet patience. If patience failed it should be abandoned. A
teacher should at least look as if she were trying. Anger, verbal
outrage, a tough manner, even if they did not bring the desired
goal, at least showed intention. If these methods all failed, the
teacher could blame someone else for the disorder — the pupil,
the parent, the administration. One had done one's best. And
together the teachers built up teacher solidarity, reinforcing this
role-image through continual verbal reiteration: "I will be tough
this year. I will not give in no matter how unfair I seem to them."

Justifying order and discipline as good in themselves, the
teachers ritualistically assumed that without them learning did
not result. The Adams teacher believed that where teachers failed
to achieve discipline, that where confusion, noise, and rudeness
abounded, no learning occurred. This assumption was never
seriously discussed, and anyone who challenged it was treated
with scorn. The older teacher laughed at the "wacky" ideas of

"self-expression" that a newer teacher sometimes brought to teaching, but usually noted with relief that she found out "in time" that these ideas were "not practical." Having assumed that disorder prevented learning, the teacher went on to assume that by producing order she had brought about learning.[9] Criticisms of Miss Tuttle for her tolerance of noise and for her expressed desire that her pupils be happy shaded over into criticisms that she could not really be teaching, that her first graders were not making much progress. With no evidence one way or the other, the teachers relied on faith.

However, even this faith concealed ambivalence. The Adams teacher wanted the pupils to like her, not just to be afraid of her. So she regretted the very methods she praised. She justified her toughness by noting the dangers of letting down the side. (Pupils might take advantage of weakness; they might divide and conquer.) She appealed to teacher solidarity, but she was ambivalent: "I have no patience. I am crabby and tough this year. You can't ever let down. You can't ever stop and have any fun with them or they take it the wrong way." "Oh dear, it is awful to get angry at poor innocent children. I wish I wouldn't yell at them." "I hope you didn't hear me yelling at them."

This ambivalence accounts in part for the confused response to the "tough" teacher. Yes, she was successful; everyone could agree that she did have complete order, that her pupils were models of decorum, but "she has frightened the Stone boy so that he has stomach aches all the time. I don't approve of that."

TEACHER AS DIRECTOR OF LEARNING

Discipline can be readily observed. Producing learning, although it was the core of the teacher's self-image, was less observable and was thus less often directly discussed or clearly expressed by the Adams teacher. It was differently interpreted by the primary and the intermediate teachers, but all the teachers considered it to be crucial.

The Adams teacher, encouraged to take a service attitude, to eschew sordid economic motivation, and to accept a small salary, believed that her abnegation was more than matched by the good she did. What higher goals could there be than to produce the mature individual, the well-rounded, grown-up person, the democratic citizen? And only the experienced teacher, one trained at the right type of institution, could know how to achieve such goals. An inexperienced or untrained layman, no matter how well meaning or enthusiastic (like the parent who tried to teach the child to read at home with "half-baked" methods), merely sabotaged her trained efforts.

However, educational goals were of two kinds: ultimate goals — vague, general, unspecified, whose achievement was impossible to measure — and highly specific goals such as that the pupils should learn the three table or be able to recite the states and capitals. Nowhere in the teacher's training or experience was a clear bridge built between these levels of aspiration. It was never quite clear to her how the achievement of specific tasks could accomplish the broader goals, and no one could define for her except in equally general terms what was meant by the educated, mature individual. Furthermore, she was only one step in the whole process. What she achieved would be of relevance only if it was built upon by succeeding teachers over whom she had no control. Should she strive to produce a pupil who knew many facts, or one who was good at problem solving, one who was skeptical and questioning, one who was imbued with the cultural heritage, or all of these, and then in what proportions? On top of uncertainty about ultimate goals were uncertainties about method. All the research on learning theory and teaching methods had not clearly told her which methods really worked best or how the results achieved through one method rather than another were related to learning in a broader sense.[10] Mrs. Crane said, "Learning is an accident." Mrs. Preston noted even more morosely, "It usually doesn't take place. You may reach one child a year if you're lucky." And from Mr. Scranton, "It is not what the teacher attempts to teach that they get."

The Adams teacher confronted this dilemma of not being able to demonstrate the connection between her means and her goals in various ways. One was to ignore the ultimate goals and to substitute intermediate goals that could be more clearly defined and were more easily related to the specific techniques she was using. So she was encouraged to obtain test scores, rankings, measurable (and thus observable) results. She then assumed that she was achieving the broader goals, that high test scores stood for maturity and low test scores demonstrated failure, carefully shutting her eyes to any evidence from "educational experts" that such might not be the case.

However, achievement of these measurable results, the intermediate goals, sometimes seemed insufficient to her. Children who did the best on standard tests often seemed the least responsive in the classroom; a pupil's ability to make high scores on multiple choice questions was different from his ability to do creative thinking. Questioning the instrumental value of the tests she began to move toward purely ritualistic performance.[11] She gave lip service to the larger goals, but tended to judge herself by her methods, her techniques, the routines of her teaching: "We cover the material; I expose them to it. If they don't know it, it's not my fault." "We cover the textbook at least." "We will *do* the four table today." This ritualistic process was frequently accompanied by "buck passing." The teacher blamed others for interfering or the children for not trying. The methods were good, but the goals were not achieved because the children did not cooperate with her or the parents put road blocks in her way.[12]

Another possible stance was to question the ultimate goals. As the teacher found the goals remote and unrelated to what she was doing, she would express skepticism about them; they were mere slogans. When glowing statements about American education appeared in press and national magazines, an Adams teacher made cynical comments. The fatalistic, slightly sour point of view was most noticeable in the older, more experienced teacher. She worked as hard or harder than her younger colleague, but she did not seem to expect as much. She was neither as hurt by failure nor as pleased by success.

Intermediate and primary teachers at Adams handled the dilemmas of directing learning quite differently, and the subgroup norms were more significant in this context than the norms all Adams elementary teachers shared. All the teachers believed that a teacher must be a person with dignity and self-respect, who maintained some social distance from the pupils. A teacher was not a mother. Even the kindergarten teacher saw herself as standing apart from any individual pupil, trying to teach him, to change him, not to love him if to love him meant to accept him as he was. However, the interpretation and refinement of this aspect of the self-image was significantly different in the two subgroups.

The intermediate teacher emphasized preparing the pupil for high school and encouraging him to be mature, grown up, and "independent" (which usually meant doing willingly what the teacher wanted). She emphasized knowledge more than skills. How much did the pupil *know* about science, social studies, literature? She took for granted that he knew arithmetic, reading, spelling, and listening, since "they were covered in the primary grades." When the fifth and sixth grades were departmentalized at Adams, the teacher's emphasis on the importance of knowing subject matter increased. As she herself specialized she increasingly demanded that her pupils show competence in her specialty. "I feel sorry for those downstairs teachers who have to teach *everything*," said Mrs. Preston. The intermediate teacher, focusing on content, was less interested in art projects, demonstrations, or music programs for the parents, and more interested in test achievement.

The intermediate teacher drew a clear distinction between her role and that of the primary teacher. The content of courses taught downstairs was derogated. When Mrs. Merrick asked in a faculty meeting for science books for the second grade, the intermediate teachers were immediately hostile. If money for new books was scarce, obviously it should go upstairs, not down. The younger children could go on nature walks. They did not need books for that.

In contrast, the primary teacher prided herself on her ability to deal with the "whole child." Although she complained about having to remove boots and unstick zippers (too reminiscent of the baby sitter role) in addition to knowing all the subject areas, she viewed her "motherlike" role as a major asset. She prided herself on her warmth, responsiveness, spontaneity toward the children. Miss Benson who had taught third grade for twenty years downstairs was not able to adjust to teaching fifth grade upstairs. She treated the fifth grade pupils as though they were third graders, referring to herself in class in the third person, as "Miss Benson" instead of as "I." The fifth graders delighted in mimicking her, none too gently, behind her back: "And can Miss Benson draw a picture too? And we will put them all up, yours and mine, and choose the best." Miss Benson's attempts to be a fifth grade teacher in the manner of a third grade teacher were rejected not only by the pupils but also by the other teachers. She was not emphasizing the important norms.

Along with the emphasis on learning subject matter the intermediate teacher "expected" from her pupils signs of maturity: independent work, good judgment, and even an inhibition of the desire to escape the classroom and go to the bathroom. This last expectation, physically symbolized by the fact that the bathrooms were not only downstairs but at the far end of the school, was often reinforced with the moral exhortation, "If you are big enough to be a fifth grader you are big enough to wait until recess." A fifth grade girl who had an accident in class was regarded with amazement by the teachers: "Old enough to menstruate but not old enough to hold it."

Events continually contradicted many of these expectations for maturity. Yet, in the face of continued disappointment the upstairs teacher clung to her belief that the simple process of walking upstairs had transformed children into mature students. When I once wondered aloud whether it was too early to departmentalize studies in the fifth grade, I was told, "Well, they all have to learn to stand on their own feet sometime, to acquire responsibility. If they don't do it now, they never will. How are they going to get along in seventh grade, if they can't do it now?"

Primary teachers also talked this way sometimes, when they stressed the requirement that their pupils must learn to be less babyish, must learn to cooperate with other children, and to share. But the lower grade teacher did not emphasize to others, or to herself, her knowledge or *what* she taught, since even to herself *what* she taught seemed rather simple. She emphasized *how*, the difficulty of getting material across to these children. She derived some security from her conviction, acknowledged to some degree by the upper grade teachers, that it was harder to teach first grade arithmetic than to teach high school mathematics, to teach a child to read than to teach Shakespeare. At the first step one was more starkly confronted with the mysteries of the learning process and one could not "cop out" as the upper grade teacher sometimes did with, "I present it. If they don't get it, that's too bad for them."

Not only did primary and intermediate teachers define teaching in different ways, but each justified and rationalized her respective definition. Just as the college teacher could feel superior to the high school teacher, and the high school teacher to her, the intermediate teacher could see herself as superior to the primary teacher because she knew more and had more information to impart to her pupils. As the fourth grade teacher said, "I would hate to teach third grade social studies; there is nothing to it; it is so dull."[13] Knowledge conferred status. Mrs. Preston, boasting of how surprised Mr. Hanson was at the quality of the science exhibit, commented smugly, "He didn't realize how much we taught over here." Even if most of the pupils did not learn, one could still be successful. What one knew counted, not how one taught.

This claim to superior knowledge was used with some hesitation, however. The rationalization of "They aren't interested so I can't teach them," frequently so useful to the high school teacher, was less readily adopted by the fifth or sixth grade teacher. If the fifth or sixth grade teacher did not find complete security in this rationalization, it was because she did not wish to invite the inevitable comparison with the high school teacher who seemed to her to be so "snobbish." If knowledge was the key to status then surely the high school teachers knew more than she. Confronted with that unarguable advantage, she might turn right around and protect herself with the language of the primary teacher. She would speak of the whole child, of understanding children, or of having to teach the unteachables whom the high school would throw out. A little later she would again be asserting the importance of her own knowledge and complaining to the primary teachers that the children she had to teach knew so little and should never have been sent upstairs: "It is hopeless. We teach. That is our job. If they don't want to learn, it is not our fault. They shouldn't be here."[14]

Although she did not have to project a different image to two different groups, the primary teacher was not much more secure in her own justification and rationalizations. Her job definition oscillated between total, comprehensive responsibility and considerably more modest and limited tasks: "I have to be sympathetic, and yet I just can't do everything."

The importance of one or the other of these emphases probably varies from one school to another. At Adams, the intermediate orientation dominated because the Old Guard teachers, who took most responsibility for socializing the new teacher and set the tone in the school, were concentrated in the intermediate grades. What was taught was more important than how it was taught, just as preserving order was more important than teaching, and discipline was more important than self-expression.

One major question, in teaching as in many other occupations, is: "How can one measure success?" The institutionalized program of standardized tests, IQ and achievement, would seem on first glance to provide such a measure. However, the dangers to her self-image inherent in these external measuring devices often outweighed their potential rewards, and the teacher found ways of neutralizing these tests through ritualization. The significance of the IQ test for the Adams teacher lay in her conviction that since it gave a true and accurate assessment of the pupil's native intelligence it reflected neither credit nor discredit on the teacher. This conviction prevailed despite the evidence that IQ scores for particular pupils were noticeably inconsistent over the years.

She had no such protection or reassurance from the achievement tests, which purported to be a direct measure of what she herself had accomplished with a class. She found them a less than satisfactory measuring device. Most children in a class progressed each year in accordance with the national average; a few jumped far ahead; a few lagged far behind. Little correlation could be demonstrated between scores and the innovative or humdrum methods of the teacher. A teacher, ready to boast of group scores in her class one year, quickly discovered, on examining the previous year's scores for her class, that she had accomplished nothing unusual. Naturally, this evidence bolstered the arguments of the traditionalists against the innovators in the school. Why change methods if nothing made any difference? Somewhat defensively one teacher joked, "Teaching isn't important. Just keep them around a year and they make a year's gain." Exposure to school was sufficient, not what she did. Certainly this kind of devaluation of test results, while in some ways a protective device, was also an encouragement of ritualism and a brake on experimentation. For the teacher of a slow class the doubtful significance of tests as a measure of her accomplishments became a strong protection against the necessity for self-criticism, while the teacher of an average or superior class was restrained from overt self-satisfaction.

The teacher at Adams neutralized the possible negative significance of the standardized tests through at least four protective devices. First she denied responsibility for the results. Since the tests were given in March rather than in September or June, they could be viewed as a measure of the success of two teachers rather than one, and, therefore, each could secretly blame the other for inadequacy. And as Mrs. Crane remarked cheerfully, "None of us was responsible for teaching study skills, so we don't have to worry about how they did on that part of the test." What many *might* be responsible for, none could be *held* responsible for.

Second, she did not publicize the results any more than she had to. One suggestion, that the teachers be evaluated in terms of the improvement their pupils made on the standardized tests, was seen as a major threat and opposed by all the teachers. No one should be required to parade poor results. However, if a teacher wished to take pride and pleasure in her high scorers she had to reveal her lower ones as well.

A third protective device was self-belittlement: "I guess I didn't teach them anything. Look at these dreadful scores. What did I do wrong?" This immediately disarmed criticism. Or more commonly: "Well, now that the tests are over I might as well take it easy and not bother to teach."

A fourth device was to belittle the tests themselves. They did not measure what was important or what the teacher knew better than any test. A teacher devalued the pupil who attained a high score on the test but did poorly in daily class work. He was "lazy" and therefore did not deserve to succeed. The Adams teacher strongly resented Mrs. Milton's reliance on the test results in placing pupils for the following year: "I know them better than she does. How can she tell when she just looks at the results?" Every effort she made to use "objective" reading scores in placing pupils in reading groups was challenged by particular teachers who considered their own personal judgments to be far more relevant: "Children are so lazy. They never check their answers. No wonder they get them all wrong." "It is artificial to base their future on how they do on one test that they may have taken when they were tired or nervous or sick."

However, de-emphasis of the tests as a measure of success did not mean that the Adams teacher had strong faith in any alternative device. With no clear alternative, she fell back upon ritual performance and underemphasis on goal achievement.

Some teachers used the tests quite self-consciously in a prestige game with other teachers or to impress parents. However, any Adams teacher so unwise as to boast of success with the tests was apt to be cut down by hints that she coached the children, ignored the time limit, or gave help in some way. In a more bureaucratic school where the administering and scoring of tests were taken out of the hands of the individual teacher, this sort of suspicion and hostility could be reduced. Although the Adams teacher enjoyed the advantage of secrecy and protection from public scrutiny, she also had the continual problem of trying to build up her image without bringing resentment and anger upon herself.

Having used all these devices to reduce the threat to her own self-conceptions, the teacher at Adams looked upon giving the tests, scoring them, recording (and then ignoring) the results as an important duty in her role as teacher. These activities could be assimilated under the more general duty she imposed upon herself — the obligation to work hard. Ritualism extended beyond displays of observable toughness and disciplinary control to the demonstration of observable effort that became an outward sign of dedication and moral seriousness.

TEACHER AS INDUSTRIOUS WORKER

The importance of working hard was a cultural value particularly emphasized by the Old Guard teachers. Whatever their religious or family training, they were all imbued with the Puritan Ethic. To work hard as a teacher was but one aspect of a wider cultural imperative: to be ascetic, thrifty, clean, respectable. The emphasis upon working hard was self-justifying, but it also served to counter the community stereotype about long vacations and the soft life and to alleviate the teacher's own anxieties about the achievement of ultimate teaching goals.

The teachers, without ever specifically talking about teaching as a "profession," thought of it as "different." "Teaching isn't like other jobs." "When you teach you have to accept certain limitations. If you're not willing to do the extra work, you shouldn't go into teaching." The Adams teacher did not ordinarily enunciate this attitude quite so clearly as Mrs. Merrick who once remarked sententiously, "One does not punch a time clock as a teacher. One works until the work is done, no matter how long it takes." At which Mrs. Crane was heard to mutter, "Thinks she's so special, doesn't she?"

Personal satisfaction in hard work was not enough, of course. One had to make the hard work visible to others, both inside and outside the school. In school, the teacher stripped some of the insulation from her classroom in order to give active evidence of her industry. She accepted extracurricular responsibilities; she ostentatiously carried home stacks of papers; she ran innumerable tests through the ditto machine, leaving samples around to confound the other teachers in the teachers' room; she showed up faithfully at faculty meetings; she complained of fatigue; and she left her classroom door open so that any passer-by could see that she was standing in front of the class "teaching."

Mere talk about working hard was discounted and balanced by banter (jokes about tossing papers downstairs to grade them, about filing one's work in the circular file — the wastebasket). The teacher demanded more concrete evidence of hard work from a colleague. Although he talked a lot about how hard he worked, Mr. Scranton was sometimes criticized by the older teachers because "he never got around to grading his papers" and was never prompt in taking care of administrative responsibilities. Mrs. Gregory commented disapprovingly that Mrs. Calhoun and Miss Tuttle were tardy in submitting monthly attendance reports. Ritual performance of duty was necessary, not just ritual affirmation.

Once the teacher had performed her duties with full outward compliance to the requirements, she was then entitled, and indeed expected to complain. Complaints ranged over every aspect of the teacher's day, and there was much grumbling about late hours and the lack of free time: "There isn't even time to pee in this job." Administrative chores were too time-consuming, leaving the teacher no time to teach. All the griping was accompanied by rejection of any practical suggestion for lightening the load: "I'm of the old school. I don't believe that one can turn any of this work over to a teacher's aide and still do a good job of teaching." "They'd still have to be supervised. When I went into teaching I recognized that I would be busy all day." Pride was taken in the fact that all this hard work had to be borne alone.

The Adams teacher did her complaining in the informal group.

With outsiders she reiterated that, of course, one must give help to children whenever it was needed. In the informal gab sessions she complained, "You shouldn't have to give up your noon hour to *those* children," or "You shouldn't have to stay in at recess with *that* class." It was the fault of the pupil or the class, some willful inadequacy, not some special need, that forced the teacher to work harder than she otherwise would have had to.

The open classroom door made it possible for the teacher to demonstrate her hard work to her colleagues. A good day of teaching at Adams was one in which a teacher graded many papers, kept strict order, lectured to the class, and became very tired. In order to communicate this to others, one's teaching methods had to show. But this invited ambivalent attack. A teacher dittoing work sheets or tests in the teachers' room could expect to be bombarded with sarcastic remarks: "You are getting yourself lots of paper work there." "You give too many tests you know. Not going to give another one, are you?" Or she might meet with feigned sympathy: "You poor thing, all those papers to grade."

Paper grading was a highly resented chore and ordinarily one that commanded respect from other teachers. However, the teacher was expected by her colleagues not to grade papers at her desk while her pupils were doing busy work. Active "teaching" was the ideal. Mrs. Crane excused herself one day for "giving so much written work. They pay no attention to oral discussion." The premium at Adams was put on oral teaching. If Mrs. Milton came to supervise, the teacher took it for granted that she should stand at the front of the room and "teach."

Finally, the image of hard worker had to be projected beyond the walls of the school and come to the attention of parents and interested community members. People had to be convinced that the teacher's lot was not an easy one. When at the meat market I ran into hints or suggestions such as: "Teachers aren't really grown up. They have short work days and long vacations," I could not argue back directly without appearing oversensitive and defensive. But I felt impelled to display such symbols of busyness as I could muster, stacks of papers and excuses for social events. Few outsiders accused the Adams teacher to her face of having an easy life, but the jokes, the gibes, and the bitter community arguments whenever salary increases and contracts had to be negotiated made the point for her. As one school board member asked, "What arguments can I use against the people in town who think you have it pretty soft?"

The rare outsider who said, "You must have the patience of an angel; I know how hard it must be to have those children all day," brought momentary balm to the teacher even as she recognized the unspoken codicil, "and you're a fool to be in that job."

To counter the community stereotype about her soft life the teacher had to indicate publicly how hard she worked at her job, showing her unlimited willingness to carry out, with moral seriousness, all the duties that were comprehended in her teacher's role. So she believed herself obligated to attend PTA meetings that she hated. And she participated willingly if not enthusiastically in the parent-teacher conferences.

The Adams teacher prided herself on her refusal to take leave, even when she was ill. Mrs. Gregory expressed dismay at Miss Tuttle's casual remark one morning that she was sick and was going to go home for the afternoon, asking, "But suppose he can't find a substitute on such short notice?"

"That's his problem, not mine," was the breezy response.

To which Mrs. Garten, listening in amazement, remarked with a noticeable lack of conviction, "Maybe we should all be like that." But she was not and neither were the other Adams teachers.

A TEACHER'S RIGHTS

Within this framework of moral duty, self-sacrifice, hard work, and ritualistic adherence to traditional ways of doing things, it is hard to imagine any room for a teacher's rights. However, the Adams teacher did believe she had rights, rights defined and hallowed by tradition and a strong belief in equity.[15] To understand the meaning of these rights we must distinguish not between the primary and intermediate teacher, but between the newer and older teacher. Rights that were seen as legitimate when claimed by the older teacher were often denied by this same teacher to a newer member of the staff. Legitimacy depended less on the nature of the right than on the claimant and the situation.

What was legitimate depended on years of service and a pattern of reciprocity often misunderstood by the newer teacher.

A teacher would accept unequal treatment if it had not resulted from calculated discrimination or if the disadvantage was reversed in another year (as in the situation of drastically unequal class size). The newer teacher, with less experience, often misunderstood the situation and demanded what seemed to her to be equity, only to find the older teacher accusing her of a demand for special privileges.

Since what had been done in the past became the criterion for the present, the older teacher was naturally in the best position to define the teacher's rights. Even respect for legitimate authority did not restrain the older teachers from challenging new rules that contravened tradition. Only by appeal to the unwritten laws of custom could the obsessively law-abiding and law-minded Adams teacher set any limits on her dedication to what she saw as her duty. As long as the customary ways of doing things were respected she complied with any order. A state law requiring that there be a special class for mentally retarded children was obviously in her interest so the Adams teacher felt no compunctions about publicly demanding its early implementation. However, until this law was put into effect, she accepted her traditional duty to teach all children placed in her classroom, regardless of their mental capacity, emotional problems, or physical disabilities (although she also felt free to complain about it). But she also felt it was her right not to have such children assigned to her more frequently or in greater numbers than to another teacher. Allocations through the ordinary classroom procedures were accepted, but when a deliberate attempt was made to place a difficult child in Mrs. Crane's class even though Mr. Hanson coated the bitter pill by explaining, "You are so good with the slow learners," the teachers believed it was unfair discrimination.

Equity among teachers in size of classes was claimed and hallowed by the appeal to "the old days." The meaning of this flexible phrase, the old days, depended on the situation in which it was used. Something more than tradition was involved in the teacher's picture of her rights to a class of a particular size. Shifts of perspective reflected a consistent and strong set of convictions as to what equity meant. When Mrs. Merrick complained that her class was too large, she appealed not to the past but to outside standards. "In some schools they don't let you have more than fifteen children in a first or second grade class. It is a crime," she complained. Mrs. Gregory, who a minute before had been agreeing with her, now immediately shifted to attack Mrs. Merrick, "You new teachers are going to have to get used to large classes. There aren't going to be any more small classes for a number of years and we are all in the same boat, so why complain?"

The older teacher criticized the newer teacher for not completely accepting the service ideal, for not taking her work seriously enough. The right to a small class or the right not to have troublesome pupils in a classroom was relative, not absolute. Each teacher should be treated alike. A teacher should not be expected to have an excessively large class if there were legitimate procedures for dividing it. But a teacher accepted a large class if everyone else had a large class or if she was to have a small one the following year. Mrs. Gregory attacked Mrs. Merrick not for demanding a small class, but for demanding it as an absolute right.

Rights claimed in relation to time and space were more clearly defined and more generally accepted by all teachers than those relating to classroom composition. A teacher considered that her school day ran from eight-thirty in the morning to three-thirty in the afternoon and that at other times, even though she were on the school grounds and busy with school work, she was not really responsible to pupils or parents. If pupils arrived at school before eight-thirty in the morning, the teachers refused responsibility for them, although Miss Tuttle did say that the children should not be penalized for their parents' lack of consideration. When Mr. Hanson finally issued a directive to the teachers that pupils who came early were to be supervised, the teachers complained about the infringement on their rights but nevertheless accepted the redefined responsibility.

During the half hour between the dismissal of classes at three and the end of her formal duties at three-thirty, the Adams teacher believed she had the right to leave her classroom as long as she did not leave the school grounds. When a high school teacher remarked with some disapproval that he could never find an elementary teacher in her classrooom after school, no defense was offered since none seemed necessary. It was a right. Even the arrival of a parent and Mrs. Gregory's annoyed comment that "the poor woman couldn't find a teacher to talk to," brought no guilt. Mrs. Crane retorted lightly, "We have a right to a cup of coffee." On another day it could just as well have been Mrs. Gregory herself sitting in the teachers' room at three o'clock, completely unconcerned about parents who might be seeking her.

So, although the Adams teacher told parents that she was glad to talk to them at any time, she did not quite mean it. Unless the teacher had asked a parent to come, she did not want or really welcome any after-school visitors, particularly on Friday. For parents to come immediately after school was dismissed as annoying but not illegitimate; for them to come late in the afternoon was wrong: "What do they think I am? I am free to leave at three-thirty. I can't hang around all afternoon. Not that she cares about her son anyway. . . . "

An Adams teacher's rights extended to place as well as to time. The teachers asserted their nonlegal but traditional right not to be shifted from one grade or classroom to another without their consent. Legally, any teacher was required to teach any grade to which she was assigned. In practice, a teacher could retain the same grade as long as she wished. Any attempt by the administration to violate this unwritten rule led to united opposition by the teachers, a usually effective solidarity.

Just as she had the right not to be moved from one grade to another, so the teacher claimed a territorial right to the classroom itself.[16] Similar rights were staked out to sections of the playground, and boundaries were also maintained between upstairs and downstairs. When the music or the art specialist taught in the neutral territory of the cafeteria or in his own classroom, the classroom teacher expressed only moderate hostility to his work "with my class." This was true even when the classroom teacher attended the session. The specialist, however, who came into the classroom to teach provoked in the classroom teacher strong feelings of resentment and hostility.

For months, Mrs. Gregory and Mrs. Preston carried on a running verbal battle over rights to their classes' territory on the playground, a battle which finally had to be settled by administrative decree, the appointment of a third teacher, Mrs. Crane, as arbitrator to set firm boundary lines which neither group was then allowed to cross.

That the classroom belonged to the teacher and not to the pupils was evident in the treatment of bulletin board displays which, although designed to be a learning experience for the pupils, were often the work of the teacher alone. Mrs. Milton objected one day that the bulletin board was not the children's work. "How can it be?" Mrs. Preston asked. "The children do such sloppy work. My room would look dreadful." Unless a teacher had a particularly orderly and artistic group of pupils she tended to direct bulletin board creation by imposing the frame on the class and then closely directing individual work to fit within it.

A heated discussion ensued over the suggestion in an educational journal that a classroom teacher should not have a desk of her own. No Adams teacher could see any merit to this idea. Her desk was her center and much time and thought were devoted to its placement and to instilling in the pupils the moral conviction of its inviolability. A teacher displayed open hostility against a pupil who touched anything on the desk, took anything off it, or worst of all, opened a drawer to look for a paper clip.

Cherishing her few rights against her strong sense of moral obligation to be the disciplinarian, the director of learning, and the industrious worker, the Adams teacher attempted to do what she saw as her job.[17] Confronted by demands and expectations from pupils, parents, the principal, and the supervisor, she responded with her own expectations of them and of herself. And it was to her colleagues that she looked most immediately for guidance, support, and protection. Her self-image was enhanced and justified by her solidarity with the other teachers, while the variations in self-image between primary and intermediate teachers, newer and older teachers were bolstered by informal colleague subgroupings within the school.

3 COLLEAGUES AND PEERS

Adams, a characteristically traditional school, through physical structure and social arrangement isolated each teacher from every other. Even a casual visitor would quickly be made aware of the teacher's physical isolation from her peers and her close physical contact with children for most of the workday. When as a teacher one learned the rules and regulations governing the job, the visitor's casual impression would be reinforced. Each teacher was responsible for her charges from their arrival in the morning until their departure in the afternoon. She was expected to supervise their play and their lunch as well as their work. Contact with one's peers usually occurred during "stolen" time. Contact with one's subordinates was the norm.

Constant legitimate interaction with her pupils did not produce an exclusive attachment between teacher and pupils since the authority of the teacher prevented equality and encouraged some awe and constraint.[1] Although over time the intensity of interaction with the class cut down the interaction with outsiders, the teacher did not thereby sever her connections with her colleagues or stop seeking contact with them. No Adams teacher accepted to any appreciable degree the formally defined limits on interaction with peers.[2]

Every teacher needed to communicate with other teachers, to turn to them for support, to "break the rules," sometimes with bravado, sometimes with casual insouciance, sometimes with strong defensive justifications. The Adams teacher was uneasy about breaking the rules, not because she expected to be punished by an unnoticing administration, nor even because of her legal responsibility to the child, but mostly because of her dedication to the ideal of total commitment to the job. She would joke uneasily about her visiting, "I'm just going to take a minute." "I know I should be in my room but I gotta go," she would comment as she entered the teachers' room, went, and then lingered to chat: "I bet they are killing themselves in my homeroom, but tell me, how can I be everywhere at once?"

This sense of strain disappeared from social interaction before and after school hours, when wandering and visiting were relaxed and unselfconscious. The teacher then would even smoke in the halls without embarrassment. At such times the child or parent was the interloper; the teacher being observed was no longer required to act the role of teacher even though she was still in the school building.[3]

The colleague was important to the teacher, maybe particularly important in stolen moments, just because of the long periods of time she had to spend with her subordinates in unremitting effort to produce responsive and adaptive behavior. Teachers interacted with other teachers whenever they could, and this interaction had very important functions for the teacher and the school.[4]

GROUPS AND SUBGROUPS

Whom did the Adams teacher define as her colleagues, as those in the same situation with herself? Although the elementary school was only an archway removed from the high school, the elementary teacher did not refer to the high school teacher as a colleague. Primarily, by colleague, she meant one of the regular teachers in the Adams Elementary School itself, with an occasional ambivalent extension of the term to include special teachers who worked with her class. Since the Adams School had only nine regular teachers, the colleague group was small, but even so all nine were rarely together (except at formal gatherings such as faculty meetings). Physical and social divisions prevented the teachers from establishing an all-inclusive teacher group. Only during the year of intensive research did such a group seem to emerge (which may in part reflect certain influences of hidden participant observation not apparent to me during the research) and it died before the end of that year, never to reappear so strongly again. However, even without informal group contact among all the teachers, each teacher defined herself to some degree in relation to all the other teachers, sought from every other teacher support and protection, and complained about the lack of true unity and group feeling.

The ideal role-expectation that any Adams teacher held of a colleague was that she show loyalty. A teacher who betrayed another to class or parent was resented. This norm, acquired to some extent during her socialization as a teacher, was primarily a verbalized response to the teacher's conviction that the school environment was hostile, that she was surrounded by enemies, and that she needed protection.[5]

Although all-teacher unity was only rarely realized in actuality and although the teachers themselves (particularly the older ones) talked rather cynically about their failed expectations, they still clung to the ideal, depended on their colleagues, looked for support, and sometimes, to their own surprise, were not disappointed. The older Adams teacher insisted that this ideal expectation was less well realized at Adams than elsewhere: "One teacher should be able to talk to another when she is upset. In *other* schools the teachers help one another. They are around when you want to blow off steam or talk."[6] But: "No one listens to anyone else or cares around here. You are on your own." I quickly discovered that it was better to believe, as a teacher expressed it succinctly, "You can't trust another teacher in this school. Whatever you say gets immediately reported," than to count on another teacher's help and assistance. During my first difficult months of teaching I asked one of the older teachers for advice and was shortly thereafter called on the carpet by the superintendent who said that he had heard I was having trouble with discipline.

During the year of the study, for a few months, this usual distrust was modified. An after-school coffee-drinking group in the teachers' room included all of the elementary teachers, except for Mrs. Preston (for reasons to be discussed later). The group dissolved in January because of new regulations that required teachers to supervise bus pupils after school. It was never re-established but, during its short existence, it had a noticeable effect on teacher sentiments. The teachers as a group engaged in many purely social activities during these months. Favorable expressions of liking and trust were frequently heard even after the group dispersed: "I do think we have the most congenial group of teachers we have had in a long time. Everyone seems to get along. I guess it's because everyone has a sense of humor." The phrases "we teachers" and "we elementary teachers" were heard for almost the first time at Adams.

While the newer teachers took this kind of amity for granted: "I love it here. Everyone is so friendly. That is why I am coming back," the older teachers had less faith in the new situation: "Yes, we are congenial because we aren't together enough to get on each other's nerves."

Far more important than the all-teacher groupings at Adams was the elaboration of an interlocking set of subgroups, somewhat divisive and somewhat conflicting. Membership in these subgroups helped to clarify each teacher's role-definition. There were more or less firm divisions into primary and intermediate teachers, the upstairs and downstairs cliques, and the Old Guard and the new teachers. Subgroup formation was importantly influenced by spatial and temporal characteristics of the Adams School. Because of the illegitimate quality of much teacher visiting, it was natural that a teacher would interact most with teachers in nearby rooms and with teachers whose schedules overlapped hers.

As noted in the last chapter, the most significant formal dividing line in the Adams Elementary School was that which separated primary and intermediate teachers. The values and role-expectations a teacher held for herself and for her colleagues were highly colored by whether she taught a primary grade or an intermediate one. One source of this distinction was certainly her teachers' college training where separate programs were offered for the primary or intermediate teacher-to-be. Whether she learned to emphasize methods or content depended in part on the courses she took, on her practice teaching, and on the older teachers she worked with. The distinction was then reinforced when she was hired to teach as either a primary or an intermediate teacher. Textbook publishers maintained, if they did not create, this distinction by publishing texts clearly classifiable as primary or intermediate in scope, level of difficulty, degree of emphasis on pictures or written text.

In the Adams School this distinction was emphasized not only by the teachers themselves but also by the subjects taught, by the in-service training programs, and by the marking system and report card. It would, therefore, seem likely that this distinction would provide the major basis for subgroup division in this school. And it did except for one complicating factor.

In most respects the physical and temporal patternings of the Adams School reflected this basic line of demarcation. Thereby they reinforced the already existing dichotomy. As the teachers were forced through scheduling of recess time and lunch and through location to interact most with those already like them, the common values and sentiments were reinforced, leading to increased activity and interaction.[7] Simple matters such as what games to suggest at recess time were influenced for a teacher by the presence of other teachers and classes on the playground. Only within her own classroom, her private sanctum, did the teacher have the freedom to pursue her own schedule, activities, and pace.

For many years at Adams the stairs provided the most important physical line of demarcation between these two groups of teachers — primary teachers downstairs, intermediate teachers upstairs. However, the increase in enrollment and the employment of more teachers led the year I was employed to the displacement of Mrs. Gregory from the heights and her ignominious relocation among the primary teachers on the first floor.

To understand the importance of this "demotion" to Mrs. Gregory, we must recognize another crucial basis for distinction between Adams teachers — whether one was Old Guard or new. This distinction was far less a matter of age than of tenure and of background. The Old Guard teachers had taught at the school for at least ten years; they were older women with families and ties in the local Adams community; they had gone through the traditional training process from normal school to classroom; they saw themselves as integrally attached to school and community, responsible for educating the Adams children in the right ways. They considered themselves aligned with a few other teachers who were not teaching in the school during the study, but whose backgrounds and experiences were similar to theirs; they considered themselves less closely aligned with newer teachers whose training at least approximated theirs and who had local roots (Mr. Scranton and Mrs. Garten and, to an even lesser degree, Miss Tuttle); they considered themselves least aligned with the new teachers, those whose backgrounds, experiences, and affiliations were most remote from theirs, those who came to the school with liberal arts backgrounds, from other communities, from jobs and experiences not directly related to elementary education (Mrs. Calhoun, Mrs. Merrick, myself, and a number of other temporary interlopers). To be Old Guard meant to share values and frames of reference, but it also meant to share gossip and experience and relationships in school and community over a number of years. Strong personal animosities and violent quarrels shook the group but did not destroy it. For the Old Guard teacher, tradition was the key symbol: "What I learned in training school" or "What has always been done." The present was always judged by "how it used to be done," since the past was far rosier than the present. After all, in the good old days supervisors supervised, principals gave orders, teachers worked harder and were more dedicated, parents cared and helped the teacher receive respect from the pupils.

At the time of this study the Old Guard teachers were all intermediate teachers (although this had not always been true at Adams). Therefore, the values and role-expectations associated with being Old Guard and those associated with being an intermediate teacher reinforced each other. However, the two groups did not perfectly match nor did either match the physical division provided by the stairs. As a result, the subgroup patternings were complicated.

Old Guard solidarity was demonstrated most clearly in the morning before school when the arriving Old Guard teachers would stop and chat in Mrs. Gregory's classroom before moving on to their own rooms. On these occasions conversation concerned the community, people who had died, the good old days, "how we used to do it," rather than strictly school matters.

Both values and physical factors influenced other alignments. As noted earlier, the primary teacher, Miss Benson, who had to spend a painful year teaching fifth grade upstairs, was never accepted as an intermediate or an upstairs teacher by the other teachers. Her ideas and her role-expectations had been fixed for too long for her to adapt. On the other hand, Mrs. Gregory, close to the upstairs teachers in position (intermediate) and in background (Old Guard) was rather effectively kept out of the most important subgroup, the upstairs clique, primarily as a result of physical and structural elements over which she had no control.

Her interaction with the others was limited to before school and the noon hour. Her recess time was different from that of the upstairs teachers, and she had no opportunity for casual informal contact during school hours. The upstairs teachers put through a departmental teaching program from which Mrs. Gregory was excluded, ostensibly because it would take too long to change classes if the pupils had to go up and down the stairs. In addition, the principal divided the teachers along the upstairs-downstairs cleavage for compiling supply lists and scheduling parent-teacher conferences.

The frequency of interaction and the low turnover of personnel led to a strong we-group feeling among the upstairs teachers against the rest of the staff. Whatever else Mrs. Gregory was, she was a downstairs teacher and, therefore, not part of the group.

Just as the distinction between primary and intermediate was recognized and verbalized by the teachers, so was that between upstairs and downstairs teachers. If Mrs. Merrick walked upstairs to get some materials from the supply closet, Mrs. Crane was sure to caution her not to faint in the thin air and to remember her place. To which Mrs. Merrick was sure to respond that it must be so easy to teach upstairs with such "grown-up" pupils. Sometimes the comments were more caustic. As Mrs. Merrick remarked to me one day, "We have so many things to do and teach downstairs. Of course, I suppose you have things to do too." Before I moved upstairs I was warned many times, "Don't get like them" (that is, cold, rigid, unfeeling).

The ingroup solidarity was demonstrated to me by the fact that after only a couple of years upstairs I was, despite my difference from the others in age and background, classified as one of them, "women of our age," "us old ones," in contrast to the "young" or "new" downstairs teachers who were in some instances neither younger nor newer than I.

Mrs. Gregory refused to accept definition as a downstairs teacher, but she was never accepted as an upstairs teacher. Old Guard in background, an intermediate teacher in her methods, her values, and her orientation, she chose to stand alone. She clung to her values as an intermediate teacher firmly against and apart from the primary teachers, insisting on a separate recess time (which she then shared with no other teacher in the school), refusing to participate in the spring field days since the upstairs teachers did not include her, and she refused to be included by default with the primary teachers. She would complain frequently to the upstairs teachers about the excessive freedom that the new teachers gave to the primary children, about noise, about drinks of water, about afternoon recess: "Mine are big enough in fourth grade not to need that." But her complaints never gave her acceptance in the upstairs group.

Physical and scheduling factors, personality clashes, levels of interaction, and my presence (Mrs. Crane to me jokingly: "Hanging around with you has made us all high hat. Poor Mrs. Gregory!"), all contributed to the isolation of Mrs. Gregory from her usual group. However, another factor was certainly contributory. Mrs. Gregory occupied the position of marginal man in this situation.[8] Her own values, reflected in the ways she taught, were too ingrained to let her be one with the group to which she felt so superior. She was denied entrance into the group whose norms and values she shared. More than any other intermediate teacher, she translated these norms and values into action. She was stricter, more rigid, more demanding of maturity in her charges, and more concerned about baby habits than any of the upstairs teachers. Her behavior became the boundary for the upstairs teachers. An upstairs teacher expressed doubt about her own values, not in countering a primary teacher, but when she was confronted with one of Mrs. Gregory's strong maxims: "Every child in fourth grade should be able to do long division." "My class has learned to work by itself with me out of the room." As Mrs. Crane said, "She is just *too* strict. I respect her order but I don't much approve of what she teaches. The children are afraid of her. I don't like that. I want respect, but I don't want children afraid." Mrs. Gregory's rigidity and firmness may indicate that, in her position, she believed this was the only way to avoid being considered merely another somewhat inferior primary teacher.

Teacher interaction at Adams was defined in terms of the subgroups, particularly upstairs-downstairs, less frequently Old Guard-newcomers, on certain more formal occasions, intermediate-primary. However, situational and accidental elements did bridge some of the chasms,[9] making possible at least infrequent communication up and down and across lines. Smoking was one of these elements, my desire to observe was another, as were idiosyncratic elements such as Mrs. Gregory's self-imposed isolation.

AUTHORITY AND LEADERSHIP

During the few months when all the teachers gathered after school for informal coffee sessions, Mrs. Preston almost invariably refused to participate. When she occasionally came in she would seem embarrassed, ill at ease, and quickly leave. Her resentment of the group revealed itself in numerous comments to Mrs. Crane and me during these months. That she voluntarily excluded herself from these gatherings, but not from the larger group when it planned some formal activity such as a going away party or a dinner, reveals something about the ambiguous authority position of Mrs. Preston in the Adams School.

Mrs. Preston was in the unfortunate situation of having once had an official authority niche, "elementary teaching principal," in the school which she had lost with the accession of Mr. Hanson to the position of principal (and thus to formal control over all the teachers). She was expected to continue to carry out all the duties of her previous position but with neither recognition, reward, nor appreciation. The position she had held gave her no extra pay, no time off, but it did give her responsibility and some authority over the other teachers. She was supposed to transmit communications from the superintendent's office, to coordinate and arrange schedules, to prepare all memoranda or lists needed by the administration. She was in charge of student records and also adjudicating any disputes between teachers. Her authority did not extend over any other teacher's methods of teaching or disciplining pupils, nor give her rights within any other classroom.

With her loss of position she became equal in all formal respects to the other teachers, but since all of these duties still had to be performed by someone in the elementary school, she was informally expected to perform them.[10] While Mr. Hanson gave her nonposition at least semiofficial status by referring to

Mrs. Preston at the first fall faculty meeting as "head teacher in the elementary school," the other teachers, particularly the other members of the Old Guard, resented her attempts to carry out her duties. They sarcastically referred to her behind her back as the boss: "Look out. We had better get in our rooms or the boss will be angry." Or they pretended not to understand why she behaved as she did: "What is she, the big cheese around here or something?" Mrs. Preston, herself, disliking her ambivalent position commented, "Not till they pay me for being head teacher, I'm not. I get not one cent. Why should I do any extra work?" but she still managed to compound the resentment by playing the role for all it was worth. She clutched to herself all possible outward symbols of power, from the only key to the supply closet, which she kept on her person at all times ("The other teachers come in and take too many things"), to the right to be the only teacher to pick up the mail in the office. This latter activity also enabled her to return with gossip, directives, and information from the administration, usually prefaced with the comment: "I'm not sure I should tell you this, but he might want you to know."

Mrs. Preston's attempts to extend her control into the classroom were resisted as illegitimate by the older teachers, but this resistance was rarely directly expressed. Vocal resentment of her "unwarranted" attempts to "take over" other teachers' duties on the playground, or her "bossiness" on the upper floor was rarely translated into action. The teacher shrugged, remarked "The boss says so," and complied. However, when the other teachers, particularly her upstairs departmental colleagues, made decisions in her absence she raised no objections, acceding to these decisions as if they had been hers. Although the other teachers always talked as if they expected her to make trouble: "I hope she doesn't bite your head off," she never did.

While grudgingly recognized as the leader of the teachers in their participation in the formal social structure, Mrs. Preston was never regarded by them as a leader in informal activities and casual good times. The other teachers carried on private conversations, exchanged personal confidences, restrained from turning to her in part because of her official manner. And she responded by avoiding the after-school coffee sessions.

There is little evidence of leadership in the more informal

gatherings of teachers. If any teacher came close to being an expressive leader, it was Mrs. Crane. On her the sentiments of warmth and liking converged.[11] Old Guard herself, close to Mrs. Preston through years of common experience, looked up to with respect as a source of ideas and instruction by the younger teachers, she was able primarily through her casual easy manner and friendliness to encourage positive in-group feeling, to reduce tensions and anxieties. When she was present, the teachers — primary and intermediate, new and old, upstairs and downstairs — engaged in banter, jocular griping, humorous talk. When she was absent, the larger gatherings broke up, replaced by subgroup and pair formations. This same role she played with the upstairs clique, deferring to Mrs. Preston on formal matters, but unifying the group in informal activities.

SOCIALIZATION

One's colleagues are very important for the teacher. Each teaching job is a new role, and no amount of formal training or earlier experience can completely prepare a teacher to carry out the special requirements of this role.[12] So the more experienced colleague acts inevitably as a socializer, a model one can imitate and a leader whose orders, comments, jokes, even sanctions tell the new teacher what is expected of her and what she should expect of herself.[13] Socialization of the new teacher was one of the important concerns of the older teachers, but like many other things at Adams it was for various reasons often more ineffective than effective, more productive of tension and anxiety than of ease and satisfaction.

During the acute teacher shortage in the mid-1950s it became possible for liberal arts college graduates with varied backgrounds to enter public school teaching without having to submit to the lengthy teacher training ordinarily required by the state. The college graduate could take on a full-time teaching position in a public school after completing a summer program at a teachers' college. Further training for these obviously unprepared teachers was provided while on the job through evening and summer courses.

It was this route that a number of us followed. I was hired in the spring to teach at Adams in the fall. I did not learn until

September that I would teach fourth grade. I requested the opportunity to visit some classes, a request that was greeted by Mrs. Milton, the elementary supervisor, with some surprise. Ordinarily, I learned, the new teacher did not come to her new school until the day before classes began in September. However, I was humored and was able to meet some of the teachers and to visit a number of their classes. I felt ill-prepared to start off as a full-time teacher.

On the day after Labor Day all of the elementary teachers attended a meeting with the superintendent where they received the time schedule for recess, lunch, and bus duty, room assignments, and class lists. I was given a copy of *The Curriculum Guide,* which listed the subjects to be taught at each grade level, and a mimeographed sheet prepared by Mrs. Milton that suggested possible time allotments for particular subjects, hints on room arrangement, and a few suggestions for conducting the first day of school. My obvious helplessness in selecting supplies and textbooks for my pupils finally led Mrs. Crane and Mrs. Gregory to take pity on me and help out. At least a week of school passed before I knew which reading books were appropriate for my class.

Operating without direction as to how to plan the day, the classes, or the transitions from one activity to another, I attempted to piece together these procedures from *The Curriculum Guide,* from suggestions in the teachers' manuals provided with the textbooks in each subject, from my skimpy training, and from as much observation of the other teachers outside of the classroom as I could manage from my self-contained vantage point. My memory of my first days as a teacher is one of confusion, even chaos, failed experiments, and insecurity.

In the weeks that followed I found no more direction, no more guidance from colleague or administrator than in those first hectic days. Mrs. Milton, whose official job I had been told was to train the new teacher, showed up only twice in the first month and gave minimal help. The superintendent visited my classroom once. So I turned to my colleagues for help and advice in matters both of discipline and instruction. I found them unresponsive, uninformative, and amazingly reticent with suggestions or even direct answers to questions. Through observation and imitation I was able at least to a degree to simulate the teacher's role in the hall, in the lunchroom, on the playground. In the classroom, it took much longer before I experienced any feeling of ease. I was on my own, confronted daily by confusions in schedule, by constant complaint from the pupils that that was not the way it was done the year before.

That I did learn, that I did become in my own eyes by the second year a "teacher," however inadequate, is certainly true. It is also true that it was a painful first year, that I often wanted to give up, that I was often amazed that anyone survived the process and remained a teacher. It is legitimate to ask how far my experience of becoming a public school teacher was typical for new teachers at the Adams School. It was certainly comparable to that of others who entered teaching the same way. For those who came through the regular teachers' college channels, or, like Mr. Scranton, merely moved into teaching at Adams from teaching in another school, the transition was no doubt easier and had more coherence. But my observations suggest that no new teacher at Adams ever found it easy to incorporate her new role.[14] As a new teacher crossly complained to me once, "Why are you all so close-mouthed? I try to get some advice on teaching the language arts and all I get is double talk and suspicious looks. You'd think I wanted you to spill your private trade secrets." The difficulties faced by any new teacher at Adams can be partially understood as a consequence of the lack of congruence between the dominant ideology operating in this school and the structural and situational conditions during these years.

Many schools provide formal socialization and training programs for new teachers, orientation sessions the week before school opens, even in-service courses for new teachers during the term. Adams as a small school with little teacher turnover in the years preceding the teacher shortage never instituted any formal training of this sort for the new teachers.

The ideology at the Adams School rested upon certain assumptions that had no basis in fact at the time I started teaching. One assumption held alike by Old Guard teachers and administration was that any new teacher's training should prepare her to teach in any elementary school in the state without more formal instruction. Another assumption was that any special problems or characteristics of a particular school could be explained, any possible gaps in the teacher's knowledge could be filled in, and any idiosyncratic aspects of a teacher's personality could be coped with by the elementary supervisor. To the degree that these assumptions were justified, the colleague was of only minor importance for the socialization of the new teacher, standing primarily as a model for manner, tone, and external characteristics. The older teacher at Adams came into teaching under these conditions. She found her training directly transferable to the new position, and she was so closely supervised that she had few decisions or choices to make. So she had "no problems," at least in retrospect.

It is hard to know if these assumptions were ever really justified at Adams. The new teachers saw the past only through the nostalgic eyes of the older teachers, for whom the good old days were so much better than the present. But if one held these assumptions the dominant ideology made sense and did not need to be questioned. This ideology included a belief in the inviolability of a teacher's classroom and the belief that it was not one teacher's job to tell another teacher how to teach. It was quite proper for one teacher to be a model of discipline and order for another to follow, or for one teacher to inform another about the school rules and her responsibilities on the playground or in the lunchroom, but no teacher should invade another's classroom when teaching was going on; no teacher should belittle or question another teacher in front of pupils or parents; each teacher should support and back up the actions of a colleague in public. No teacher should attempt to direct the methods or content of another teacher's classroom work, unless explicitly asked, and probably even then only very circumspectly, since one did not want to seem to be interfering.

What was the basis of this ideology? In part, the physical arrangements of a school encouraged privacy for the classroom teacher. In part, the fact that only one teacher taught a particular grade, typical in the experience of the Adams teacher, meant that no teacher was directly involved with the pupils or the classroom work of any other teacher. This ideology derived from the contradictory desires of the teachers, first to ensure their solidarity against the outside enemy (parents, in particular) and, second, to win prestige over the colleague in the eyes of the same enemy. As the school increased in size and more than one teacher taught at the same grade level, this desire for prestige increased. This was not competition for higher pay or for an advanced position, since neither of these avenues of mobility was open to the Adams teacher. But it was a desire for honor in the eyes of the outsider, for some recognition of achievement, or, negatively, a desire to prevent any other teacher from achieving special recognition not accorded to oneself. So an ideology of noninterference in a neighboring classroom was functional. It enhanced teacher solidarity against the outside by preventing divisiveness and cutthroat competition. Since each teacher had to keep her teaching to herself within her own classroom, she could not display it gaudily or individually to parents or administrators. If one teacher did not interfere with another she neither showed off her own successes nor threatened the shaky security of another. When Mrs. Gregory and I both taught fourth grade, our relationship was strained and tense. I was new, odd, and therefore potentially threatening. Mrs. Gregory gave me no help or direct advice and was as close-mouthed as possible about her own methods, although she did like to show off her results. Once I became a sixth grade teacher, Mrs. Gregory became warm, friendly, even expansive about subjects she had not discussed with me the year before: how to teach math or how she managed to get through the social studies curriculum I never quite completed. Mrs. Preston, on the other hand, who had ignored me the first year, became hostile, noticeably competitive, secretive, and yet boastful, as soon as she had to share the sixth grade with me.

I found these elementary teachers insecure about their own dignity and defensive about the image held of them in the community. The most common reaction to this insecurity was not to listen to what another teacher reported about her work.[15] Interest, as Mrs. Calhoun noted, was only pretense, and Miss Tuttle's wistful belief that "if you have two people teaching the same grade then teachers could talk to one another" and care what you were doing seemed less realistic than did minding one's own business.[16]

Because of the changes in the methods of teacher training and the decline of supervision in the Adams School, the Old Guard teacher found that the new teacher did not slip inconspicuously into the traditional pattern. Although the Old Guard teacher espoused the ideology, it was not as successful in cutting down teacher rivalry and producing conforming colleagues as it had been in the past. The new teachers, with their unfamiliar and varied backgrounds, appeared to adhere to strange methods of teaching and even to set themselves somewhat different goals. In so doing they challenged the traditional methods and upset the ritualistic security on which much of the Old Guard philosophy rested: "It doesn't make any difference how you teach, since nothing works."

As a result of these changes the Old Guard teacher began to fear that the parents might be influenced by all "this silly falderal" and might even expect similar strange behavior from her. She feared the loss of her own prestige in the eyes of the parent, as well as a dangerous decline in sound order and discipline. She herself felt secure as a disciplinarian, far superior to the new teacher. Here at least she could lay down the law, but in the classroom she was less confident. She doubted the efficacy of the "new ways," but had no way to prove the efficacy of her own ways — no appeal except to tradition. Her response to this threat was to cling to the ideology, to hide behind her own classroom door, and to conceal her own knowledge and techniques from the newcomer. If she did not interfere or help, the new teacher would finally accept defeat: "She'll learn." Until the new teacher could talk her language, could look at teaching in her terms, she could not be trusted or confided in. But, on the other hand, suppose the new teacher went too far in upsetting the old order, as she might without enough supervision? Maybe something had to be done by the Old Guard teacher to socialize her. From these contradictory pressures to interfere and to keep hands off emerged a pattern of indirect training through innuendo and hint, accompanied by strong hostility when this approach failed to change the new teacher's behavior. It was this pattern of indirect socialization of colleagues that characterized the Adams School.

Despite her qualms about interference, then, the Old Guard teacher took on some responsibility for socialization of the new teacher, strongly resisting any efforts of newer teachers to interfere. She restricted her activities to her own subgroup — upstairs or downstairs — and she attempted to operate indirectly rather than directly.

Mr. Scranton and I were primarily socialized by Mrs. Preston with Mrs. Crane's help. Mrs. Gregory concentrated on socializing the primary teachers on her floor, as she had attempted to socialize me during my first year of teaching. Here she was handicapped by being the only Old Guard teacher on the floor and therefore having no assistance in her activities. She refused to accept help from any teacher who was not Old Guard, so that she greatly resented Mrs. Calhoun's rare attempts to instruct Mrs. Merrick during the first few months of the year. Finding Mrs. Calhoun trying to show Mrs. Merrick how to teach pennmanship one afternoon she watched in cold silence until Mrs. Calhoun faltered to a stop, turned to her, and asked meekly, "That's right, isn't it?" Then she took over by herself. Actually, Mrs. Gregory worried not just at the usurpation of her own authority but also at the bad influence that a newer teacher like Mrs. Calhoun might be on a neophyte: "Mrs. Merrick is going to be just like Mrs. Calhoun. She just follows her. Of course, Mrs. Calhoun keeps going in and telling her what to do. I thought she was going to fit in, but she is going to be just like that one and go her own way. It's too bad."

It was difficult to carry on indirect socialization without allies. My memory of my first year of teaching is of how little Mrs. Gregory did to help or guide me, how often she turned off my questions with a shrug. It is only in looking back that I can see how she attempted to direct me through indirection. I started a class newspaper that the children took home. I was pleased with my enterprise here as with other of my nontraditional activities such as a class trip, a choral speaking program, a party for the first grade. I learned finally through a few of the parents that the other teachers resented my behavior and believed that I was showing off. To have to use the parents as allies shows how desperate Mrs. Gregory was to inform me without informing me directly. In addition, other Old Guard teachers began to make veiled critical remarks to me, or in my presence, quoting what someone else had said. I began almost unconsciously to cut back gestures of independence, concealing my odder methods within my classroom.

Later from my upstairs vantage point I saw the difficulties Mrs. Gregory faced in trying to instruct without instructing. She expressed her annoyance with the new primary teachers — their failure to keep to the schedule, their tolerance of noise, their sloppy dress ("These young teachers don't realize how they look when they wear sleeveless dresses and forget their stockings. They do set a bad example.") — to the upstairs Old Guard teachers, but she was unable to let the new teachers clearly see what she objected to. All her glaring, her noisy door shutting, her vague comments at the lunch table completely missed their targets. Her isolation from allies and her acceptance of the ideology countered her strong feeling that something had to be done before there was complete deterioration in the standards of the school. The upstairs Old Guard teachers were somewhat more successful. Since there were two of them, they could support one another as well as use their interchanges as signs to the new members.

Indirect guidance took various forms. One teacher would make a "private" comment to a second about a third, which someone invariably repeated to the third. So I learned from Mrs. Crane that Mrs. Preston did not want me to teach upstairs "because she doesn't want to have to discipline all your children as well as her own." So Mr. Scranton found out from me that "Mrs. Crane thinks you let them walk all over you because you are too nice."

Or a teacher made a criticism in the guise of a compliment. It took time for the new teacher to sense the difference: "I have far less patience than you do. I wish I could ignore them the way you do." ("You are too considerate, too willing to listen to them, but you are not nearly as nice as you used to be.") One learned to recognize that what seemed like compliment was criticism; what seemed like criticism was compliment.

The Old Guard teacher might criticize something done by a teacher not present in order that a teacher listening could learn what was wrong. So Mrs. Crane said in Mr. Scranton's presence that Mrs. Calhoun was too lax, too casual in the classroom. She felt much more strongly about Mr. Scranton's casualness than she did about Mrs. Calhoun's. Unfortunately, he failed to get the subtle hint. Teachers no longer with the school, those who had become symbols of one or another kind of failure, were often mentioned in this kind of conversation, their failings supposed to be warnings to the new teachers.

Mrs. Preston was the only teacher at Adams that I ever saw flatly ignore the ideology of laissez faire, the indirect approach. She frequently interfered rather directly, even inside another teacher's classroom. During my first year upstairs she entered my room a number of times despite my presence to quiet the class, or to instruct me in front of the pupils. She followed a similar practice with Mr. Scranton throughout his first year. However, even she, despite this aggressive approach, did not offer help or advice on the content of his teaching. Her interference looked far more like an attempt to preserve her slim status superiority as the dominant teacher in the school than an attempt to socialize the new teacher.

The indirection was most apparent when the new teacher appealed directly for help. Requests for advice usually brought forth only facetious comments from the teachers in the teachers' room: "They're acting up? Beat them, just keep them out of my hair," or ambiguous answers: "We have discussed this problem a lot. We cannot decide how to handle it," or no answers at all. As one older teacher told me once, "You don't want people to think you are interfering. They take comments as criticism instead of as help."

Rather than directly respond to requests for help, the Old Guard teachers carried on undercover criticism of the new teacher for doing the wrong thing. Miss Tuttle asked for guidance on grading standards from the other teachers at a faculty meeting. This led to a long general discussion about grading, but she received no answer. The next year the Old Guard teachers were furious at the marks she had given her pupils: "How could she give twelve of those first graders straight A's? That is ridiculous." It was Miss Tuttle's responsibility to know how to do the right thing without being helped, at least by the older teacher.

So, although all the Old Guard teachers disapproved of and gossiped to one another about Mrs. Merrick's habit of making her second graders finish their work during the noon recess, none ventured more in direct answer to her request for policy than the general hint: "Of course, every child should have some outdoor play." When she responded defensively, "We all go out for recess. I am giving up my lunch hour for the children," no older teacher said anything. Each defined the situation as none of her business but the responsibility of the supervisor. When the supervisor took no action, the teachers were angry — not at her but at Mrs. Merrick who should have known better.

When the new teacher was herself indirect, she was more

successful in getting help. A superficially boastful remark often turned out to be an indirect request for response and so for standards: "I have to keep so much discipline with twenty-eight of them. I hate to but otherwise...." Sounds of approval from the Old Guard teachers would confirm Mrs. Merrick in the rightness of her action. A new teacher who brought sets of papers into the teachers' room, ostensibly to show off what good work her pupils were doing, hoped to have her notions of quality confirmed by someone more experienced, and this she usually achieved through careful listening.

Rather than ask directly for help, the new teacher learned to turn the problem into a humorous story, playing down the anxiety it caused her. Then the Old Guard teacher could respond in general, rather than to the specific problem: "When that boy, Tom, in my room does not finish his work I send it home with a note for his mother to sign. That brings him around." Or an Old Guard teacher would recollect something that happened the first year she taught, emphasizing how she handled a similar problem. By such means the Old Guard teacher avoided any appearance of direct interference, but she made her point.

Even in the more intimate informal groups and in response to direct requests for help, indirect socialization was more frequent than direct instruction. Despite the older teacher's awareness that direction was needed if the traditions were to be preserved, the ideology of noninterference was too strong to overcome all the old patterns. However, as the Old Guard teacher was made more and more aware that the attitudes and behavior of the newer teachers seemed to deviate further and further from her ways, her tone became shrill, defensive, hostile. Her dominance seemed less secure and her methods of preserving dominance less adequate than in the past.

Socialization did take place at Adams. Even the "odd ball" like me learned to feel like a teacher, to behave in ways congruent with ways of the others, to respond as they did to parents, disobedient pupils, outsiders, and administrators. During my first few weeks of teaching I was constantly aware that I was play acting, wearing the mask of a teacher rather than being a teacher. I emotionally identified with "disobedient" pupils rather than with the reprimanding teacher. The manner and actions of the other teachers seemed to me artificial, contrived, and even in some situations laughable. When Mrs. Preston stood waving her finger vehemently at defiant Johnny, exhorting him to feel guilt for pushing a little girl on the playground: "What would your mother think of such behavior? Aren't you ashamed, a big boy like you? How would you like it if . . . ?" I could not believe she took herself seriously or that Johnny would not laugh in her face. But I imitated and watched myself imitating. I recall taking my class to a play during the second month of my first teaching year, sitting relaxed and watching the play and then becoming aware that other teachers were glaring at me because some of my boys were misbehaving. I had to force myself to scold them as I had seen the other teachers do, terribly afraid that my artificiality would show, and then had to force myself to stop watching the play in order to keep alert for further signs of trouble. By the end of the year I played policeman with the others without particularly noticing myself doing it. I began to forget that I was wearing a mask. I found it harder to stand aside and watch myself being a teacher. The emotions I had simulated I began to feel. Johnny's behavior in the lunch line now annoyed me inside and not just because Mrs. Gregory would glare at me if Johnny acted up.[17]

So the process did take place, even if less effectively than in "the good old days." But the failure of the ideology to fit the situation, the difficulties faced by the Old Guard in instilling values earlier ensured through supervision and training, meant a heightening of in-group tension, a sense of outrage and anger among the older teachers toward the newer teachers and the newer toward the older. And on neither side was there any clear understanding of why. The Old Guard teacher thought the new teacher insensitive and even deliberately resistant to her guidance. The new teacher found the older teacher unhelpful and nonsupportive. Each interpreted the behavior of the other as personally threatening and calculated, rather than as a product of the situation.

SUPPORT FROM ONE'S PEERS

A teacher's colleagues were important to her in other significant ways. Each teacher clung to her expectation that the informal groups would protect her as well as support her in dealing with pupils and outsiders.

Although lines of communication were very inadequate at Adams and downstairs teachers continually complained that information of importance to them was lost on the upper floor, there was a reasonably effective defensive communication system. When Mrs. Milton arrived, every teacher learned about it almost at once. The message, "the redcoats are coming," quickly spread through the school. A parent on the prowl for a teacher was quickly noticed and the teacher warned. Although Mrs. Preston voluntarily separated herself from the group that gathered after school in the teachers' room, she did not betray its members to the parent who came looking for them. She would hurry downstairs to tell the group that a parent was waiting, after offering some high-sounding excuse to the parent.

Similarly, criticism from outside or threatening gossip moved very rapidly through the teacher group, although some of it did not cross the upstairs-downstairs line. Any outside threats or attempts to split the group were met with defensive solidarity by all. The teacher took it for granted that no other teacher would betray her or undermine her in the parent-teacher conference, and when there was evidence of such betrayal each teacher was surprised as well as distressed. Strong hostility was expressed against Mrs. Wilson, an ex-teacher, because she gave away in the village many secrets that she had shared with the other teachers while on the staff.

However, the teacher expected more than that the group should merely passively defend her. She expected colleagues to help her release her own aggressions as well as to help her justify her feelings and her actions after hostile encounters with parent or administrator.[18]

Miss Tuttle, snubbed by Mr. Hanson when she requested a day off, took her anger to the teachers' room, and was soothed by support from all the other teachers, upstairs and down. They discussed his unsatisfactory character: "I've known the family for years!"; they recalled other examples of his "pettiness"; they compared the Adams School unfavorably to friendlier, more understanding neighboring schools; they offered sympathy and humor.

Mrs. Merrick, although a new teacher, showed no hesitation in expecting support from her colleagues against complaints from parents to Mrs. Crane and Mr. Hanson that she was too strict. She assumed that the other teachers would reject any appeals the parents made to them. Although the teachers at first wavered, her faith was justified. The teachers banded together in common hostility to the enemy.

Mrs. Calhoun, fresh from a difficult and ego-threatening conference with a hostile father, turned at once to her colleagues for reassurance. She expressed all her suppressed resentments and reiterated to this sympathetic audience all the arguments she had made to the father and some that she had not dared to offer.

Each teacher consciously recognized the importance of this norm of support and protection and verbally stressed it. If a colleague departed too radically from this standard she was treated with coolness and even temporarily ostracized from the group. In a more subtle way of which the teachers were less conscious, the informal colleague group bolstered the teacher's self-image. Through casual contact, discussion, and banter, the shared sentiments were reinforced. Only in the informal group could one teacher expect to talk to another who understood how frustrated she felt after a face-to-face encounter with an "interfering" and "condescending" parent. Only a colleague knew what it meant to have "wiggly" pupils on a long rainy afternoon. Only with her upstairs colleagues did the upstairs teacher find support for her belief that the knowledge she had more than compensated for the teaching skill of the primary teacher; only downstairs did the primary teacher find support for her conviction that being able to deal with the "whole child" was of crucial importance. The congruence of one teacher's attitudes and behaviors with the other teachers was increased by her contact with them. As she listened to the comments about pupils and the experiences of others, she found justification as well as standards.

Talk among the teachers tended to be light, superficial, rarely serious. One teacher listened only sporadically and half-heartedly to another; subjects changed easily; much of the talk seemed to be mutual soliloquizing. Many conversations hardly touched upon school matters; those that did rarely focused on teaching methods, educational philosophy, or the content of class material. But even these casual conversations allowed the teachers to reduce guilts and displace their aggressions.[19] No teacher believed that she could allow herself to take out on the pupil the anger and hostility that his recalcitrance produced in her. If she did take them out on him she must then assuage her guilt through some group support. As Miss Tuttle said, after a group discussion in which each teacher humorously told how cruel she had sometimes been to her pupils, "I feel much better about how I behaved. Just sitting around talking and eating makes it all seem much less awful."

Banter, jocular griping, and exaggeration dominated informal conversation,[20] rather than serious complaining. As Coser and Blau have suggested, the personal problem or the really disturbing incident tends to be saved for the clique, the pair relationship, the in-group. In the larger gathering complaints become jokes and jocular griping.[21] I found this true at Adams with certain qualifications. Seemingly close pair relationships of teachers, such as that between myself and Mrs. Crane, characterized by high interaction, frequent communication at school, and shared confidences about home affairs and pupils, did not necessarily encourage an exchange of confidences about the immediate teaching situation. Rivalry between teachers on the same or similar grade levels cut down the intimacy possible in such a pair relationship. I talked to Mrs. Garten about my hostilities and anxieties about teaching. Mrs. Crane talked to her sister, a teacher in another school. Neither Mrs. Garten nor the sister, because of physical and social distance, presented a threat, a danger of betrayal, an ability to take advantage of a confidence.

Also, the assumption that jocular griping was the norm in the large group must be qualified by recognizing that the individual teacher with a serious complaint did not always start off in a jocular manner. She might really try to bring her problems to the group, but the group never allowed this. Someone, and any teacher might make this her responsibility, always restated the complaint, exaggerated it or generalized it so that discussion inevitably became banter and was supportive rather than threatening. This happened whatever the subject of complaint, whether pupils, personal problems at home, illness, money, or alcoholism.[22] A teacher entered the teachers' room and complained that one of her pupils had taken off his shoes during class and put them in his desk. At once, another teacher responded by recalling a class she once had where the children *all* took off their shoes; someone else recalled still another equally

absurd situation. The original complainer was chaffed, joked
with, brought into the silly exchange. The complaint had been
defused.

Or a teacher, starting off with a specific complaint about a
rude pupil, herself generalized and exaggerated it to indicate that
all the pupils were constantly rude. Since no one was supposed to
believe this, all could joke about it. Angrily describing a boy who
spit tobacco juice out of the classroom window, a teacher quickly
reworded her problem into a caricature in which no one could
believe, but at which everyone could laugh. That which was
exaggerated did not have to be taken too seriously.

Even illness did not make the exchanges among the teachers
any less bantering: "What do you mean by staying out; you are
pretty lazy, aren't you?" "Did you have a nice holiday?" "I wish I
could take off time the way you do. So you were out with the boy
friend?" Verbal flippancy was sought: "Don't let it get you
down," at almost any cost.

As Rose Coser has pointed out jocular griping has important
positive and negative functions. Through expanding personal
experience into general experience, the solidarity of the group was
enhanced and individual weakness was overcome. The group's
bonds against the outside were strengthened through quick
consensus.[23] Jocular griping thus provided both support for the
teacher against outside threats and social distance from her peers
in a situation rife with anxiety about her own achievement and
status.[24] No teacher felt really safe with the other teachers. Each
one wore a self-protective mask. No teacher wished to be swept
down by the misery or failure of another. If one teacher started
to drop the mask, the others at once helped her replace it.

A teacher who disdained jocular dissembling or refused to wear
the mask of inscrutability and invulnerability baffled the other
teachers. They never quite knew how to handle Mr. Scranton's
openness and willingness to disclose himself, not only to them but
to outsiders. Freely he confessed his problems, his inabilities to
manage his class, his sense of inadequacy, leaving the other
teachers disturbed and confused.

"Mrs. Milton knows I can't handle them. Why does she come
visit me? I don't even try to tell them what to do any more."

The other teachers found it hard to believe that he was serious,
but they also began to refuse to support him against pressures

from Mr. Hanson and the parents. Anyone that candid was a threat to them as well as to himself.

Jocular griping may be dysfunctional both for the individual and for the organization.[25] Complaints minimized by banter were not corrected. The teacher who was really unhappy or anxious found no real therapy, no real answers. If she could take her serious problems to a sympathetic colleague in a pair relationship she sometimes found aid. But for a teacher who had no such outlet and no close tie to another teacher, the complaints and problems festered without alleviation. One teacher at Adams left during her first year of teaching. Unable to cope with severe discipline problems, she was hurt rather than helped by the jocular treatment accorded her requests for help or advice from the other teachers.

Most of the Adams teachers stayed on the job. But morale was low and tension high. Banter and joking concealed the problems of the teachers, but they did not eliminate them.

SPECIAL RELATIONSHIPS

The Adams teacher was related in a somewhat different way to teachers who played a special if peripheral part in her role-set because they taught her class. While she and these others shared some common expectations as teachers, there were also particular expectations in these relationships. With the departmentalization of the fifth and sixth grades the Adams upstairs teacher found herself having different relationships to colleagues from those she had ever experienced before. In the primary grades and before departmentalization, educational authority over a specific group of pupils belonged almost entirely to the homeroom teacher. The upstairs teacher at Adams now had to share this authority with others. She also had to share her authority with certain special teachers in physical education, art, and music, arrangements that required the definition of expectations on both sides.

Relationship with the physical education instructors was least complicated and least important to the classroom teacher. The physical education classes were held in the gymnasium, away from the scrutiny or observation of the homeroom teachers. So observability was kept to a minimum through physical arrangement and through the fact that the physical education instructors, concentrating most of their attention on the high school, had no contact with the classroom teachers, rarely discussed particular pupils with them, and did not even give individual grades. In their turn, the pupils rarely discussed their physical education classes with the homeroom teachers.

When a pupil or a parent did complain to the homeroom teacher of some inequity practiced in the physical education class, the teacher might express sympathy or concern, but she managed to avoid any entanglement in the issue because she was physically removed from it, and because the physical education program, in existence at Adams for a long period of time, had acquired a traditional sanctity in her eyes.

The departmental program, although shorter-lived, was the product of a request by the teachers that had been translated into action by the school administration. Therefore, it too had legitimacy in the eyes of the four teachers involved. Time periods and the movement of each group of pupils from one class to another were formally scheduled, but since there were no bells some informal juggling took place in the length of class periods. This occasionally led to hostility, against the "rate buster" who was in too much of a hurry in the morning to change classes, against the teacher who held a good class five minutes too long, and against the one who dismissed a slow class five minutes early.

Areas of teaching were specified and each teacher was too busy with her own teaching to worry a great deal about what was going on across the hall. Some hostile whispering went on, but each one attempted to mind her own business. Protective norms quickly emerged in the departmental system regulating the way in which one teacher could ask another to stress a particular topic in her class. Politeness and indirection were crucial. Even so, such requests were frequently interpreted as criticisms or attempted superiority. Mrs. Preston told me that the fifth grade was having trouble with the three forms of the word "to." She also just happened to have a mimeographed assignment sheet on that topic. Would I like to use it? I took it and used it, inwardly seething at the implication that as the English teacher I had failed to inculcate such an obviously important skill. I resolved to find a way for rapid retaliation, which was to suggest in a day or two that her pupils were not doing enough outside reading for their science reports.

The most touchy area of contact involved homework. Under the departmental system, each teacher began to assign a great deal of homework, and while the reasons given were numerous, the crucial factor seemed to be the attempt by each teacher to stress the importance of her own subject. And each teacher was critical of the homework given by the others. One reason for the touchiness in this area was that unlike the insulated classroom activity, homework was observable by the homeroom teacher. Each teacher complained about the unreasonable assignments of the other teachers while increasing her own assignments. A heavy burden of arithmetic homework one night led to an increase in English homework the next. A required report for science was almost immediately followed by a required report for social studies.

The four departmental teachers shared common goals in teaching their pupils, even when they competed with one another. Their common values were many, and they shared the in-group loyalty of occupational members against the outside. But their relationships with the specialists, Mr. Trumpet, the music teacher, and Mrs. Charles, the art teacher, were more complicated. There was little clarity about the spheres of control, little role-consensus about teaching goals, and because there was also less insulation from observability and less territorial independence, the problems of legitimacy became central.

The specialist usually invaded the teacher's classroom for the class period. He was "on my ground," "messing up my things," "getting my room in a terrible mess and then just leaving." That the only free periods a teacher had during the week should be ruined either by a need to assist with discipline or by the time she must spend in cleaning up afterward compounded her resentment about the invasion of her room. However, she verbalized this hostility not by directly criticizing Mr. Trumpet or Mrs. Charles as incompetent since they were specialists in an age of specialization. How could she be expected to judge them? Instead, she compared each one unfavorably to the teachers who had taught before them. Mr. Trumpet was criticized as inferior to Mr. Anson, who was criticized in his day as inferior to Mr. Jones. When Mr. Trumpet left, his successor was compared unfavorably to him. Mrs. Charles was criticized as inferior to Mrs. Barrett, the volunteer art teacher of an earlier day, but for the same failings once attributed to that lady — who had been criticized more easily because she had been "only" a volunteer and, therefore, not a professional specialist. Both Mr. Trumpet and Mrs. Charles were looked upon as somewhat dangerous. They gave the pupils too much freedom. They gave too little direction, allowed too much enjoyment, and encouraged the production of "ugly" pictures and awful sounds. What underlay the criticism were both a general suspicion of change, the feeling that the new must be worse than the old just because it was new, and hostility toward the interloper.

Mr. Trumpet's classroom music periods were formally scheduled and his rights to assign homework and to expect cooperation from the teachers were clearly stated by the administration. Although the teachers complained about his discipline, about the noise, about his inferior piano playing and failure to teach three part singing, they were generally willing to cooperate with him here. But they were much less willing to accept his program of instrumental instruction, which was approved but not formally scheduled by the administration. All the accumulated objections to Mr. Trumpet were funneled toward this program that allowed him to take pupils out of classes for band practice and instrument lessons. His struggle for acceptance took five hard years, subjected as he was throughout to indirect harassment that included teachers scheduling tests during his music lessons, refusing to send the pupils, asking them to return to classes during band practice, refusing to allow a pupil to play an instrument because his grades were too low, and even on various farcical occasions hiding the instruments when the pupils forgot to take them home to practice. Although the latter was verbalized as support to Mr. Trumpet: "Poor Mr. Trumpet, he works so hard and then they don't care," it was no gratification to him when he had to come and search for the mysteriously lost tuba or trombone. By the end of five years he was finally a fixture, and his program was accepted with only minor grumbling. If the administration had stood more firmly behind him from the beginning, his path would have been easier since an Adams teacher obeyed official decrees but resisted informal arrangements that suggested any diminution of her own authority, slight as the diminution might be.

Another factor that contributed to Mr. Trumpet's final success with these touchy teachers was that he was always in trouble with the high school. Attempts by Mr. Trumpet to put on a Christmas operetta with all the elementary school pupils met with strong resistance at first, but resistance melted when it was clear that the high school was trying to sabotage this unusual program: "You'd think they would give up a gym class just once so we could practice without that noise, but no, nothing we do is important." Hostility toward him as an outsider in the elementary school was reduced because the high school staff and administration treated him as an outsider in the high school. He became a colleague by default and began to be treated as an ally, even being encouraged to have coffee with the teachers after school.

The position of Mrs. Charles in the school was even more anomalous. She was the first paid art teacher ever employed at Adams, and there were no clear role-expectations defined in relation to her. Also, since she had never taught art in a public school she had no understanding of her position or of what she might expect of others. The administration set her no guidelines beyond scheduling an art period once a week for each grade, four and above.

Because there was no art room, her class was conducted within the homeroom teacher's territory. At first, Mrs. Charles insisted that she could manage the class without assistance, which was satisfactory to the homeroom teacher since it gave her some free time and also insulated Mrs. Charles from observation. Unfortunately, even from outside Mrs. Gregory could not stand the noise, confusion, and mess in her usually orderly and neat domain. After one session she refused to be deposed and then strongly imposed her views on the other Old Guard teachers who followed her example. Mr. Scranton and I, who cared much less about the noise and disorder as long as we were not responsible for it, were constrained to follow suit. The result was a constant, tension-producing confusion over who was in charge, who was responsible for discipline, for instruction, for housekeeping. In addition, the lack of congruence between the philosophy of art instruction learned in teachers' college by the Old Guard teacher and the freer and more modern methods of Mrs. Charles was enormous. The Old Guard teachers were convinced that Mrs. Charles was doing everything wrong as well as doing it noisily, messily, and with deliberate provocation. Here as elsewhere the teacher assumed that failure to keep order must be voluntary. She could have kept them in order if she had wanted to, and therefore she must not have wanted to: "I'd go in and holler at them but she likes them to be free." So rather than feeling sorry for Mrs. Charles and defining the situation as one in which the regular teacher could be of help, she saw the problem as a dispute between philosophies of teaching — hers, which was right, and Mrs. Charles's, which was obviously wrong. While the homeroom teacher could not set herself up as an art specialist, she could justify her annoyance and resistance to Mrs. Charles on the basis that she was a poor disciplinarian, a dangerous disrupter of the order so tenuously maintained in the classroom.

Mrs. Charles was criticized for what she did and for what she did not do. She was criticized for failing to claim the authority she should claim and for failing to take on the responsibility that was hers. Without clear specification of spheres of control, responsibility, and duty, with the trespass on private territory and the lack of insulation from observability, the situation would have been difficult even if she had taught art in a traditional way. The Adams teacher did not go out of her way to be slighted or misunderstood. She would have put up with a different philosophy of education if it had been clear what responsibility was hers and what belonged to Mrs. Charles.

The Adams elementary teacher held all of these colleagues, regular and special, around herself in her contacts with the other members of her role-set. Physical isolation from her peers during work hours was not allowed to become complete social isolation. She needed and sought out contact, intimacy, and response, since it was only with her peers that she could find a common frame of reference, an identity of interest. These she had to cling to despite the rivalry, competition, and hostility she might feel toward some of her colleagues and despite her confusion about defining the meaning of success, the relevance of her methods, and the degree to which she achieved her goals. The barriers between upstairs and downstairs, Old Guard and new, regular and special, primary and intermediate teachers were all important, but all of those became somewhat less important to the teacher than her unity with her colleagues when she was face to face with the important members of her role-set — the pupil, the parent, or the administration.

4   THE PUPIL
AND THE CLASS

"Pupils are the material in which teachers
are supposed to produce results."[1]

Without pupils a teacher cannot play her role; without a
teacher pupils cannot play their roles. The teacher's relationship
with the pupil constitutes the core of her role-set.[2] Her other role-
partners focus on this relationship, not on her, expecting her to
behave in ways that result in pupil learning, just as she expects
them to behave in ways that facilitate rather than hinder her
teaching. The central expectation is that she must teach (change)
the pupil, leading him toward a particular level of academic
success.

Though complementary, the relationship of teacher and pupil is
not equalitarian. Authority rests with the teacher, obedience with
the pupil. The significant components of the relationship are what
the teacher expects of the pupil and how he behaves; what she
demands and what he gives; her rights and his duties; her
sanctions and his responses.

For the role of the teacher to be justified, she and her role-
partners must believe that the change expected in the pupil will
only occur through her active intervention. Pupils are only
semisocialized; they are recalcitrant. The norms relating to
learning are not sufficiently internalized for them to carry on
without her. The teacher must thus first produce behavioral
conformity in her pupils. Only over time will the proper attitudes

emerge; meanwhile the behavior of the pupils must be directed and guided in line with legitimated values and norms. The teacher must do more than just instruct them in skills; she must ensure their appropriate behavior in pursuing and acquiring these skills.[3]

The Adams teacher had to be in charge, her authority had to be accepted, and she had to expect her commands to be obeyed. Therefore, she punished any gestures or actions by pupils that expressed overt hostility or a refusal to recognize her authority. But in her position as traffic cop she was limited to dealing with that which was observable. As Mrs. Preston said furiously to Lewis when he talked back to her on the playground, "I don't care what you think. Just don't say it and don't look it." Or Mrs. Crane, "I wish Joe wouldn't always insist on the last word. If he would just not argue I could ignore him." As long as the pupil conformed outwardly, as long as he did not defy her directly, the teacher could be in control.

The goal sought by the teacher, that the pupils learn, that they achieve a definite academic level during the course of the school year, was basic, but its accomplishment was only justified in the teacher's eyes if it was achieved through the legitimated means of docility and effort.[4] And the use of these means, too, was measured by what showed, by what the pupil did or did not do, not by what he might be thinking. Neither rudeness nor restlessness constituted appropriate behavior. The pupil must be made to work hard, do his assignments, listen attentively in class, as well as to take orders and obey the classroom rules.

If the pupil did not put forth obvious effort the teacher believed it was her fault, unless she could translate this into a failure to "care," a subjective state that she could blame on the parents although it continually perplexed her. It was easy for her to blame the family that was "different from us": "It isn't Johnny's fault with parents like that, but at least he could do his work at school whatever his home is like." But she found it harder to blame the family that shared her social position, values, and outlook. In this situation she would point to changing times: "Things were different when I was young," to a general decline in moral virtue, and to the erosion of respect for older people. So she grieved over the willingness of pupils to "turn in any sort of paper rather than work hard," and their failure to "have any sense of pride in a job well done." She was convinced that too many of the parents "would rather put obstacles in our way all the time than help us," expressing that conviction not only to her colleagues but even to some of the parents (those who understand and are "like us"). Although such complaints relieved some of her own hostility, frustration, and even guilt, they did not relieve her of the self-defined requirement that she turn out docile, striving pupils who succeeded. Even if the parents were to blame, the teacher still had to "teach all the children," however enormous the difficulties others placed in her path.

A child's failure to care might be the parent's fault. Preventing boredom, restlessness, and rudeness were the teacher's responsibility. She must not bore the pupils, since boredom led to restlessness which led to disobedience. Her training had supposedly provided her with techniques to make school work interesting and to preserve classroom order.[5] So she was forced to believe, as she did about Mrs. Charles, that any teacher who had a disorderly class must want it that way. "A teacher always has the kind of class she wants." But the training school had given the teacher no foolproof techniques to conquer indifference or to inspire motivation toward hard work and struggle. The Adams teacher did not understand children who seemed to lack such motivation nor did she willingly consider the possibility that other drives and desires could be important to her pupils.[6]

Concentrating on what showed, on what the pupil did or failed to do, nevertheless the teacher still interpreted what the external behavior signified and imputed motives. To interpret behavior was one way to control it and to manipulate the pupil. To decide how to handle a pupil, a teacher had first to interpret his behavior as docility or insubordination, as effort or laziness, as success or failure. No teacher could completely redefine what she observed in terms of what she would have liked to observe; pupils and their behavior were "out there," recalcitrant reality, not figments of her imagination. Nonetheless, as shall become clear, the system was much more in her hands than even she often realized; she could and did manipulate pupils, interpreting their behavior so as to bring it in line to some degree with her own interests. For the teacher to impute to a child a failure to care was for her also to define his lack of trying as disobedience. Consequently, she would then impose sanctions that might not have been used if the pupil's failure to try were attributed instead to a lack of intelligence, or understanding, or middle-class motivation. Similarly, the pupil who tried extremely hard might be defined by the teacher, bothered by such straining against the limits, as an overstriver, as arrogant and smug, as a bad rather than a good child. In addition, when the pupil's effort failed to produce satisfactory school work, the teacher often attempted, sometimes to no avail, to redefine his obvious effort as an absence of effort.

SEX AND SOCIAL CLASS: THEIR INFLUENCE ON THE TEACHER'S TREATMENT OF PUPILS

Not only did the teacher interpret the behavior of pupils in ways that made it possible for her to manipulate and direct them, but she also interpreted the seemingly similar behavior of different pupils in different ways. So, a teacher might judge one child who failed to do his homework as lazy, another as incapable, a third as confused, a fourth as defiant. She would define one child who continually interrupted a class discussion as rude, another as eager, another as disruptive, another as interested. In part, the way in which the teacher interpreted behavior depended on her estimate of the pupil's past behavior and personality. In part, however, it depended on his sex and social class position. The Adams teacher did respond differently to boys and to girls, and to lower-, middle-, and upper-class children.[7]

The elementary school was dominated by women. There had never been more than one male teacher on the staff at a time. The men who did teach in this school were usually considered to be less than manly by the women teachers, who themselves shared the stereotype of elementary teaching as a woman's job. The feminine emphasis resulted in the paradox that, while unanimously professing to prefer boys to girls as pupils: "They are more direct, less sneaky," all the teachers were more severe with and more demanding of the boys, kinder and more forgiving with the girls. The boys frequently complained that the teachers liked the girls better and treated them more fairly. This accurate assessment, however, conceals a significant difference in the expectations the teachers had for boys and girls. Since a "normal" boy was mischievous, noisy, messy, and troublesome, the teacher expected a "real" boy to be somewhat disobedient. A girl who misbehaved might for a long time escape being defined by the teacher as a troublemaker; she was given far more rope, but once she was so defined she was more severly condemned and more severely castigated. The Adams teacher accepted without question the simple stereotypes that obstreperous boys were normal boys, obstreperous girls were "hard" or "fast."

Ethnic and racial categorizing was not important in the teacher's differential treatment of pupils, not because all was tolerance at Adams, but because of the lack of ethnic diversity. There were three Jewish families in the town and no Negroes. The teachers usually knew the religious and ethnic backgrounds of most of their pupils, but this information was far less important in their judgments of pupils than was social class standing. Adams teachers ordinarily did not use specifically social class terms, but they knew who belonged where. The distinctions they made were residential, economic, and social. The people "above us" lived on the Hill, were snobbish, had money and spent it, were lax in manners and morals, and looked down on us without justification. But they ran the town and had to be propitiated. Those "below us," from the shacks along the River Road, were shiftless, had too many children and unstable jobs. They had crude manners and low morals. Their children were not clean, were not interested in school, were repeaters, truants, smokers at ten, the focus of pity and resentment. The majority of people in Adams were "just like us," residents of the Hollow, not too well off, but thrifty, hardworking, modest in home, income, and way of life (tradespeople, small professionals, farmers), anxious to get a little ahead, satisfied with the town and its ways, devoted to cleanliness and the American flag, and deeply suspicious of outlanders, the overeducated, the rich, and the sophisticated.

Most of the Adams teachers had taught in the school long enough to be able quickly to place pupils at the right level. The newer teachers, who in a larger town might have taken a long time to comprehend the local social structure, learned rapidly from the older teachers. The definition of a pupil's social class position was important for the teacher in interpreting his behavior and deciding how to handle it. A teacher did not anticipate that a lower-class child would be docile or would try very hard. If he did, he was looked upon with some wonder, and he received more praise for trying and for good behavior than did the middle-class child whose good behavior was taken for granted. When a lower-class child failed to do his homework, he had not showed effort; when he was rude or disobedient, he was nondocile. Such actions confirmed the teacher's anticipations, even while challenging her expectations, and each subsequent apparent infraction, even one that she might have ignored if a middle-class child had committed it, was readily defined as confirmation of her original judgment — a clear illustration of the working of the self-fulfilling prophecy.[8]

On the surface, the Adams teacher seemed to anticipate the same docility and hard work from the upper-class as she did from the middle-class child. She expressed disbelief, surprise, even dismay at signs of rudeness or laziness. Yet her surprise often masked a malicious delight. Deviant behavior from the upper-class children merely confirmed her convictions about their parents. It was obvious to her that children of such irresponsible parents could not behave well or try hard. So she was quickly ready to pounce on the first sign of deviance and then to interpret all subsequent suspicious actions as deviant.

She bent over backwards in the opposite direction for the middle-class child. She assumed as long as possible that he shared her values, that he responded to the same cues, the same appeals. So, she overlooked and even justified behavior that in another child she would have classified as disobedient or lazy. If he slipped from grace, she assumed that it would be easy to bring him back. If his actions became too persistent to be overlooked or nudged back, she responded with righteous indignation, haranguing and scolding the child, calling up all her moral force to persuade him of the error of his ways. She also assumed that the middle-class parent as her ally would accept her definition and assist her in disciplining the child: "If you don't behave, we will march to the telephone and call your father. He can take you home." This was often an effective threat. The legitimacy of her authority over the child was reinforced by her ability to make coalitions with these parents, whose authority bolstered rather than challenged her own.

However, she made no such assumption about the parents of

the lower-class child and usually tried to turn punishment and confrontation with his parents over to the administration. In the classroom, she relied on threats, a visit to the principal's office, and detentions rather than on emotional appeals to his conscience. She knew that her usual appeals were ineffective. The child who responded to moral exhortation by saying "Why should I go to school? My mother went through sixth grade and she gets along all right," or "I'm going to work on the roads like my father; why should I learn arithmetic?" was not expected by the teacher to have parents to whom she could appeal for aid. She did not feel surprised when such a child defied her: "What can you expect? He is a Wingdale; they are all like that." "I'm afraid Tom is getting like the rest of the family. It is too bad. He was a nice little boy, but after a while all of them. . . . " The teacher's sense of the futility of appeals to the parents was reinforced by remarks from hostile and frustrated lower-class parents: "I'll bash your head in if you hold my kid back." "You ain't got no right to give my kid a detention." "Everyone is against us; he is a good boy. You don't treat him right." Mr. Hanson, who was appealed to for help in dealing with Richard, a troublesome lower-class child, often seemed unaware that the other pupils sometimes misbehaved. "There are lots of others who are just as bad as Richard," protested Mrs. Crane.

"Well, I never see them in the office," he said in surprise. The ones he did not see were those middle-class children whom the teachers handled themselves or handled with the help of the parents.[9]

The impact of the teacher on the lower-class child tended to be slight, in part because she invested less emotional force in her appeals and in part because her expectations began to be lowered as she experienced continued frustration in achieving them: "If I can just get Richard to sit still this year, I will consider it an accomplishment. I don't mind if he doesn't learn anything, but I wish he would be quiet so he doesn't set a bad example for others."

The Adams teacher also turned to the administration for help in controlling the misbehavior of the upper-class child. She was apprehensive, resentful, and a bit afraid of these parents. However, the administration rarely acted for her in such situations, and she retreated to sarcasm, ridicule, and complaints to her colleagues.

DOCILITY PLUS EFFORT EQUALS SUCCESS

Although her anticipations and handling of infractions varied depending on sex and social class, the Adams teacher applied common expectations to all the pupils she taught. For them all, docility and hard work were the only legitimate means to the legitimate goal of academic success. The requirement for docility was a requirement for order. The pupil was to do as he was told, to follow orders, to be quiet in class, to listen to the teacher, to do his assignments when he was asked to do them, not to fool around, not to argue with the teacher, not to fight with his classmates. The extent to which a teacher demands total docility and a lack of individual initiative depends on the school, the administrative demands, and her background and training. Teachers vary tremendously in the degree of flexibility they encourage, the amount of disagreement, banter, or noise that they allow. They differ in the extent to which they suggest rather than order, insinuate rather than command, whisper rather than scream. Mrs. Garten once punished a little boy for being fresh because he had a peculiar look on his face, "as if he was laughing at me." Another teacher allowed a pupil to imitate her walk in front of the other children and then joined in the laughter. The philosophy shared by the teachers of the Adams School was more restrictive than that found in the more "progressive" schools, but all schools and all teachers demand some degree of docility, some recognition of their own self-respect and dignity.[10] Whether or not a pupil may argue with the teacher or wander freely in the classroom or reject a particular suggestion varies from one school and one teacher to another. Schools frequently differ not in the requirement for order but in the nature of the sanctions imposed for lack of conformity. In Adams, because docility was highly stressed, failure to conform was rather vigorously (though usually only verbally) sanctioned. The teacher attempted to instill a sense of shame and guilt and whether or not the pupil acquired these proper feelings, he did learn quickly to display the appropriate response. He learned not to shrug his shoulders, not to talk back, not to smile significantly at the wrong moment: "Wipe that smirk off your face!" He even learned to cry a little, convincingly. Rudeness was the cardinal sin at Adams where overt disobedience was infrequent. Rudeness was a deep threat to the teacher's self-image of dignity and authority and had to be stamped out immediately.[11] Mrs. Crane's tone revealed deep shock as she told me one day, "Richard almost defied me, but luckily he thought better of it." Rudeness had many guises that the teacher learned to recognize. It included a flip response, a too casual answer to a teacher, calling Mr. Scranton "Bud," or Miss Benson "Clarabelle" (even behind her back). A teacher often could signal out no particular action that she found offensive and yet condemned a child for his "attitude," which usually meant his facial expression or tone of voice.

Sometimes a teacher attempted to justify her disapproval of rudeness on the grounds that it harmed the children: "It is bad for children to defy teachers, bad for their characters." But usually the teacher worried more about the harm it did to her than about its effect on the children.

Docility then was necessary to preserve the teacher's own self-image and also because it was the most observable outcome to others of her role-performance.[12] While the insulated classroom concealed her teaching from others, it did not as effectively screen any failure to keep order. Noise could be heard through the walls and shoving, yelling, talking back, and fighting were easily observable on the playground, in the hall, or in the lunchroom.

Not only docility but effort was required of the pupil, and again the teacher was concerned primarily with outward expression, not with inner feelings. The pupil had to show that he was trying. Education was not a right but a privilege which must be earned through hard work. Knowledge acquired without effort was not as valuable as knowledge one had to struggle for. This remnant of the Puritan Ethic is an important tenet of the middle-class orientation of the American elementary school, bolstering the built-in requirement of the teacher's role that she be an active participant in the process of learning, not just a bystander. The teacher reiterated all the familiar dictums: by the sweat of one's brow; leisure encourages laziness; earned income is better than inherited; idleness is sinful; daydreaming is dangerous. She applied all of these familiar clichés to her own role as well as to that of the pupil. If the pupil could breeze through his courses with little effort, the teacher felt herself useless. Her importance in the education of the child was demonstrated when the child had to work hard and when the limits of this hard work were defined by her. The pupil had to try, but not too hard. He should not ask for extra work or suggest that particular assignments were boring. To do so was to be called "fresh" and be given extra homework as punishment. The pupil was never to question the teacher's knowledge, the relevance of her homework assignments, or to try to use methods other than those defined as acceptable by the teacher. Such extensions of effort (overstriving) constituted a lack of docility as threatening as the rude answer or the noisy classroom.

It seems clear that with this emphasis on effort the teacher did not automatically value very high intelligence or think it was sufficient for success. Similarly she rarely explained a pupil's failure on the grounds that he was stupid. Only occasionally did the Adams teacher suggest that a child might be unteachable in the public school: "All I asked him to do was copy from the board. Anyone can copy from the board." Rather than stressing the stupidity of the academic failures, she commented with wonder on their practical intelligence: "Richard can't do anything in class but you should see that scheme he worked out to make money by renting his bike!" Academic failure was more often blamed on willful disobedience than on inability. If the pupil was teachable, and most Adams children had high enough IQ scores to be considered teachable, then the teacher had to believe she could teach him. Since she was responsible for achievement, she could not use stupidity as an excuse for a child's failure nor could she attribute academic success to high intelligence, an innate quality for which she could take no credit.[13]

She responded to the more intelligent child with ambivalence. A pupil who never had to try, never had to listen, never had to do the exercises in the book and yet learned seemed to achieve regardless of the teacher. This diminished her accomplishment that had to be linked to the achieved results. The more closely she could make a connection between her effort and his achievement the easier it was for her to be rewarded for success, but also the easier it was to blame her for failure (to make her a scapegoat).

A class of bright children might be more stimulating to teach, but it was also more threatening. A teacher's frequent response was fatigue and hostility rather than pleasure: "Tim confused the whole class by asking some stupid question about what if the moon were bigger than the earth, then what would happen to the solar system. I soon put him in his place." "All they do is ask me silly questions about unimportant details rather than try to learn what is in the book. They ask what color Alexander's horse was and that sort of thing." The teacher's tension after such sessions was increased by her own feelings of inadequacy and the possible damage to her own dignity if the pupil should ask her something she did not know or challenge some statement she made.[14]

Just as the Adams teacher did not directly attack the specialist, so she did not criticize the intelligent child for his intelligence. Instead she criticized him for being cold, arrogant, lazy, and insensitive to others: "Intelligence isn't the only important quality. One has to get along with others in this world." She reduced the importance of intelligence by indicating more in sorrow than in anger that it was of no value unless it was accompanied by other more adaptable and conformist personal qualities: "It is all very well for John to be quick, but if he goes through life picking on others and being mean to the other children, it will be no good to him. He will have a hard time in the world, I'm afraid."

The Adams teacher then was not only director of learning and traffic cop but also "gatekeeper." It was she who proclaimed the equation to the pupils: through docility and striving you will succeed academically, and without them you will fail. For her to succeed as teacher she had to promote most of the pupils, had to see that they completed the work of the year. In any school, a teacher has some autonomy in this gatekeeper role, some opportunity to define success as well as to measure it. It is she who is responsible for filtering up to her superiors or out to the parents her estimate of the achievement of the pupil. The nature of the class (slow learners or fast) and the nature of the school (ghetto or suburban) may influence the level of success expected, but however it is defined the goal is the same and enough children achieve it to validate the teacher's expectations. In no school does the teacher lack all control over success, nor is there any school in which her autonomy and power are so complete that she can assure that all pupils will fit the simple equation where docility and striving produce success, nondocility and nonstriving produce failure.

The Adams teacher had a great deal of autonomy and freedom from external control. But her autonomy tended to lead her to traditionalism rather than to innovation. She used her autonomy to manipulate the placement and promotion of pupils in consistent and predictable ways.

To the degree that her success as a teacher was measured by the academic success of the pupils, the Adams teacher could be considered successful. Most of the pupils in this school learned enough to be promoted to the next grade. Most of the pupils also displayed enough docility and striving to fit the equation of means and end that she considered legitimate. The teacher at Adams did not find herself faced with the problems of control and discipline so prevalent in many American urban schools. She rarely encountered real defiance. Most pupils did what they were told with at least an external show of willingness. Although the teachers talked to one another as if rudeness and freshness were great problems, in practice this was not true. The expectation for docility was fairly realistic, being usually met with appropriate behavior.

Her expectations for visible hard work were less often clearly fulfilled. It was, of course, much harder for the teacher to measure effort. She had to infer hard work from the behavior she could observe. Frequently, then, she used success or failure as presumptive indicators of effort or laziness. A pupil with low academic marks on the report card almost always received a low mark for effort. The teacher assumed, in line with her expectations, that failure to work led to academic failure. Although she tried also to assert a similar connection between conduct and success, she far less consistently marked conduct specifically in relation to achievement, since conduct was clearly a more independent variable. A pupil who failed academically but who was obviously quiet and well behaved in class usually received a high mark in conduct. In fact, he was often more rewarded by the teacher than the academically successful pupil who caused her trouble.

Since most pupils at least minimally succeeded, since conduct on the whole was reasonably satisfactory, and since the teacher usually was able to tie effort to achievement, the equation between the legitimate means and the defined goal was for the most part demonstrated at Adams. However, despite the teacher's ability to manipulate and her need to demonstrate the validity of this equation, there were always exceptions and deviant cases.

My observation of the other intermediate teachers and my own experiences during my teaching years at Adams can be most usefully summed up in Figure 1. The categories of pupils that the teachers recognized and responded to are real, although the

names are my invention. At least a few pupils in any class were
to be found in each of the categories, and the Adams teacher not
only attempted to explain the reasons for this deviation from her
expectations, but also tried to move pupils from the undesirable
categories into the desirable ones.[15]

	Success		Failure	
	Effort	Absence of Effort	Effort	Absence of Effort
Docility	Winners	Aristocrats	Ritualists	Wallflowers
Lack of Docility	Troublemakers (Innovators)	Magicians	Soreheads	Losers (Rebels)

1. Typology of Pupils as Classified by Teachers

The Winners succeeded legitimately through docility and hard
work. For the other academically successful pupils, the
Aristocrats were docile but lazy, the Troublemakers disobedient
but hardworking, the Magicians neither obedient nor
hardworking. For those who failed to achieve academic success,
the Losers failed legitimately, demonstrating neither obedience
nor hard work, the Ritualists failed despite conformity to both
means, obedience and hard work, the Wallflowers were docile
nonstrivers, and the Soreheads were nondocile strivers. Only the
Winners completely met the teacher's expectations. To some
degree the success of Aristocrats, Troublemakers, and Magicians
was unearned. The failure of Loser, Sorehead, and Wallflower
was deserved, but the teacher's picture of her own role was sorely
threatened by the failure of the Ritualist, the pupil who used the
requisite means but still missed the goal.

Winners were predominant at Adams despite the teacher's
continual complaints. The Adams teacher also labeled more

pupils as Aristocrats than as either Troublemakers or Magicians. Since it was important for the teacher to treat all failures as total, she classified more pupils as Losers than as Wallflowers, more as Wallflowers than as Soreheads or as Ritualists. The small number of pupils she classified as Soreheads and Ritualists reflected again the weight of the ideology: effort unrewarded by success soon became lack of effort. It is also clear that among the unsuccessful lazy pupils, more girls were Wallflowers, more boys, Losers.

1. *Winners:* The Winners cooperated, did their work carefully, showed effort and a desire to learn. They did well on tests, completed their homework, were quiet when it was time to be quiet, or helpful when it was important to be helpful. However, they were not perfect. Occasional naughtiness, mischievousness, messiness, and laziness were anticipated and made the teacher's role important. It was her job to encourage the pupil, and she had to expend effort to keep him docile, hardworking, and successful. A very bright child could be accepted and even rewarded by the teacher as long as he showed her that he accepted her definition of classroom learning and was cooperative and obedient. It was important that success not go to his head making him casual, indifferent, or arrogant. The bright girl frequently played this role quite effectively, although the teacher was aware that sometimes even the bright girl became an Aristocrat, still sweetly obedient but terribly lazy. The teacher was more frightened of the very intelligent boy who, just by his existence, seemed to challenge her definitions, to be a Troublemaker rather than a Winner.

2. *Aristocrats:* These successful pupils were well behaved and cooperative in the classroom, but did not seem to work hard. Although the teacher often found them smug, she did not display overt hostility toward them, since they were obedient and verbally noncritical. However, she took every opportunity to show them that the failure to work would have adverse results in the future. She could not prevent such pupils from passing, but she could say in sorrow rather than in anger, "Sally, you would have done so much better if you had spent a little more time on your paper."

The interpretation of a failure to work varies from teacher to teacher, but also from one school to another. If a particular teacher considers any failure to work to be a challenge to her and a denial of her authority, a nonstriver is also considered nondocile, and the teacher will see no Aristocrats in her class, only Troublemakers and Magicians. In a school in which striving is defined as unlimitable, in which the more the pupil challenges the more he is rewarded, success will also be unlimitable. In such a school there would be no Aristocrats or Magicians, since no lazy pupil would be considered successful. The only successful pupils, besides the Winners, would be Troublemakers, those who interfered with the smooth running of a class through noise, mischief, or disobedience. However, at Adams, with its definitions of limited, measurable academic success, the teacher did have to cope with pupils she defined as Aristocrats or as Magicians. She handled these pupils either by trying to prevent their academic success, or if this was not possible, by denigrating it as less significant in the long run than their personality failings.

3. *Troublemakers:* At Adams there were two kinds of Troublemakers. The first were those pupils who were disobedient in class or on the playground. The second, the Innovators, were those whose nondocility showed up in their handling of the academic classroom requirements. The teacher resented and belittled the child who was "too smart for his own good," because he learned things too easily, seemed to know more than she did, questioned her, challenged her, asked for more work, or claimed the work was boring. Since at Adams to question the teacher was to be rude, the Innovator was a Troublemaker. He tried, but too hard and in the wrong ways. He challenged the orderly acquisition of knowledge by the average pupil, and he challenged the teacher's authority to define what he should learn. The Adams teacher resented the successful Innovator far more than she resented the other Troublemakers. After all, a boy who flew paper airplanes around the room during library period was a nuisance and must be strongly reprimanded, but if he worked hard and learned, he was not challenging her superior knowledge or her gatekeeper role. He did not endanger her self-image nearly as much as the pupil who implied that she did not have the qualifications to teach him. Most Adams teachers shared the sentiments of Mrs. Gregory who said, "I would rather have average pupils in my class any day than the bright ones." Complaints about disobedience and laziness were more common among the intermediate than among the primary teachers at Adams. Because of the limitations on striving, some of the brighter children may have become bored and frustrated in the

early grades, turning them by fourth or fifth grade from easy Winners into Troublemakers, Innovators, and a few into Magicians.

4. *Magicians:* Few pupils were placed in this category in the intermediate grades. Some Winners did become Magicians, but the teacher did her best to propel such pupils into a failure category rather than admit her lack of control over the legitimate avenues to success. It was hard for nondocile nonstrivers, however brilliant, to succeed for very long.

5. *Ritualists:* Just as there were few Magicians, given the value system, so the teacher defined few as Ritualists in the Adams School. Ritualists in the primary grades usually became Soreheads, Wallflowers, or Losers in the upper grades. However, sometimes an intermediate teacher was confronted with a pupil who had been a Winner in the primary grades, who had succeeded as long as the academic requirements were oral and concrete, rather than abstract and written, but who no longer could succeed. Such a pupil became a Ritualist, still good, still hardworking, but failing to achieve. In time, such failure would begin to undermine the docility and the hard work.[16] How long can unrewarded conformity persist?

Since a Ritualist, like a Magician, challenged the teacher's expressed expectation that cooperation and hard work must be rewarded by success and their absence by failure, she assumed that, appearances to the contrary notwithstanding, the pupil must not have really tried. So she could then label the seeming Ritualist as a Wallflower, a docile but nonstriving failure. This proved that he was lazy and so undeserving of success. When she was confronted by a genuine Ritualist, a pupil who obviously tried, who obviously cooperated but still failed, she was disturbed. In such a situation the Adams teacher might timidly ask whether her standards, values, and goals might be inapplicable to some children. In a school oriented as Adams was to grade achievement, however, she herself was in no position, even if she wanted to, to change the dominant ideology. All she could do was to pass on to the next grade the docile pupil who tried and failed, with the only partially satisfying justification that for him to repeat a grade would do him no particular good, and anyway, the "chairs in my classroom are too small for him." She was much more likely to promote such a child than one who did not try.

6. *Wallflowers:* The Adams teacher did classify some pupils as Wallflowers. Although these pupils did not try, they also did not cause her trouble. They represented a most useful kind of deviant, a clear illustration to the other children of what happened if one did not try hard. There had to be Wallflowers, either present or recollected, for the teacher to point to when she exhorted her pupils to effort.[17]

7. *Soreheads:* The Soreheads were a thorn in the teacher's side. They did have didactic use, since lack of docility did seem to produce academic failure, but because they worked hard they unfortunately demonstrated that hard work did not necessarily lead to success. A teacher's resentment of the Innovator, and her attempts to trip him up and to catch him out, might result in his becoming a Sorehead rather than a Winner or a Loser, either of which would have been preferable to her.

8. *Losers:* Presumably, an Adams teacher should have expected that any pupil not a Winner would be a Loser as a salutary example to other pupils, a valuable "I told you so" category. As a bad example, the Loser was important, but, because of his disruptive influence on other pupils, she preferred to have Wallflowers than Losers in her class.

Some Losers were classifiable as Rebels. They differed from the other Losers in that they denied the legitimacy of the system, rather than failed within it while accepting it.[18] For a teacher to consider that some pupils were challenging the system and thus were Rebels was to interpret their behavior, verbal and nonverbal, as threatening. Often, she made this judgment on the basis of the social class position of the child. A middle-class child who did not try or cooperate and did not succeed was considered by the Adams teacher to be misguided and probably savable if the parents would cooperate with her. However, the lower-class child who did the same was often defined by her as threatening the legitimacy of her position and, therefore, fit only for expulsion. The upper-class child was similarly judged as a threat, but the impetus for removing him from the school more often came from the parent than from the teacher.

The teachers at Adams, even without the use of these labels, obviously classified pupils into these eight categories. However, they did not necessarily classify particular pupils in the same way, and pupils considered to be in one category at one time might be reclassified at another, either as a result of a change in their behavior or as a result of a redefinition of the behavior by the teacher. The teacher did have some autonomy and control over the pupil and what happened to him. When a teacher considered a pupil to be an Aristocrat or a Magician she challenged the accuracy of his exceptionally high achievement test scores. She did the same with the low scores of the pupil she defined as Winner or Ritualist. She attempted then to prevent these scores from being used to represent the "real" achievement of the pupil. Since she had a significant voice in determining pupil promotion or retention and even more authority in deciding whether a pupil should be placed in the fast or slow division of a grade, her definition of his category was as important as were his objective test scores. As a result, she was sometimes able to push a pupil who had threatened her own definitions by being classifiable only as an unacceptable success, Aristocrat, Troublemaker or Magician, into becoming a Loser. The attempts by Mrs. Preston to move Stan, an intelligent lower-class boy, from success to failure by refusing him promotion to the seventh grade despite his high test scores because he never did his assigned work and was disruptive in class did turn him from a Magician into a Loser. As soon as Stan was sixteen he dropped out, never to go through high school. His failure was in part a function of his social class position.

However, the teacher was not always successful in such attempts. The middle- and upper-class pupils were better able to withstand a teacher's pressure than the lower-class pupils. So, Walter, son of a local doctor, another Magician, remained a Magician, defiant of authority (but not to the extent of getting himself expelled), lazy, but academically successful. He added insult to injury by making both aspects of his defiance obvious, and the teachers sputtered and complained about him. Mrs. Crane burst forth, "I asked if he would like to take over and run the class, and that didn't even faze him. He is impossible!" His usual unrepentant academic success was a distressing sign to the teachers of their own failed expectations. But ultimately, the teachers could believe that they had won even with Walter. He left the public school in ninth grade for a private school. This decision pleased everyone: the teachers believing that he was impossible to handle; the family believing that the school did not provide enough challenge.

The outcomes for Stan and for Walter show the importance of

social class position. Stan, a boy with no encouragement from home toward education and with no protection against arbitrary teacher action, became a Loser and quit school. Walter, also a nonconformist, remained a success as long as he was in school, protected by his family and his class position.

I suggested above that the different Adams teachers did not always classify pupils in the same ways. However, the differences were much less significant than I ever expected when I started teaching. One September Mrs. Crane and I smugly agreed that we found Timmy no problem even though he had caused Mrs. Gregory interminable headaches the year before. However, by October she and I had to admit that he was as difficult as Mrs. Gregory had claimed, sneaky, lazy, disruptive, an obvious Troublemaker.

When Mrs. Gregory told me that Kathy was nervous and erratic, I was convinced that Kathy was just frightened by Mrs. Gregory. However, in time I too began to find Kathy nervous and erratic.

A pupil known as a Troublemaker in kindergarten or first grade carried his reputation through the grades. The complex process of interaction among the elements of personality, treatment by teachers and peers, and role-expectations assured that once he had been identified as nonconformist his reputation preceded him, and his subsequent behavior was interpreted as nonconformist. Once labeled, a child might become alienated from school and increase the antisocial behavior that first led to his becoming so labeled. A child considered in first grade to be sloppy, lazy, careless, or rude was usually found to be even sloppier, lazier, more careless, or ruder in the fifth grade. It was rare for a sixth grade teacher to have a "problem child" who had not already been so identified by previous teachers. Conversely, it was rare for a child to be "discovered" by a teacher. Every teacher liked to believe that she had discovered or waked up some child. Usually, she found that the child had been waked up each year and had then gone back to sleep. Occasionally, of course, an individual teacher did have a real influence on a pupil and was able to make contact with him in ways no other teacher had. Personal likes and antipathies did make a difference. If a teacher formed a strong personal attachment to a pupil defined by the others as "bad," she could through indulging him and overlooking his disruptive behavior significantly change him.

However, such an attachment often affected her classroom control and produced visible resentment among the other teachers: "All she does is baby him and he is no better." "I wouldn't put up with such rudeness. Why doesn't she treat him like the others? It is disgusting."

I found in the departmental arrangement on the upper floor only small personal variation among the four teachers in their estimations of pupils. Personal likes and dislikes influenced the teacher's ability to manage a pupil in the classroom, but not usually her ability to encourage him to learn. All four teachers found Bob a nonlearner and a troublemaker. Mr. Scranton who actively disliked Bob was unable to control him in class. The other three could manage him even though they could not teach him. Similarly with Richard, no teacher in the school was ever able to manage him until Mrs. Crane was able to like him. He behaved for her and for no one else. As Mrs. Cornhouse had said when Richard was in her class, "Every day I come in resolved to like Richard and every day I fail." With none of these teachers, however, did Richard or Bob progress academically.

The absence of significant differences among the Adams teachers in evaluating and responding to the pupils can in part be explained by the common norms inculcated during their training. The Old Guard teachers agreed with one another more often than they agreed with the new teachers. The traditional view that the social class background of the teacher is the crucial determinant of her attitudes toward and treatment of the pupils, that she, being middle-class in origin and upwardly mobile,[19] inevitably discriminates against the lower- or working-class children,[20] is far too incomplete to explain the consistency of outlook among all of these teachers, even those few with different social backgrounds. The demands of the teacher's role at the Adams School did have an independent importance in influencing her behavior. The role was defined within a middle-class context. Whatever her own background and upbringing the teacher had to adopt in action the framework of values acceptable in this school if she was to work in it. Those teachers who remained in the profession found themselves at least minimally constrained by these values.[21] What these teachers required of pupils — docility and striving, crowned by academic success — have helped to produce the results noted by earlier students of American education.[22] Public school education in Adams as elsewhere was integrated willy-nilly with the class structure, not only because the teachers were middle-class themselves but also because the roles and structures were a product of the class system. Troublemakers and Aristocrats were encouraged to become Magicians, who were in turn pushed into becoming Losers (leaving school voluntarily or through pressure). Who were left by high school? Among the successful pupils, mostly Winners; fewer unsuccessful pupils, and of these, more Wallflowers than Soreheads or Losers.

LESS CRUCIAL OR CONSISTENT EXPECTATIONS

For the teacher to succeed as a teacher, she believed that these expectations for the pupils were necessary. She had other less central expectations that were more dependent on the situations she faced and on her own social background (such as those relating to sex and social class or ethnic group).

The intermediate teachers shared some expectations for pupils that separated them from the primary teachers. Old Guard values were revealed through these expectations as well as the desire of the teachers to mark clearly the boundary between teaching primary and intermediate children. Whatever their backgrounds, pupils should be mannerly, clean, and neat: "He doesn't even wear an undershirt." "I didn't expect my job would mean I had to teach them not to drink their soup." "She could at least comb her hair." The annoyance sometimes seemed quite genuine; in other instances it seemed to reflect a displacement from the annoyance that a pupil was too fresh, or too clever, or was "looking down on me." Ken frightened the teachers with his intellectual superiority, but they could neutralize the threat by noting how sloppy, badly dressed, and unkempt he always was.

There were desirable personality characteristics implicit in being a "good" pupil that mattered beyond sheer school performance. Children should at all times be good tempered, cheerful and agreeable: "One thing you can say for John is that he is always good natured, always has a smile, even if he hasn't much upstairs." Girls should be ladylike, which meant being modest in action, restrained in speech, and not tomboyish or suggestive. No child, boy or girl, should be too different from the others either in opinions or in talents. Lew was continually reprimanded for drawing cartoons in library period instead of reading his library book. For a pupil to be an exceptional cartoonist, while interesting, was also somewhat threatening to the teacher. It escaped from the teacher-defined role: "He should put some of his effort into his school work." The Good Citizenship Award never went to a pupil who was particularly distinctive in any respect, intellectually or artistically: "He will be rewarded in society anyway, while June who is so helpful and normal never will get anything for it." So the Good Citizen was the child who was helpful, docile, and usually a girl.

The intermediate teachers talked a lot about "maturity." They talked to one another and to their pupils as if they really believed that to become a fourth or fifth grader meant to acquire a sense of responsibility and to respond "maturely" to a teacher's requests. These expectations of the teacher were continually frustrated and seemed unrelated to her anticipations. Maybe it was only through reiterating her disappointments here that she could show how necessary she still was as traffic cop, how necessary was her unremitting watchfulness. Finding the pupils continually "silly," "immature," "unreliable," or "sneaky," anticipating that they would fool around in line, would talk if she left the room, would steal drinks or make noise when they went to the bathroom, she had to remain continually alert, allowing very little opportunity for the pupils to escape her watchful eye. Only the obviously docile ones could stay upstairs at recess time to work on a play production; only the obviously docile ones could go to the library in small groups by themselves. Mrs. Gregory and Mrs. Crane carried on periodic campaigns in the lunch room, unable to eat themselves, in their unremitting endeavor to catch the pupil who hid his food under his napkin, who put carrots in his pocket, who took two oranges, or who bought ice cream without finishing his beans. As Mrs. Gregory told me very early, "You have to keep on guard. They will try to get away with anything they can."

These same teachers, with all their talk about the value of maturity, did not intend this word to imply sexual maturity or emerging adolescence to which they responded with exaggerated horror or amused prurience. Any interest in the opposite sex, as expressed by the pupils through writing notes, rough playground games, or whispering, came in for extensive disapproval and often sly comment. Maturity seemed to be valued as it was useful for teaching these pupils, not in itself.

EXPECTATIONS HELD BY THE PUPILS

The teacher's authority over her pupils at Adams was ambiguous. Her subordinates did not choose her as their leader; they were involuntary participants in the system, and she had the tools with which to exert her dominance over them despite their wishes. So, to that extent, their attitudes of hostility or antagonism did not matter. However, she also knew that much of her effectiveness as a teacher involved persuasion, that what she was attempting to do, even against resistance, was to instill knowledge and values, and that this could not be done entirely through force, threats of force, or the sanctity of her position.[23] Also, she felt insecure about her own status in the eyes of her superiors and the world outside. Hostility hurt her; criticism undermined her; dislike wounded her. The teacher continually tried to prevent not only the expression of negative feelings by the pupils but also any awareness in herself that such feelings could be held. Even certain seemingly innocuous questions from pupils were threats to the legitimacy of the system and her place in it. Certain things should not be expressed. The slow learner who asked innocently, "If I work, what difference will it make?" could not be answered truthfully. So he should not have asked the question, and rather than being answered he learned that to question was to be rude or fresh.[24]

Thus the teacher kept herself in the dark, seeming to be really surprised and shocked by any evidence of hostility and yet continually fearing this hostility.[25] And pupils early learned to conceal their feelings and to give the teacher what she wanted. They learned to write down the acceptable platitudes in reminders assigned for disobedience: "To be good in school you should keep your mouth closed and listen to the teacher and watch your book and be sure to listen to directions and not talk in class and you should sit up straight and not make paper airplanes or fool or talk with the person who sits next to you. . . . "

So the pupil hid his hostility, and the teacher hid from herself, if possible, any awareness of it. Mrs. Merrick quoted in dismay the second grader who said to her, "I hate this rotten work, I hate you," but she quickly consoled herself with "Of course he didn't mean it. He was just angry."

While the pupils learned to hide hostility, they also learned to manipulate the teacher by playing on her need for liking and approval. In this way, they were able to achieve some of their expectations of her, despite their formally subordinate position.[26] Just as the teachers socialized their colleagues through indirection, so a pupil manipulated the teachers indirectly, subtly pointing out the kindness of one teacher, the privileges showered on one class, in order to bargain with a less receptive teacher for similar privileges.[27] These manipulations were indirect since a direct challenge usually backfired,[28] reinforcing the teachers' unity against the threatening pupil. Sometimes, however, the maneuver that failed to achieve its immediate objective had later success. Although Bill was strongly reprimanded for telling Mr. Scranton that the class should be allowed to work together in study period because "Mrs. Preston lets us do that," a week later Mr. Scranton let his boys work together in study period.

The Adams teacher did take pupil expectations into account (positively and negatively) more than she probably realized herself during the year: "I'm not going to show film strips any more. They don't even look at the screen." "The children get so restless when we do poetry. I guess I will have to stop having it." "I can't play games with them all year." "I will just let Five B read the rest of the year since they hate written work so."

Even Mrs. Gregory, concerned as she was with her own dignity and her dominance over that recalcitrant class which she had to tame, recognized that the pupils had expectations of her and that some of these expectations were legitimate. The barriers to free communication between teacher and pupil meant that no teacher really knew all the expectations held by the pupils, and in fact she might misinterpret certain gestures and behaviors as signifying demands other than those intended. But these expectations, accurately or inaccurately understood, did compose a significant aspect of the teacher's role-set. She responded to them in different ways, accepting some, rejecting some, defining others in her own terms.[29]

One expectation recognized by the teacher as legitimate, in part because she helped to inculcate it to make her own job easier, was for order in the classroom. Many teachers insisted that this demand was part of the child's nature, not just a product of habit and school experience: "Children are natural conservatives." This was why progressive schools and "newfangled" methods in education that encouraged spontaneity and disorder could never work. I discovered for myself the strength of this expectation my first year at Adams. Believing that the pupils would prefer variety, I adopted a flexible, changing schedule. As a result I found myself continually battling restlessness, confusion, and overt hostility from my pupils.

The order and predictability sought in the classroom were also demanded from the teacher. While the other teachers said Mr. Scranton was "too nice" to the pupils, the pupils accused him of being "mean." I too was a mean teacher, while Mrs. Crane and Mrs. Preston, far more authoritarian and much less permissive than I, were considered nice. With the more rigid teachers the pupils knew what the limits were. The teacher's behavior was predictable. Mr. Scranton and I confused the pupils through lack of assurance and vacillation, thus encouraging them to challenge the rules and our attempts to enforce them. My duty period on the playground was a continual confrontation, with arguments and disputes as to what was allowed and what forbidden. Mrs. Crane, Mrs. Gregory, and Mrs. Preston rarely encountered this type of attempted manipulation. Simply enough, with me it often worked; with them it not only failed to work, it often backfired against the pupils.

Another central expectation was for fairness, usually verbalized as a demand for complete fairness. That the pupils might have had more realistic expectations underneath this absolute, idealistic demand, is possible, but it was the idealistic that they presented. The rules had to be fair, the teachers had to live up to the rules, and everyone should be treated equally, regardless of extenuating circumstances. Pupils, at least through the sixth grade, rarely accepted a teacher's argument that the slower learner should have easier work, that the handicapped child should be excused from physical education.[30]

Almost any action of a teacher could be and would be labeled unfair by some of the pupils. It was unfair to give too much homework, to give homework over the weekend, to forbid a pupil to ask another teacher for help, to fail to help a pupil, to make the sixth graders do fifth grade work, to complain about a pupil to another teacher, to assign work not in the textbook, to treat pupils as babies.

The pupils who most often complained about unfairness were those who were less privileged, less successful, and often less well behaved. Since the teacher saw these pupils as unfair to her, they no doubt were more insecure in the classroom and less likely to anticipate fairness. Any negative gesture toward them was an anticipated deprivation.[31] If I stared at Walter in class with no particular intent, he would soon remark truculently, "What did I do? I didn't do nothing."

For these pupils requisite fairness had almost unlimited scope. It was unfair of the art teacher to be late to art class. It was unfair to make the boys follow the girls to lunch. It was unfair to have school at all on hot days. The playground rules were unfair: "We can't do anything outdoors." Even concern for a pupil's health was suspect: "She had no right to tell me to go to the doctor." And it was particularly unfair to be reprimanded or punished, since someone else had done something worse.

However unfair these pupils considered the rules, they were the first to demand that the teacher adhere strictly to the rules when it was to their advantage. "You aren't allowed to hit me," said Walter, forestalling what he saw as an imminent attack from an angered teacher. Richard responded to Mr. Scranton's threat to keep him after school and thus force him to walk home, "You have no right to."

Accusations of unfairness were less inhibited than other negative responses to teachers, because the teachers themselves recognized the legitimacy of the claim. No teacher wished to be considered unfair. But her definition of fairness and her view of pupils' rights often conflicted with theirs. While each child insisted that he had the "right" to use the bathroom at will, the upstairs teacher often rejected this demand since pupils took advantage of this "privilege" and sneaked drinks of water while out of the classroom. A drink of water was not a pupil's right. However, the teacher was uncertain about how to handle the request to go to the lavatory since it was so hard to determine true need and occasional accidents encouraged her to be cautious.

The right to get a drink of water was considered legitimate by a teacher only if the pupil had hiccoughs or had just lost a tooth. Otherwise drinks were a privilege granted only as long as no pupil assumed it as a right. However, if one teacher let her class have drinks, then the other classes claimed this as their right and in this situation most teachers capitulated. The rights of a class were often perceived as different from the rights of an individual pupil.

Many of the girls in the Adams School claimed the right to go to the nurse at any time. The teachers varied in their recognition of the justice of this claim, and its corollary, the right to take a friend. Mr. Scranton, in particular, found it difficult to refuse, since he found it embarrassing to ask why. However, Mrs. Gregory made no bones about saying that she refused this privilege most of the time: "They just want to get out of work. Nothing wrong that I can see with them."

The teacher and the pupils disagreed rather fundamentally on what was meant by "reasonable help" which both considered a legitimate pupil right. This disagreement did not seem to arise with the primary teachers where the standards of "reasonable help" seemed to be consistent. But the intermediate teacher believed that the pupils were too dependent and asked for more help than she needed to give them. She stressed individual responsibility, self-help, standing on one's own feet in response to the pupil's, "Teachers are supposed to help you; that is what they are for." This expectation was a product of what the teacher did rather than of what she said, since despite her protests and complaints she usually gave help when asked. Not to help was in some way not to be teaching, even though she believed that too much help prevented independence. Mrs. Gregory complained, "They don't want to learn. They want you to do all the work for them and don't want to do anything for themselves." The ambivalence in the teacher's response illustrates her contradictory self-expectations. Teaching must be active, but the demands on her time were enormous. She had to have an influence, but she also had to move the child toward maturity and independence. Confused, she helped and then complained. Her confusion and her resentment were increased when another teacher gave help to a child whom she had refused.

The pupils' expectation that a teacher not punish a class for the actions of one or a few[32] was rejected by most teachers on pragmatic grounds. When I kept a class in from recess because some were misbehaving, I was told by one of my aggrieved ·pupils, "We didn't do it. It isn't fair to those of us who didn't do it." Naturally, my justification was primarily expedient. How was I to find the culprit in any other way? Mrs. Merrick once asked the other teachers how to apprehend the child who spilled ink on the back counter and was told to punish the whole class: "Then you will find out." And because of a lack of class solidarity in the second grade she did find out.

Despite the manipulation of teachers by pupils, the teachers' competition for affection, and the pupil's jealousy of his individual rights, the pupil rarely anticipated or expected that one teacher would protect or support him against the hostility or commands of another teacher. Such an expectation was only voiced in situations of dire provocation. Richard, with whom I constantly disputed when he was in my homeroom, only once turned to me for support against another teacher. On this occasion Mrs. Wilson had struck him in the face for a minor rule infraction, and he came to me in tears. Although I gave him comfort and agreed with him that it was unfair and wrong, I took no action against Mrs. Wilson. More important than fairness to the pupils was the solidarity of the teacher group, and a teacher hesitated to challenge the authority of another teacher over the pupils. A teacher who showed partiality for a pupil or for a particular class was resented by the other teachers, since this partiality meant that the pupils had a way to manipulate a teacher and break down group solidarity. As Mrs. Crane said resentfully one day, "There is no point in my asking Mrs. Preston to bawl that class out; she will just tell them how mean I am."

THE TEACHER AND THE CLASS

Although one pupil usually failed to weaken significantly the united front of the teachers, despite sometimes successful manipulation, the class was much more effective in breaking down teacher solidarity. Any one pupil was part of the out-group, the *they* for the teacher, and each teacher expected other teachers to support her in dealing with the pupil, as in dealing with parents or administrators.[33] But a teacher related to her class in a more complex way. A class had power,[34] not a great deal, but more than the pupils at Adams either realized or attempted to wield.

As Waller has pointed out, "The fundamental problem of school discipline may be stated as the struggle of students and teachers to establish their own definitions of situations in the life of the school. . . ."[35] The kindergarten teacher had one of the hardest jobs in the school.[36] She had to mold the children, unfamiliar with what was expected of them, from an unorganized mass into some kind of group that could be taught. Mrs. Garten saw kindergarten as the place to familiarize the children with routine and regularity to prepare them for first grade: "That's why we need kindergarten — to save the first grade teacher all that stuff." At Adams, the group constituted in kindergarten remained almost unchanged throughout the elementary years. Working and playing together 180 days each year they developed a sense of group identity and consistent patterns of behavior and expectation. Long before junior high school, they thought of themselves as a group and were so considered by each teacher.[37] The teacher talked to her class as to an individual and praised it or blamed it as she did the individual pupil: "You should set a good example to the rest of the building. Now you are grade five, you know." And in loving approval: "If you are not careful, you will get to be the best class on the floor."

Just as the teacher encouraged competition among the pupils in her room to spur them on to hard work and greater achievement, so she pitted one class against another in spelling bees and geography quizzes. Rainy day recess periods were occupied with contests and games among the upstairs classes, instigated by the teachers.

Over time each group acquired its own label. There were "good" classes (hardworking and eager) and "bad" classes (lazy, disobedient, negative). The "eager fifth grade" resulted from the spur provided by the enthusiasm of one pupil. A wide gap between the top and bottom students in a class or a predominance of average pupils produced a group the teachers called "dull." Three troublemakers with strong leadership qualities and a sense of mischief turned one group into "that difficult sixth grade."[38]

A group labeled as good usually was able to keep its label, to continue to receive the accolade, "the nicest class I ever had," or "the only group whose seats I never had to change." A group labeled as bad was pushed by its label toward further "bad" behavior. Labels were hard to outgrow. The members of a class considered to be the noisiest, laziest, worst-behaved on the upper floor referred to themselves in this way. Years later their reputation as that "difficult" class preceded them through high school.

Except for the kindergarten teacher, every teacher had to confront what was already a group with its own standards, patterns of behavior, and expectations, the complex product of earlier experience in school and constant classroom association over time. And each teacher had then to make this group her own and define the "teacher dominant situation," by incorporating its standards to hers, its expectations to hers. The experienced teacher knew what she had to do in the first few weeks of the new school year.[39] The new teacher, with less idea of what she wanted and less knowledge of how to get it, operated with less conviction and less sureness, but she too established some modus vivendi with her class during that difficult month of September. No teacher completely accepted her class's definitions. She always had some changes to make, if only to show that she was in charge. To the frequent pupil objection, "But that's not the way Mrs. Smith did it," she would respond, "But you are in the fifth grade now. We do it this way," or, "Fourth graders don't need afternoon recess. They are too grown up."

However, most Adams teachers were grateful for the patterns that had been established. Standard classroom procedures could be taken for granted. Since the traditional rules accepted as sacrosanct by the pupils became quite rigid over the years, it was to the teacher's advantage to accept what had gone before as right. The conservatism of the pupils was encouraged by the conservatism of the teacher. To break pupil habits, particularly those of a whole class, required effort and every teacher had to decide how important any change was to her. Redefinition took time and energy she might be using in other aspects of her teaching.

As the teacher molded her class and was molded by it, she began to identify herself with it.[40] Because of the status and power difference between her and her pupils this identification never became complete, but her relationship with her class moved from the impersonal to the personal, and social distance between teacher and pupils was reduced.[41] The original separation of interests, the class as *they,* as the out-group, began to fade away and the formerly impersonal rights and obligations became imbued with affect. The teacher, spending six hours a day with her class, began to see the world through its eyes, its interests as her interests, even as she continued to be separate from the pupils because of her authority and the requirement that she must teach, judge, and control them.

An Adams teacher usually taught at the same grade level each year. Each September her new class, a group unused to her ways and to the work she expected, suffered in comparison to her previous group, a group trained by her, familiar and comfortable in mutual adaptation. No matter how willing she may have been in June to get rid of a class, by September it had taken on an aura of virtue, infinitely more attractive, intelligent, and docile than the new, awkward, confused group which she had to mold. I heard every Adams teacher at some time say in September, "This is the worst class I have ever had." But no teacher seemed to remember having said it before.

September was a gruelling month as the teacher learned to know the children, to discover their clique relationships, to determine which child could be trusted, who should not be given responsibility, who should sit near whom. She had to be careful not to respond too quickly to those pupils eager to attach themselves to her, since often these were the marginal members, those least likely to help her establish her control over the class.[42] Finally, she had to cope with what seemed to be total ignorance and the insistence by the children that "we never had *that* before."

During the first few days of the new school year no teacher referred to "my class" or "my homeroom," although she might talk of "your class" or "your homeroom," particularly if she wanted to inform another teacher of her responsibilities: "Your class is acting up on the playground." Before the end of September she did talk of "my class" but usually only to compare it unfavorably to other classes she had had. During this time, she would level indirect attacks against previous teachers who were responsible for this confused mass of ignorance. Only Mrs. Merrick openly accused a previous teacher of incompetence and this was a teacher no longer teaching in the school: "My class can't even count to five. Seriously, what did they do in first grade? That I can't see." But, by implicitly blaming the group's defects on someone else, one remained a good teacher, saddled with a badly prepared class. Sometimes a teacher even asked the teacher she was indirectly criticizing for support and sympathy in her difficult situation.

Only early in the year and at the moment of parting did the Adams teacher express worry about what the following teacher would think of her class. This was not, as might have been expected, a major source of anxiety for the insecure Adams teacher, possibly because her identification with the class became too complete for her to imagine anyone else teaching her pupils. But in September a teacher might warn the teacher of the next grade not to expect too much the next year. Mrs. Preston carefully informed the junior high teachers that her class was worse than any class she ever had before and that if the pupils were promoted it would only be because "I was forced to do it."

So for a few weeks the teacher held her class at a distance, denying that its work or its behavior had anything to do with her. But then a subtle change began to occur in each teacher, more rapidly if she had an intelligent, well-behaved, and likeable group of children, but eventually even with a slow and difficult group. A simple illustration of the change is Mrs. Merrick's description of her noisy second grade. In September the noise was *out there*, done by *them*. By May it was done by *us:* "Did you hear us today? We didn't mean to disturb you upstairs, but we were having a wonderful time learning a new dance."

The transformation of Mrs. Gregory during the study year was typical. In September she said to me, "How can these children manage departmental work next year? You will have to treat them as fourth graders. If you think the group you have now is bad, wait until you get this crowd."

In October she remarked, "This is the worst class I ever had. They can't reason."

Even in November she asked me desperately, "How can I get them up to fourth grade standards? Children must have changed over the years. This is the worst fourth grade I have ever had."

But despite her vocal complaints she was molding the class to her image even in September, bringing it up to the standard of order she demanded, and as she did so she began to accept it.

I never heard Mrs. Gregory criticize the class as a whole after November. While she might say that a test had to be repeated or that the children were lazy, she usually boasted about "my class." She was calmly smug about their achievement test performances. She talked no more about placing half the children in a special class. She even flared up at Mrs. Preston who suggested that some of them might need remedial reading help. And in addition she demanded for her class all the privileges of every other class. Although angered when a child asked for a Christmas party ("uppity"), she decided to have one since "I couldn't have them left out."

Having watched and fully participated in this process of identification with a class over a number of years, I was struck by the ways in which the departmental system in operation for such a short time on the upper floor subtly changed it and introduced ambiguities. One distinction between the elementary and the high school teacher had always been: "We have to teach everything and really get to know the children. They just know one aspect, so they can't really get to know them." With the introduction of departmentalization, the upstairs teachers had a double identification to handle, identification with a subject area and with a homeroom class. The transition from a parent-teacher role in which she was responsible for the total school life of her class to a subject-teacher role in which she was responsible for teaching one subject to four different groups of pupils was difficult and confusing, and each of the four upstairs teachers made a different kind of adjustment. The differences were more striking partly because the groups were divided by ability as well as by grade level. Mr. Scranton and Mrs. Crane had as homeroom classes the slower divisions, Mrs. Preston and I the faster divisions.

Mr. Scranton, finding his pupils failing to obey him and treating him with some contempt, identified less with his group than did any other teacher I ever observed. For him, the departmental arrangement became a good excuse to avoid identification beyond the minimum, and any time another teacher talked about the class as his, he rejected the imputation.

Mrs. Crane took an opposite approach. Hostile toward her homeroom for the first two months, making only critical remarks about carelessness, restlessness and noise — "You can't expect this kind of class to have a library period. I can't expect them to study. They never know what subject they have next"; "If they could just learn to be quiet, it would be enough for the year" — she moved first to grudging acceptance of them. No matter how angry she became with them, they were *hers,* and it was her job to manage them. And finally she began to praise them more than to criticize them: "They have improved so much since they came up here." Even: "This is the best class I ever had, and they did it all on their own. Nobody helped them."

It was not easy for a teacher to identify herself with a group of low achievers, low strivers, and troublemakers. It was particularly difficult when a teacher did not have the group under her watchful eye all day. So for Mrs. Crane love and identification required that she supervise her homeroom group as much as possible even when they were not under her direction. She made the children correct the errors in their compositions before I saw them: "I didn't want them to think you would accept such sloppy work." She followed them to the other rooms to see that they sat down quietly, and she asked the other teacher to refer to her any who misbehaved.

One result of this constant supervision was that while Mrs. Crane herself had little trouble with the group, the other teachers had a great deal. The other teachers both resented her interference: "It made me sick. I walked out," and recognized and envied her success. Resentment here was modified by awareness of how hard it was to identify with a slow class. No such modification of resentment occurred over the identification by Mrs. Preston and myself with the fast classes.

I quickly accepted my homeroom as a nice group and went around telling the other teachers so all year, to their barely concealed annoyance. Mrs. Preston did the same but did it so ostentatiously that the other teachers began to fight back. They began to criticize her group, telling her the pupils were stuck up and lazy. They frequently reported to her the misdeeds of her class, annoyed not only with her but also defensively with the intelligence of her group. When she began to give her group special privileges and to help them with their homework in other subjects, while commiserating with them about the unfairness of some of the assignments, the other teachers were furious. As Mrs. Crane burst out, "Why should one group be treated so specially around here?"

Both teachers and other pupils responded negatively to this degree of identification,[43] since it threatened the expectations for fair treatment. Mrs. Preston's behavior, of course, seemed particularly outrageous just because it was exposed. Ordinarily when a teacher identified with her homeroom and no other teacher had frequent contact with the class, comparison was not easy and competition was mild. But, in the departmental system, the obvious superiority of the A groups to the B groups was clear and competition became cutthroat. The A group teachers seemed to gloat, and the B group teachers were under constant pressure to keep up.

Every departmental teacher, except for Mr. Scranton, clung to some degree to her identification with the homeroom class even while beginning to enjoy being a specialist. But the sense of subject identification began to flower. Mrs. Preston joined a science association; Mrs Crane attended special mathematics meetings. Each teacher pretended ignorance of the subjects taught by the other teachers: "I don't know how to teach English." "I'm certainly glad I don't have to teach science." Such comments inevitably brought gibes from downstairs colleagues: "Since you have taught fifth grade for years you should be able to teach all the subjects." Little by little, contacts were initiated between the upstairs teachers and the junior high school teachers of the same subjects. Such contacts began to break down a little the strong anti-high school sentiments of the Adams intermediate teachers. Little by little the upstairs teacher derived more of her identity and self-image from her subject than from her homeroom class.

Over time a common identification with both a subject and a homeroom class became less possible. But, at the time of this study, identification by each teacher with her class was strong, an identification that had some important functions for her and for the school.

First, identification tended to encourage respect for tradition, to reward conservatism, and to penalize the new enthusiastic teacher. A teacher's attempt to undo established habits of writing book reports, to unteach faulty knowledge about space, to encourage individualized reading programs produced resistance and confusion in the class. Often it was far easier to carry on the old ways. For the older teacher this seemed self-evident since she usually shared with the lower grade teachers standards of classroom management, as well as of teaching methods and academic performance. For the newer teacher who might consider the weight of tradition an obstruction to her own ideas, the desire to change was greater. But, unfortunately, she was also less able to keep order, to set up the teacher-dominant situation. So the newer teacher too began to settle for the "tried and true."

It was a rare teacher who persisted and succeeded in redefining the traditional order, since the experienced teacher who might have had the skill to do this was usually too accustomed to the traditional ways to consider overthrowing them.

A second function of this identification with the class was that the solidarity of the teacher group tended to be weakened. A teacher now had an ally in her competition with or jealousy of another teacher. This occurred, however, even among teachers who taught different grades and thus had some insulation and autonomy. The continual territorial disputes on the playground illustrate the teacher's concern for her class's rights and her hostility to other teachers who might threaten these rights. A dispute between the second and the fourth grade teacher as to who had the right to the baseball field at noontime led finally to a name calling contest, avidly enjoyed by all the pupils in both classes.

A third function of identification was that it provided the teacher with a symbol, a way of representing her role to the outside world. It was only her class's proclaimed achievements and perceivable deportment that represented to others her success or failure. At times, the teacher might prefer to reject the picture of herself provided by her class, but, at other times, this picture provided her with the only measurable tokens of her success, at least her success in her expectations for producing docility and order.

Criticism of her class by others became criticism of her. She might know that her class needed to be reprimanded: "If they are bad, please feel free to punish them," but she resented any other teacher actually doing this. Any interference, however graciously accepted, was soon followed by an unpleasant remark about the interfering teacher. And the interfering teacher was usually very careful to apologize: "I know it was your class and it wasn't my business, but since I was right there I spoke to them."

With the class as her symbol, each teacher attempted to procure benefits for it and resented seeming slights against her class as slights against herself. So she was alert not to get cheated out of any available supplies for "my class," protesting angrily that "she took the books that were obviously meant for third grade."

Through this symbolization the teacher sometimes began to

resemble her class. Associating with a group of children continually and with her peers only occasionally, identifying her interest more and more with these children and standing with them against the world, she began to think and act as her pupils did.[44] The elementary teacher might even display certain childish characteristics, similar to those of her class. So Mrs. Gregory fought for a playground field as if she were ten, not fifty-five. Mrs. Cornhouse and Miss Tuttle regaled the other teachers with first graders' jokes. Identifying with her class and letting it symbolize her to the world, the Adams teacher gradually and unwittingly came to resemble the children in that class.[45]

Finally, identification enabled the teacher to augment the authority she had in teaching and molding her class. The teacher wanted love and approval from her pupils,[46] maybe more in the primary grades than later on when she was more concerned about her dignity. The love she sought and gave could also be used as a way to manipulate the pupils, to obtain in the unstable classroom situation the leverage she needed for control, leverage beyond that provided by her formally constituted status. As has been noted in various studies, this may become a two-edged sword; the teacher may be able to manipulate pupil conformity, but at the same time she leaves the way open for pupil and class manipulation of her and of her expectations.[47] Having identified with the class, with its emphasis on order, its need for a champion, the teacher responded to its expectations in part because they had become her expectations. The power of the class over her went unnoticed as long as it was subtly wielded.

The importance of the pupil in the teacher's role-set is clear. Toward the pupil were directed the teacher's most crucial expectations; from the pupil came important expectations with which the teacher had to deal. That these expectations were not always congruent was obvious even from my vantage point as teacher, and it was also obvious that no teacher could succeed as a teacher by attempting to impose her expectations in toto on the pupils and thus mold them to her image. However, she was more successful with them than she was with that other most important member of her role-set, the parent.

5 NATURAL ENEMIES: TEACHERS AND PARENTS

A parent of a first grader complained to me one day that her son's teacher was unfair. Her son, she told me, was insecure and sensitive, afraid of school and the teacher: "He needs confidence and so he should have an A on his report card." She could not understand why Miss Tuttle refused to change his mark after finding out about his needs. When Miss Tuttle heard about the complaint, she was as sincerely puzzled as the parent: "Doesn't she understand that I have to follow the rules and use standards? I can't give Timmy an A just because he is sensitive."

"To wish a child well" does not mean the same thing to parents and teachers,[1] and the fact that both are concerned with socialization, education, and the best interests of the child does not eliminate the fundamental difference between the primary relationship of the parent and child and the secondary relationship of the teacher and child. The parent has particularistic expectations, the teacher, universalistic expectations.[2]

This difference, it must be emphasized, lies in the definition of the roles within the larger social order and not in the expressive styles of individuals. Some teachers at Adams were cool and impersonal with their pupils; others overwhelmed them with love and affection. This variation did not merely reflect the grade level of the teacher. Mrs. Preston (sixth grade) used frequent terms of endearment and talked of her closeness to her pupils. Mrs. Calhoun (third grade), on the other hand, was distant and matter of fact with her class, although not unfriendly. Whatever the teacher's style, her universalistic relationship to the pupil is central to her role. Even when, as Jules Henry pointed out, the teacher seems to use "love" to teach the pupils, she still has the brakes on, is still not involved: "If this were not so, children would have to be dragged shrieking from grade to grade and most teachers would flee teaching, for the mutual attachment would be so deep that its annual severing would be too much for either to bear."[3]

This universalistic orientation, of course, does not preclude a teacher's concern with the personal problems and backgrounds of her pupils. The Adams teacher was certainly frequently aware of extenuating circumstances for poor school work or failure to pay attention in class. When Mrs. Preston commented that Joey was doing poor work in science, Mrs. Crane responded, "You can't really blame poor Joey. His father is drinking again and beats him up every night." Such interchanges were frequent. The teachers all agreed that this was why it was important to know the families of their pupils: "The teachers in a rural school can know the families and thus understand why the kids behave the way they do." However, to know extenuating circumstances increased sympathy and concern but rarely affected grading. As Mrs. Crane put it, "It's all very well to know about the family background, but if the administration demands that we grade on a standard, it doesn't do any good to know these things, does it?" The child then was not blamed for his failure, but he still failed.

Although the teacher's role is always to some degree universalistic, it is least so in kindergarten and becomes progressively more so through the grades.[4] The difference between the teacher's role and the parent's role is least noticeable at the start of the child's school experience. As Waller commented, "Women teachers, especially in the early grades, find it a very convenient technique to play the part of the mother to their pupils. . . . "[5] So the kindergarten or primary teacher is less concerned about teaching subjects and more concerned about the child as a person, focuses less on ranking and more on the individual. But even in kindergarten, the teacher must judge, evaluate, and compare each child with others. She must decide whether a child is ready to go on to the first grade. She starts to think of him as a pupil, and this process becomes more specific each year. The child begins to be expected to complete items of the curriculum, to work for passing grades, and to take standardized tests.

The first grade teacher each year at Adams was the focus of more parental concern than any other teacher. Most requests for private conferences came from parents of first graders. In these conferences the parents revealed shifting moods of anger and respect. They asked for particularistic treatment and for special consideration: "He's just a child, you know," against the teacher's attempt to apply universalistic standards, even while they showed tremendous anxiety about whether the teacher was helping the child to succeed: "Will he pass? Has he learned to read?"

The upstairs teachers were ambivalent about departmentalization, since they were not sure that even fifth graders were ready for impersonal universalistic treatment. A parent who accused the upstairs teachers of forgetting that the pupils were children touched off a long series of soul-searching discussions on the upper floor.

OVERLAPPING SPHERES OF CONTROL

The basic difference between the parental and the teacher role existed at each grade level, and it was this difference that neither parent nor teacher at Adams wished to confront directly. Each was hostile toward the other, with the teacher believing that most parents were deliberately obtuse and willfully made her job more difficult. An important reason for the tension and the hostility was the lack of clarity as to the boundaries marking off the spheres of control over the child. The child became the territory in dispute, and since each, parent and teacher, had some authority over this territory and each wished to do something different with this authority, conflict arose. Both spheres of control were legitimated, but the areas so legitimated were not unambiguously defined.

For example, one ambiguous area was that of "out-of-school." The parent usually insisted to the Adams teacher that her control was limited to school hours. Some parents believed that the teacher had neither the right to keep the child after school nor the right to expect homework to be done if there were more pressing home obligations. Parents wrote notes to the intermediate teachers asking that a child be excused from doing homework because the family had to visit a relative, or he had to do chores, or he was sick. In each of these instances the teachers complained about interference, but they always complied with the parental requests.

Most of the parents also seemed to believe that school attendance should be under their control, keeping a child home not only because of illness (legitimate from the teacher's point of view), but also frequently because he had to go to the dentist, because "he was so tired I let him sleep," or because the family was going away on a trip. In this as in the question of after school time there was annoyance, but rarely overt disagreement between parents and teachers. The teacher usually accepted the parent's definition and rights.

There was less agreement and more hostility generated over the frequent parental attempts to control certain in-school matters. A mother sent a note requesting that her child be excused from outdoor recess since he had a cold. The teacher's response was typical: "If he has a cold he shouldn't be in school. If he is able to come to school he should be able to go out for recess." A mother requested that her child be allowed to ride home on a different bus in order to visit a friend. A mother sent a note giving her child permission to walk over to the village at noontime. Some of these requests contravened established school rules, others merely the informal arrangements of the teachers. Each request was handled by the particular teacher in such a way as to avoid conflict. If the request directly flouted the rules, she usually rejected it; if it merely challenged an informal arrangement she usually complied but complained. The clear imputation by the parents that such requests were perfectly legitimate, that their authority over the child did extend to these matters, angered the teacher far more than the inconvenience of the particular request.

Only within the classroom did the Adams teacher believe that she clearly had the authority to give the orders and direct the child. But how far did this control extend? Over his manners, his morals, and his play relations as well as his school work? The teachers did not always agree with one another, but usually they acted as if all of these matters were within their jurisdiction. However, they tended to claim the authority over manners and morals as adults rather than as teachers. While a pupil might complain, "It ain't none of your business," the parents did not usually interfere in the teacher's assumption of control here.

The day-to-day routine of the classroom, the materials taught, the grades given were controlled by the teacher, and she knew that the parents felt helpless to interfere in these matters. As one parent said, "What can a parent do? You bring up your child as well as you can and then you send him off to school. He has all kinds of teachers — cruel ones and ones without any experience — and when you try to object to something, they give you the runaround. It is frightening."

Even Mrs. Gregory, the terror of the fourth grade, was reluctant to object to what she considered unfair treatment of her daughter in the high school: "I would like to complain to Mr. Hanson but I don't dare. Mr Scoville will just take it out on May."

Although the teacher acted as if she expected the parents to criticize continually her methods of teaching and the marks she gave, this rarely happened. The teachers began to joke when the report cards were sent out: "I had better go out tonight before the parents start calling me up." "I will take the phone off the hook." "I'm going to really get it this time." But I never was called, and the other teachers rarely reported being harassed by parental complaints. Any parent who did call usually wanted to question a low conduct mark rather than an academic mark.

While marks in academic subjects were rarely a source of overt dispute between parents and teachers, promotion and group placement did raise questions about the spheres of control. Usually the parents were consulted if the teacher planned not to promote a child to the next grade. Also, as every Adams teacher knew well, if a parent objected, the child was usually promoted. The Adams teachers also knew that Mr. Hanson usually yielded to a parent's objections about group placement if the parent was "important" or "noisy" enough. The teachers were convinced that in reality, even if not in law, the parent retained the final authority, delegating and withdrawing portions of it at will.

Two factors that contributed to the Adams teacher's lack of

assurance as to the extent of her control over the pupil and her anxiety about the encroaching parent were her low social status and the absence of institutional buffers between her and the parent. The low social status of the American teacher has been attributed by researchers to a low respect for intellectual endeavor, the preponderance of women in the occupation, the low degree of professionalization, and the lack of either professional autonomy or authority in the gatekeeping role.[6] The elementary teacher, in particular, has suffered from low prestige and restricted authority. Forty years ago Willard Waller attributed the low social standing of the American teacher to low financial rewards, to a lack of congruence between the teaching profession and our commercial culture, and to the commonly held stereotypes of the teacher, as despot, as adolescent, as too pure for the rest of us, and as a failure.[7] Whatever the crucial factors now and then, it is clear that the social status of the teacher has not significantly improved since Waller wrote and may even have declined relative to other professional groups.[8] And at Adams as elsewhere the teachers were aware of their position and felt insecure and uncertain in attempting to maintain authority when dealing with parents.

The elementary teacher identified herself with the average people in the town, with those in the Hollow, rather than with the "snobs" on the Hill or the "riffraff" along the river. Although she had more education than many of her neighbors and associates in the community, she saw herself and was seen by them as like them because of her own background, her husband's occupation, and the status of being a teacher. As a result, the Adams elementary teacher could not often use her social position as a weapon in dealing with threatening parents. She considered only one group really inferior to herself, the lower-class fringe.

Not only did the Adams teacher lack protection through status, she also lacked institutional protection. Unlike the teacher in the private school who usually has little direct contact with parents, and unlike the teacher in many public schools who is protected from parental interference by administrative or procedural barriers, the Adams teacher had direct contact with the parents. There were no formal provisions to mediate the complaints of the parent or the teacher through the principal or administration.[9] (See Figures 2a and 2b.)

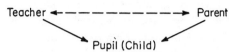

Principal

Teacher ←— — — — — — —→ Parent

Pupil (Child)

2a. Formal Relationship of Teacher and Parent, Adams

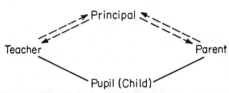

Principal

Teacher   Parent

Pupil (Child)

2b. Formal Relationship of Teacher and Parent, Other Schools (such as the Chicago schools described by Howard Becker and Miriam Wagenschein)

Howard S. Becker, "Schools and Systems of Stratification," in *Education, Economy and Society: A Reader in the Sociology of Education,* ed. A. H. Halsey, Jean Floud, and C. Arnold Anderson (New York: Free Press of Glencoe, 1961), and Miriam Wagenschein, "Reality Shock" (M. A. diss., The University of Chicago, 1950), pp. 63-64.

This is not to suggest that the teacher had frequent contact with the parents. She did not; parent-teacher conferences were instituted primarily because there was little contact, but what she had was unmediated.

CONTACTS BETWEEN TEACHERS AND PARENTS

The PTA during the year under study had lost whatever importance it may have had in the "good old days." Except for the first supper meeting in the fall, few parents and few high school teachers attended (although the elementary teachers considered it their "duty" to show up each time and to make many critical remarks about the absent high school teachers). No one wished to hold office in the organization, and winter meetings were finally discontinued for lack of attendance. It was not considered "proper" at the PTA meetings for parents to talk to a teacher about a child's problems. According to unwritten teacher protocol, if a parent wished to talk he should make a formal appointment, and the teachers usually managed to convey this idea to most of the parents. However, some parents did use the PTA meetings to catch the teachers and demand on-the-spot conferences. A teacher usually was polite at such times, but she invariably made some hostile remark afterward or made a point of warning the other teachers to "look out for Mrs. Smith. She will nail you if she can."

Parent-teacher conferences were scheduled fall and spring, the only formal arrangements in this school for the teachers to talk to parents. The teachers had serious doubts about their usefulness, remarking that the conferences did no good, that the parent you wanted to see never came,[10] that parents did not listen to you and did not want to help you, that they just wanted to boast about their children. As a count one year showed, the attendance of parents whose children were doing satisfactory work at school was high and the attendance of parents whose children were having trouble academically and socially was very low.[11]

Formal contacts then were rare but so were casual, informal contacts. Those that did occur were initiated by either parent or teacher, but usually by the parent. Although the Adams teacher talked a great deal about the importance of communicating with parents,[12] she made few direct efforts to do so. Mrs. Crane's response to the suggestion that a teacher should contact the parents if their child was doing badly in school, was to complain, "Isn't that what the report card is for? I have enough to do. You'd think Nancy could tell her mother she is failing."

A teacher did occasionally write a note or telephone a parent about disciplinary matters. The report card and samples of poor work sent home with the child were believed to be sufficient warning to the parent of academic difficulties. The papers sent home were supposed to be returned, signed by the parent. The teacher believed the parent would then make some effort to encourage the child to try harder and do more competent work. This procedure rarely had the desired effect. The papers would be returned signed, but no change in the pupil's work seemed to occur, and few parents seemed to understand the subtle message being transmitted by the teacher.

Casual contacts between teachers and parents in stores, on the street, or at parties ordinarily did not lead to discussions about school problems. The role definitions as parent and as teacher tended to be kept separate from the role definitions as acquaintances, and conversation, while it might touch upon the school or other children, rarely focused on particular difficulties between the teacher and the pupil. This restraint was clearest when the teacher and the parent knew one another outside of their teacher and parent roles. For example, I had a casual but friendly relationship with Mrs. Jones whom I saw frequently at the store and at club meetings. Although her son, Tom, was a constant thorn in my flesh in school, we never discussed Tom's behavior when we met. When it seemed necessary for me to have parental aid in dealing with Tom, I would call Mr. Jones from the school.

Similarly, the upstairs teachers had a casual bantering relationship with one of the cooks in the kitchen, a relationship they all kept quite distinct from the more formal relationship they maintained with her in the conferences where it became legitimate to discuss her son's failings. Both teacher and parent seemed to resent and resist any attempt to carry the occupational role into the nonschool situation.

Usually parents telephoned the teacher, wrote her notes, or visited the school during school hours only in response to reported mistreatment of their child. Since such contacts resulted from hostility, the ensuing confrontation was tension producing for both the teacher and the parent. The day after one of the fifth graders was jumped by a gang of other boys on the playground, his mother called up not only all the upstairs teachers, but also Mr. Hanson, asking in turn, "What are you going to do about it?" Since by the time she called there was little one could do, the result was nagging irritation with the mother for her question.

A teacher could and often did counter the accusing parent by referring the problem to Mr. Hanson, noting that the particular incident was not within her jurisdiction. This was the usual way to handle complaints about trouble on the bus, a frequent source of parental complaints, and this was one kind of delegation to the principal that the teacher found successful. For other complaints the teacher usually found the problem back in her lap, unmediated by the principal.

Parents did, occasionally, come to see the teacher after school, sometimes making appointments, often just wandering in. The ostensible reason for the visit might be to ask for special help for a child whose marks were low or whose behavior was disturbing. But such requests for help were often reinterpreted by the teacher as backhanded criticism, which made her defensive and hostile, or as true humility, which encouraged her to humiliate the parent even more. The teacher was usually put on the defensive in a parent-initiated contact, and the parent was put on the defensive in a teacher-initiated contact. Rarely did a teacher seek out a parent to praise a child. Rarely did a parent come to school to compliment a teacher. Since contact, except in the formal conferences, was primarily the product of problems on either side, there were few positive, warm, and simply friendly interchanges between teacher and parent. Contact thus tended to lead to overt or covert blame by each against the other.

PARENTAL EXPECTATIONS

The Adams teacher was frequently made aware of one parental expectation for her behavior, the expectation that she should be a strict disciplinarian with little humor or flexibility, but with the capacity to keep order and allow no nonsense. She should be like the teachers the parents had had: "She taught us a lot because she kept order." "When I was in school we had to work." "I got slapped for talking, and I never talked again." "She was tough but people really respected her. You learned in her room.""

In fact, if more teachers were like this today, said some parents, the world would be better: "Bring back the tough teacher and you will improve education which has gone soft."

However, this expectation did not usually seem to be seriously held. It was idealistic, stereotyped by nostalgia or hostility converted into irony.[13] What the parents in practice expected of the teacher was particularistic treatment: "Be firm but not harsh." "Keep order but forgive my child." So: "I walked all the way to school and thought nothing of it. Children are soft today." But: "Don't make my child walk all that distance. It is cruel." Mrs. Merrick held universalistic expectations for herself as teacher, keeping firm discipline, forbidding her second graders to talk at all in the classroom, but as parent she was outraged by the sixth grade teacher who disciplined Mrs. Merrick's daughter for talking.

The parent did not expect to control the curriculum or determine what should go on in the classroom. When academic questions were raised by parents they usually related to the amount of work or the difficulty of presentation rather than to the content.[14] However, the parent did expect the teacher to accept extenuating circumstances for an individual child and to seek out these extenuating circumstances without being prodded by the parent. "Be fair to my child" then had to be translated, discovered the teacher, into: "Show my child special consideration" or "Make the work easier for my child." Some parents asked for less rigid academic standards. One parent complained to me that since the sixth grade arithmetic book covered material not in the required curriculum, the children should not have to learn this material: "It's unfair to give advanced work and then give low marks." Another parent objected that the test questions in social studies were too hard and her daughter did not need to know all those things, since "Sally isn't going to go to college anyway."

A parent rarely asked the teacher to give the child more work or criticized a teacher for giving the child marks that were too high or for being too lenient. Only the parents of kindergarten children pushed Mrs. Garten to teach their children how to read: "They do it in Moose Head." On the other hand, parents of first graders complained that Miss Tuttle tried to go too fast and graded the children too strictly. Once the competition became real and grades began to matter the particularistic emphasis appeared.[15]

When parents did criticize the curriculum it was usually for departures from the tried and true. A parent rarely praised innovations: "Why don't children have to learn their tables any more?" "We used to learn how to spell in school." "What is this newfangled modern math anyway? I can't even help my kids at home now." The important subjects for most parents in the elementary school seemed to be penmanship, reading, arithmetic drill, and spelling; other subjects drew little comment or interest.

Some parental expectations for her that the teacher considered to be legitimate included her responsibility to protect the children on the playground, her responsibility to encourage, assist, and teach each child, and the parent's right to make decisions about the child's health needs. But she rejected as illegitimate expectations for special consideration, exemption from punishment, or a degree of watchful supervision that was impossible to sustain.

What the teacher responded to from the parents were expectations that may or may not actually have been held by the parents.[16] Often seemingly innocuous comments led her to impute all kinds of "impossible" expectations and then to respond defensively to these "impossible" expectations. Even when she rejected certain clearly present expectations, because she was convinced that she was right or that she was following established rules and policy, she did not feel easy about her actions. Following the rules I refused to let a first grader enter the school building one morning before eight-thirty. When the child's father violently castigated me for having no consideration for his child, I was defensively hostile toward this father for many days thereafter. I did feel that I was in the wrong despite the rules.

Mrs. Minny called up to say that her child had missed the bus: "Why aren't the teachers on duty to see that everyone takes the bus?" Although we all knew that this demand was impossible, that we could not be sure that every child in the building got on the bus, and although we all knew that we had fulfilled our legal responsibilities by doing our bus duty, we all felt guilty anger. For at least a week each of us went through an exaggerated and lengthy routine to check the departure of all the bus pupils. The impracticality of this procedure and complaints from the bus drivers led to abandonment of the new surveillance. As long as no parent complained again, we were safe.

A mother stormed at Mrs. Preston after her son had been injured on the playground, "After all, you only have them five hours a day." Countered by Mrs. Preston that there were two hundred children to supervise at once, she was unmollified, "But there are two teachers out there." Mrs. Preston's response to this criticism was typically mixed. She was amused at the parent's unreasonableness, but she was also angry and guilty: "Let her come and take over. Let her watch all these children at once."

For a time supervision and attentiveness on the playground increased. Soon it returned to its normal level.

Defensive guilt was also the teacher's response to implied criticism by parents. For a parent to ask the teacher to provide extra work for the child or to make suggestions as to how the parent might help the child at home was to criticize the teacher for ineffective teaching, unless the teacher had gained the upper hand by calling the parent in for a conference. Although any Adams teacher responded to such requests and gave help, she was quick to tell the other teachers about the child's failure to cooperate with her, his laziness, his lack of effort and appreciation for her extra work: "This is the last time I will bother to help children and try to explain things to the parents. They don't care." The bitterness engendered against particular parents thereafter colored the teacher's response to any other parental request, however innocent or sincere.

This bitterness was most apparent in relation to assignments requested by parents for children who were ill. Too often the teacher spent hours preparing these and then found when the child returned that none of the work had been done, or that what was done was careless, incomplete, and useless. Again, the teacher blamed the parent. It was the parent's job to supervise the work done at home. Each time the teacher angrily said, "Never again," and each time, despite her anger, she did it again, because she somehow defined it as part of her role and a legitimate parental expectation.

Most of the Adams teachers were convinced that many parents considered the school and thus the teacher to blame for any failings of the children. Although the teacher was rarely directly challenged with this accusation by a parent, she accepted as true any indirect allegations to this effect. So when Mrs. Bolster, a parent, said that Mrs. Hamilton, another parent, blamed the school for her son's failure to learn, this was proof to the teachers of the unfairness of parents.

The parent-teacher conferences often increased bitterness and hostility against parents rather than understanding. A teacher was sometimes able to gloat over the parent whom she chastened and humbled by outlining the deficiences of her child, but hostile and defensive comments were more common: "All they want to do is chat and tell you stories. They don't want to listen to your suggestions." "They say to you: 'Make Dennis work.' 'I hope you can make David mind. You have my permission to clobber him. We don't know what to do with him at home.' How do they expect us to do in one year what they haven't been able to do in ten?" "Don't ever say anything to a parent. Whatever you say gets repeated everywhere and garbled. I told her Brian wasn't working as he should and it came back to me that I couldn't handle him."

When the teacher rejected a parental expectation or demand as illegitimate, she was defensive and guilty about it. When she grudgingly acknowledged the legitimacy or the innocence of the expectation, she was still hostile, annoyed by what she considered "interference," and yet afraid to express this hostility. While unreasonable demands, "They want us to do what they can't," should be resisted: "Don't let the parents browbeat you," the parents also had to be propitiated in order to obtain their appreciation, their interest, and their respect:[17] "Whatever you do is wrong with the parents. You have to be so careful what you say. I won't give any more F's. It's not worth the struggle with them."

TEACHER EXPECTATIONS

Although the teacher wanted support and respect, her own expectations for the parents made it impossible for her to give the parents what would produce this support and respect. The core of the teacher's expectation was that a parent respond as the teacher did, to be universalistic, which meant to be objective, rational, and realistic about the child. The teacher believed that few parents lived up to this basic demand. Typical comments about parents were: "You can't get anywhere with Mrs. Closey. She thinks everything he does is okay." "She *pretends* they can't see anything wrong with John at home." "We can't work with these children. The parents always stand up for them. It's no use." "Why do the parents always believe the child first and jump on the school? Then they find the child lied."

Much more rarely was there praise: "Mrs. Hamlin is cooperative. She knows what's wrong with David and tries to help." "I like Mrs. Joplin. She is sensible. She knows her children's faults."

Ramifications of this core expectation included both idealistic stereotypical demands and more realistic but more strongly felt demands. Just as the parent often built up an image of the teacher of the "good old days," so the teacher recreated a picture of the parent of the "good old days" (in her youth, however long ago that was). The parents in the past cared. In the past they rushed to help teachers whenever they were asked. They backed up the teacher's authority and taught their children to show equal respect. The parent often punished the child more severely than the teacher did for a school infraction. But this time had gone. Parents cared no longer. Children were too free; they did not respect anyone, and the parents were to blame. They had undermined the teacher's authority. Parental interest in the school now was interference not help, an effort to prevent the teacher from doing her job as it must be done.

The idealistic expectation held by parents for a teacher who was tough turned out frequently to be the obverse of the more realistic expectation for a teacher who was like a parent. The idealistic expectation held by a teacher for a parent who cared was an exaggerated stereotype of the more realistic expectation expressed regularly in day-to-day conversation that the parent should work with the teacher not against her, that the parent should encourage the children to obey, and, most important of all, that the parent refrain from criticizing or undermining the authority of the teacher: "You'd think parents wouldn't go out of their way to make trouble for a teacher." The parent should supplement the teacher's efforts by encouraging hard work, by supervising homework, by not allowing outside home activities to encroach on the child's school work.

The teacher was ambivalent, however, as to the degree of responsibility she wanted the parent to assume. She criticized the parent who did not supervise homework: "His mother says she goes over his work but it is a lie." But she also frequently talked about how important it was for parents to encourage independence in the child. On the one hand, she believed that the parent should care and should pay attention to the child: "If his mother cares so little about her children that she goes away to work, he will deserve to fail." "If my child were failing I would want him to stay after school and get help. I wouldn't mind letting him walk home, but what can you expect from that kind of parent?" On the other hand, if the parent came to school too often, showed too much interest and concern, the teacher began to ask the opposite: "With kids like the Snoops and their parents what can one do? They interfere in everything I try to do." The visits of one parent were dreaded by all the upstairs teachers: "She tries to tell you how to teach." A frequent plaint in the teachers' room: "If it weren't for the parents I could teach. There are too many outsiders trying to tell us what to do and interfering."

The most extreme expression of this hostile reaction was the heartfelt comment of Mr. Scranton after a particularly disturbing day: "The only answer is to put children in dormitories and take them over completely from the parents. Then we might get somewhere."

However "realistic" the teacher insisted her expectations for the parents were, she revealed more than a touch of casual cynicism in her anticipations of parental compliance. Most of the teachers found few parents who were like teachers, who cooperated and cared: "Parents talk a lot about being helpful and backing us up, but they don't carry through."

So even when a teacher talked beforehand with great optimism of the parent-teacher conferences: "When Mrs. Lynn comes we shall straighten out Sally," her hostile response to the uncooperative parents afterward rarely included an expression of surprise.

The teacher saw the parents as cooperative, indifferent, or critical. A cooperative parent was one who acted like a teacher. She criticized children and asked for advice on educational matters. Cooperative parents were rare, but the teacher found some at each social class and achievement level. The indifferent parent ("She was just blah") had nothing to say, often did not bother to come to the conference, and displayed no reaction to a teacher's critical comments about her child. She was the one who would discuss everything with the teacher except the child. The critical parent either challenged the teacher directly: "Why does Susie have so much homework?" "John never had any trouble in school before," or indicated indirectly that she was challenging the teacher by expressing worry about the child while refusing to look at him "objectively." The Adams teacher believed that most parents were indifferent, attending the parent-teacher conferences because they were expected to, not because they wanted to help. The teacher did not look for reasons for this apparent lack of concern. What might be inarticulateness, or a parental defense against the power held by the teacher over the pupil's academic life, or even espousal of other than academic values: "I have taught my girls there are three things that are important — clothes, looks, and manners. If they get by in school, that's enough," was seen simply as indifference and thus as an implicit challenge to her goals. But since the challenge from the critical parents was direct, it was more threatening.

A few of the critical parents had children who were doing well in school. The Adams teacher occasionally had to counter the criticism that the school was not doing enough for the academically successful child: "Why isn't Tom at the top of the class? You don't seem to expect much of him." More frequently, parents were critical because their children were failing or just getting by. Some of these parents were from the lower end of the social scale and saw no hope for their children to move up from this level. They resented the philosophy of the school and the attitudes and methods of the teachers, believing them responsible for the children's failure. Other critical parents, in the middle or upper social classes, used their own background, education, and social position as weapons with which to challenge the school and its teachers, either as inferior and therefore incapable of judging the child fairly and making him do his best: "He's bored. That's why he doesn't do better," or as irrelevant: "He will be going away to school soon and then he will become interested and do well."

A parent whom one teacher found cooperative might be considered indifferent, even critical, by another. How a teacher saw the parent depended on a number of factors: the level of work the child was doing for her; the social class and education of both the parent and the teacher; and informal ties between the parent and the teacher outside of the school. I found that I often differed from the Old Guard teachers in my response to particular parents. Parents with whom they interacted easily and whom they saw as cooperative, or at worst indifferent, often seemed negative and cautious to me. A parent considered by them to be critical often struck me as interesting, responsive, and cooperative. However, I shared with the other teachers the experience of dealing with about the same proportions of cooperative, indifferent, and critical parents, even though I pinned on the labels somewhat differently.

DEVICES TO HANDLE CONFLICTING EXPECTATIONS

The Adams teacher, confronted with strong parental expectations that seemed to her to threaten her sense of dignity, her ability to teach, and her authority over the pupils, took refuge in a number of protective devices. One that she used (and one which was sometimes used against her) was the search for coalitions with pupils, "cooperative" parents, and other teachers. She also sought coalitions with Mr. Hanson against importuning parents, but she strongly believed that he would fail her. Since, as I noted before, there was no institutionalized administrative buffer between teacher and parent, any evidence of contact between the parent and Mr. Hanson tended to be construed by the Adams teacher as a double cross, not as a protection: "She is just two-faced. Why didn't she come to complain to me, not to Mr. Hanson, if there was something wrong?" Although Mr. Hanson may have protected the teachers from some parents' complaints, the Adams teacher knew only of the occasions when he refused to do so. He usually informed a teacher when parents called up to complain, and although he told the teacher not to worry about the call, he did not tell her how he handled it. Therefore, she always suspected that he had not supported her. The teacher knew that parental pressure on Mr. Hanson for promotion or for moving a child from one group to another was often effective against the wishes of the teachers. She grudgingly admitted that he did not usually repudiate her in a three-way conference among teacher, parent, and himself;[18] in fact, he occasionally firmly backed a teacher against the parent. And the teachers cited often, with surprise but pleasure, the story of the time he "put Mrs Smith [a prominent citizen] in her place" when she tangled with Mrs. Gregory over her problem grandson. "He backed me up," said the amazed Mrs. Gregory. "He said I had a lot of experience and knew what I was doing."

The Adams teacher occasionally turned to the pupils for coalition against parents. The class did provide some of the affection and support she needed, and she might use the interests of the whole class to persuade some recalcitrant parents of the importance of a class trip or the need for parental cooperation in a play production. However, when the teacher tried to work with a single pupil against a demanding or indifferent parent, she usually failed in her efforts, since the pupil was quite powerless.[19] I tried to persuade the mother of Richard, an intelligent but nonachieving sixth grader, to give him help at home in arithmetic. I found that my interest in Richard was regarded with suspicion rather than appreciation and that Richard's mother thought I was attempting to come between her and her son by encouraging him to want things he would never have.

Coalitions with parents themselves were frequently sought, but often proved disappointing. The teacher made this attempt usually only with those parents with whom she identified herself, the middle-class group, those who shared her convictions about the values of hard work and achievement. And it was continually galling to her to find how many of these parents were either indifferent or ineffective: "What shall I do with him? I can't make him work at home. You make him work," throwing the problem back in her lap. It was particularly frustrating that the parents who she believed should share her expectations were as likely as the others to make particularistic demands upon her: "He believed his daughter when anyone could see she was lying. You know what he said, really: 'She's only my little girl'." "Why are parents such liars; why do they defend their children?"

For even among the middle-class parents, the Adams teacher found few whom she classified as truly cooperative. And she slipped easily into suspecting the supposedly cooperative parent of being biased or of being unsympathetic to her work with the child: "I think Mrs. Arthur doesn't like me any more since I told her her son tells lies. But you would think she would want to know."

The Adams teacher rarely tried to find support for her efforts from the lower-class parents. Instead she anticipated trouble, and if it came she used her superior status to neutralize any parental accusations. The teachers turned aside without too much anxiety a hostile father's complaint about unfairness by agreeing that the mother "was obviously Italian," that the family were "troublemakers. That's why they move so much. They are no addition to the community."

The parent from the poor section of town who adopted a humble and obsequious manner toward the teacher received approbation and was likely to be sought out for coalition. Such a parent who agreed with whatever the teacher recommended was rarely encountered but was always appreciated. Unfortunately, this parental humility sometimes led to unfortunate misunderstandings. The teacher, grateful for the parent's admiration and respect for her as the true gatekeeper to mobility, often found it hard to tell the parent the truth about the child's capabilities and performance. She encouraged him to believe that the child must succeed with all this help, and the reality of ultimate failure was sugar-coated. The parent's unawareness of the brutal truth stemmed also from the fact that he often did not understand the teacher's terminology. (The use of dissembling jargon as a status weapon has been noted for many professions.[20]) So that when the parent came face to face with his child's failure in later years he naturally felt hostility toward the subsequent teacher. Quite often, the intermediate teacher blamed the primary teachers for not being honest with parents of the slower children, thus causing the intermediate teachers to be defined by parents as the villains who had cut off the chances of these children to succeed.

The Adams teacher's relations with the upper-class and more highly educated parents revealed less an attempt to seek coalitions than an attempt to narrow the status gap and to reduce her own feelings of status inferiority.[21] Relations between the teacher and these parents were distant and tentative. Any chance to score against such a parent was cherished and the encounter relived in the teachers' group. Any slight, snub, or stated expectation was threatening and was countered by strong defensive attempts to rebuild the self-image. An angry mother from a wealthy old family in town, after criticizing Mrs. Gregory to her face for the way she handled her son, sending Mrs. Gregory into a tantrum of rage that expressed itself against her class and any teacher unfortunately within reach, telephoned to apologize for being wrong. This story was told and retold, embellished, and gloried in.

One reason for the doubts about Mr. Hanson's loyalty to his teachers was certainly the fact that he seemed particularly subservient to the "people who count" in town. He was less strict with their children: "You know why Mr. Hanson let Bill get away with that. He is Mr. Alton's boy." The teachers accumulated evidence that he tended to slight their complaints about the upper-class children and that he responded most favorably to the requests from the Hill parents for special treatment, group placement, and promotion. So, when a teacher could punish such a child without his interference or even sometimes with his backing, she was particularly gratified.

The attitudes of the Adams teacher toward the·upper-class parents is partially revealed by her response to alcoholism and "immorality" at the different social class levels. Alcoholism was a serious problem in the town of Adams. The teacher's response to it varied radically depending on the social level.

The alcoholic mother or father from the middle-class group (our friends) was pitied. The children were treated with special consideration, kindness, and understanding. But alcoholism among those at the bottom of the social scale produced angry condemnation and among those at the top, jeering contempt. The lower-class parent who drank was severely condemned. The family problems, the difficulties with the children, the disgrace were occasions for moral outrage. The teachers often expressed the warmest and most sincere concern for some of the more difficult lower-class children when it seemed clear that their behavior was a response to being beaten by a drunken father or to the parent's confinement in the local jail. But no sympathy was ever wasted on the parent whose basic character defects were so clearly portrayed in his drinking.

The teachers joked contemptuously about the upper-class mother or father who drank too much. Much pleasure was derived in the teachers' group from exchanging anecdotes about the outrageous behavior of Mrs. Wiggins when she visited the school to consult about her daughter. The comments of the teachers were similar to their gibes about the upper-class mother or father who ran around and had affairs: "Did you see what she was wearing when she came to school today? Guess she has tired of her latest and is trying to vamp Mr. Scranton. Better watch out; she chases them all, you know." "What is Susie's last name now? It's hard to keep track between the husbands and the casuals her mother goes around with."

While drinking and promiscuity were considered by the teachers to be amusing aberrations of the upper class, the failure of the upper-class parents to take their children's education and upbringing seriously were considered morally reprehensible. When a Hill family took its children to Florida during the school year, Mrs. Gregory said disapprovingly, "They don't think their child is important. They don't care what happens to her, whether she learns anything or not." This reaction can be contrasted to Mrs. Crane's pleased response to the similar trip taken by the son of the local Hollow doctor, "He is having such a good chance to see things."

Criticism and disapproval of the Hill parents were often couched by the teachers in terms of sympathy and concern for the children: "Don't parents have any sense? How can they be so cruel to their children?" "No wonder Walter is such a problem with his mother fooling around with other men and ignoring him." The comments were sympathetic but patronizing: "Poor filthy Annie." "Poor Pam, she never has any breakfast." "Poor Debbie, she has to get up and feed all those children because of her mother's wild life."

The sympathy, however, was less manifest than the hostility toward those children whose parents had patronized the teacher: "At the time of the flood the Mcintyres did nothing to help me although I taught all their children in school." This hostility expressed itself in comments that the children were "less intelligent than you would expect," or "failed to take advantage of their opportunities," or were "lazy" or "stuck up."

The most intense hostility was directed, not against the wealthy parents toward whom the teachers obviously felt somewhat ambivalent, but against those living on the Hill who were "different" and who seemed to be claiming the right to superior status without the proper qualifications. So the writers, the artists, and other "queer eccentrics" were roundly condemned by the

Adams teachers for contributing to the moral decay of the society. Everything they did was criticized, even activities that were ignored when done by someone else. And the teachers lost no opportunities to recount stories that confirmed their convictions that such ways of life inevitably produced problem children. A favorite tale concerned Mrs. Rozinsky (an artist's wife) who sailed into the fourth grade class one day during the singing of the Star Spangled Banner and, hand dramatically over her heart, joined in the singing in a loud and tremulous soprano. The teachers did not consider this behavior merely an example of the eccentricity of Mrs. Rozinsky, but saw it as typical of what one should expect from artists who have low moral standards, have incomprehensibly superior attitudes toward us, and who always do strange and odd things.

The attitudes I have here described were reflected primarily in the conversation of the Old Guard teachers who set the tone in the school. Certainly not all the teachers talked this way, nor did all the teachers agree about the characteristics of particular families. However, the newer teacher, of necessity, derived most of her knowledge about the town and the parents from the Old Guard teachers and in so doing she absorbed to some degree their attitudes toward these families.

Coalitions with the other teachers were much more often sought and tended to be much more reliable sources of support for the Adams teacher than those with administration, pupils, or parents.[22] As was pointed out in Chapter 3, the teacher had to believe that her colleagues stood behind her in dealing with parents,[23] and she looked to her colleagues for the sympathy and understanding she needed when she encountered hostility from the parents. Much of the casual talk among the Adams teachers was devoted to parents, their failings, their oddities, and ways to circumvent them.

What the teacher had to counter was any pressure from outside or defection from within that might split the teacher group, divide loyalties, or let in the "enemy." Just as the teacher sought coalitions with others, so often did the parent. And this danger had to be constantly guarded against. Mrs. Lender attempted to use her friendship with Mrs. Crane as a lever against Mrs. Merrick's "unfairness" to her second grade child. Her appeal to

Mrs. Crane for help was a flattering request to which Mrs. Crane at first responded sympathetically. After all, Mrs. Merrick was a new teacher. Although Mrs. Crane did not approach Mrs. Merrick directly: "It is not my place to interfere with what another teacher does," she did show concern and went so far as to recommend that Mrs. Lender take her problem to Mr. Hanson. However, when Mr. Hanson stood firmly behind Mrs. Merrick and even subtly suggested to Mrs. Crane that it was wrong for Mrs. Lender to attempt to interfere with school matters, Mrs. Crane shifted ground and within two days she no longer supported Mrs. Lender's appeals. In fact, she virtually accused her of being a liar.

For her part, Mrs. Merrick unhesitatingly assumed that the teachers would support her against Mrs. Lender's accusations, and although the teachers were somewhat reluctant, again because Mrs. Merrick was new and a bit "pushy," they did support her. While the teachers might waver in their group loyalty, while they might criticize one another to friends, they usually stood together against any direct pressures.

The departmental arrangement on the upper floor led to some attempts by parents to use one teacher against the others. So a parent would quote one teacher to another, often inaccurately: "Mrs. Crane says she has no trouble with my son in class. Why do you?" "Mrs. Preston says Sally always does her *science* homework, and it's very neat." (Implication: "If she doesn't do her English, there is something wrong with the English teacher.") "Her marks are good in all the other subjects." Usually, the teachers reported such remarks to one another and therefore were able to join ranks against these false allegations. However, even when they knew the stories were falsifications, some residue of suspicion remained, and tension was built up by the rumors. The importance of in-group solidarity and loyalty led to strong negative feelings against the teacher or ex-teacher who broke ranks. Some gossip, never verified, that Mrs. Preston was spreading false information to parents led the other upstairs teachers to defensive solidarity against her. As Mrs. Crane put it, "It's hard enough to do this job without having a traitor in our midst." But the greatest hostility was directed at Mrs. Wilson who was taking a year off from teaching. Even while she had been teaching in the school, she had been criticized by other teachers for acting as if she preferred to be accepted by the parents rather than by her colleagues. After she left, the rumors began to spread that she was telling tales to parents, that she was revealing in-group secrets to outsiders. That a teacher, even one who never fit in, would betray them deeply upset all the other teachers: "She should know better. Where is her loyalty? After all, she is a teacher. She should know how hard it is without making it worse."[24]

The Adams teacher sometimes used the rule book to preserve her authority against parental encroachment. The school regulations and *The Curriculum Guide* came in handy as sources of legitimation. As one teacher told a parent concerned by his son's poor handwriting, "But we don't teach handwriting in the sixth grade. Look at *The Curriculum Guide.* By sixth grade the children should know how to write." However, if the parent directly challenged or ignored a rule, the teacher usually backed down. The regulations, although codified, had never been specifically endorsed by Mr. Hanson or by the school board and so did not provide the teacher with the support necessary to combat a parent convinced of his rights.

The Adams teacher rarely sought support for her authority from the professional association and the professional codes.[25] She turned everywhere else first: to administration, to school rules, to colleagues, and, in particular, to her years of experience. Mrs. Garten was the only teacher who specifically cited her training as a justification for her methods. Criticized for failing to teach reading to her kindergarten pupils, she countered, "I was trained in kindergarten work." However, even she ultimately used the unshakeable argument, experience: "I know children; their muscular and eye development have not progressed far enough for reading."

The Old Guard teacher then was at a distinct advantage in seeking legitimation. She had years of experience with children to support her against parental pressure. To the mother who took a six-week reading course and then criticized Mrs. Gregory's methods of teaching reading, Mrs. Gregory responded, "I have taught for years. I know that this is the right way to do it." The younger and newer teacher found herself at a disadvantage in this atmosphere where the premium was placed on experience and the folk wisdom so slowly and painfully acquired. Miss Tuttle, rather than cite her recently completed teacher training for support, retreated in some confusion from a parental challenge: "I can't tell him why his son behaves that way. I haven't taught long enough."

So it was the older teachers at Adams who fed the common parental stereotype that a young teacher or a highly trained teacher was less adequate than an older, more experienced teacher: "What kind of education will my child get with these young girls who have only had two or three years of experience?" Or, as another parent remarked on learning that the kindergarten teacher in a neighboring town had a Ph.D., "How ridiculous! What good will that do her?"

The teacher, by appealing to her experience, was utilizing a powerful form of insulation that made her independent of evaluation or criticism by other than her peers.[26] This insulation took on a particular coloration depending on the level at which one was teaching and the group from which one sought protection. The protective ideology, focusing on *how* one teaches rather than on *what* one teaches, used by the primary teacher against the intermediate and intermediate against the high school teacher, was adopted by the teachers at all levels against the encroachment of the person most concerned to limit and question her authority, the parent. Within the school the primary teacher talked most about the special skills involved in teaching. Confronting the parents, all the teachers adopted her arguments. This protective cloak was more functional than the cloak of knowledge of subject matter, particularly in dealing with the better-educated parents.

However, the most dangerous parents were not those whose education was greater than the teachers, per se, but those who were also teachers and thus privy to the secrets of the trade, the backstage regions one wished to hide. If these were high school or college teachers one suffered some tension, some insecurity, but one could use this cloak with some success, just as the elementary teachers used it against the high school teachers within the school system. If one was dealing with parents who were also elementary school teachers, one could not use this cloak and responses toward these parents became particularly ambivalent. On the one hand, it was satisfying to be able to talk to one who "understood" one's problems, who could empathize; on the other hand, it was awkward to have no way to create social distance through the usual devices, since the parent-teacher understood and used all of these devices herself. Backstage then perforce became front stage with all the attendant difficulties of incorporating a stranger.

This use of the cloak of special skill by the teacher against the encroachment of the parent helps to explain what might seem ambiguity in the parents' response to the school. Although parents are more completely involved with the children than are the teachers, this emotional intensity does not entail any real concern with the immediate school environment in which the child spends his days nor any great desire to have more frequent contact with the teachers.[27] This lack of interest seems to be a product of a number of factors. In a work written from inside the teacher's role I can only speculate about the elements that composed the parent's response. One element was the parents' stereotypical picture of what elementary education was all about, based primarily on what they had experienced. Reading, arithmetic, and spelling were the core. Other subjects — social studies, science, hygiene, art — were peripheral, even frills. I found it hard to persuade many parents that what the child learned in these areas would be important for his future education. Even a well-educated parent was undisturbed to learn that false information was being presented in sixth grade science and that the textbooks were ten years out of date. Another found more amusing than disturbing a teacher's misuse of the English language. This indifference was not universal; some parents became intensely interested in what was being taught and how it was being taught, but in my experience most parents did not show interest as long as the traditional curriculum was being presented. Other aspects were irrelevant and at best kept the child occupied and disciplined.

Another element was that the parents willingly accepted the ignorance imposed on them by the insulation of the classroom from observation and the norms that restricted parental snooping in the school. By preserving their ignorance they could avoid having to confront the challenges to their ultimate authority over the child posed by their delegation to the school of the right to educate him.

The protection provided by ignorance was threatened by change. The parents became anxious when changes in the curriculum occurred, when modern math became a new subject, when spelling mysteriously disappeared from the report card and language arts appeared, when the children brought home strange assignments in subjects about which the parents had in the past felt easy and familiar.[28] They protested; they wanted to know what was happening; they talked wistfully of the good old days and what they had learned. So to knock down the protective screen of ignorance was to force the parent to ask, "What are they doing in that school to *my* child?" Since the Adams teacher, particularly the Old Guard teacher, was no more interested in novelty than the parent, such a traditional approach satisfied her too. All the teachers discovered that the best way to avoid parental interference was to preserve the appearance of the old even when smuggling in the new.

It is evident that the barriers to observation of what went on in the school were functional for both parents and teachers. Physical barriers and social norms provided this insulation.[29] Although no official regulation prohibited parents from visiting the school and classroom during school hours and teachers told parents to come any time, the tradition was rather firmly established that parents were not welcome unless specifically invited or after hours.

This insulation was also increased by a firmly established pupil tradition. What went on at school was not reported at home, and what went on at home was not reported at school. The pupils kept their two worlds separate, thus insulating both parent and teacher from one another. "Show and Tell," institutionalized in the primary grades in many schools such as Adams, unwittingly became one formal device for encouraging the child to reveal details of home activities. Ordinarily, however, what the children told did not expose family secrets and home life. When it did, most of the children as well as the teacher found the experience unsettling. When Connie regaled the fourth grade with the account of her father's drunken trip to the city, they enjoyed listening but seemed embarrassed, refrained from asking questions, and none attempted to match her story with one of his own.[30]

In part, this reticence exemplifies how people handle roles they play within different social structures. Particularly if the complexity, degree of structure, and values are significantly different, they compartmentalize them and put up barriers between them. At home children learned early what was considered private family business, not to be discussed outside. And the child early learned from experience or was taught by his peers that to attempt to carry the school world home, to explain what had happened at school with its complex structure of roles and expectations among peers, teachers, and administrators might possibly expose him to parental interference in his school world. The parent could not correctly interpret an incident in its larger school context; his reaction was particularistic, "my child"; he made personal issues out of complex universalistic interrelations of marks, ranking, status in classroom and group. For a child to ask his parent for assistance then was to expose himself to rejection by the peer group, to allegations of dependency, of being a baby, to threaten the uneasy balance, however unpleasant, of his place in the school culture.

Similarly, the fifth or sixth grader, as I noted earlier, did not tattle to the homeroom teacher about problems he encountered in his physical education classes. In the world of high school, the adult world of competition and struggle with older boys and girls, one's status and place would be threatened if one complained to one's homeroom teacher about mistreatment. From one's place in this world, the elementary school and the elementary teacher seemed more particularistic, more like home and mother, and any retreat to home had to be avoided.

I in no way suggest that no child ever talked at home or that no child ever asked the homeroom teacher for help against the physical education instructor, but such occasions were rare. Ordinarily this insulation was preserved. I was continually struck by how unfamiliar parents were with their children's school experiences, even those which might seem to reflect credit rather than discredit on the child.

Faulty communication is a common explanation for the failure of the teacher and the parent (or for people playing any roles that hold contrasting expectations) to understand one another. The problem is reduced to a simple matter of improving perception and opening channels.[31] It is certainly true that there was a communication gap between teachers and parents, widened by the teacher's deliberate effort to protect her role from too much external scrutiny. However, this is not a sufficient explanation for the lack of congruence. Even when there seemed to be plenty of evidence to show the teacher that her expectations for parents were not going to be met, she clung to them.[32] This happened even if the same person played both roles, teacher and parent, at the same time. Of course, such double role-playing did bring about some modification in the behavior and expectations for each one. Mr. Scranton said that after becoming a parent himself he expected less from other parents. A parent, recently turned teacher, said that she now expected less from the school than she had before. But this did not change the way in which both of these teachers responded to the parents of their own pupils. While acting as teachers they incorporated the teacher's expectations of parents. While acting as parents they embodied the parental expectations. I was able to discover no evidence that playing these two roles caused any teacher-parent to feel inner conflict or incompatibility. The definition of the situation as parent or as teacher seemed to eliminate any tendency to operate simultaneously with the opposing definition.[33]

What happened if a teacher had to teach her own child? Under such circumstances would internal conflict not be inevitable? Teachers whom I queried insisted that in this situation they demanded more from their own children than they did from the rest of the class. They applied the universalistic norms to their own children in a more exaggerated fashion than they applied them to the other children. In this way, they could avoid being accused of "favoritism." To mitigate possible internal conflict, then, a teacher would move toward the expectations of one role at the expense of the other. However, where the two roles were separable by time or definition, the teacher seemed able to shift from one to the other without seeming strain.[34]

The discrepancy between anticipations and expectations was functional for the teacher. One way to protect her own self-image, her sense that she could never realize her educational goals considering the material she had been given to work with, was to throw the blame for failure on to someone else and parents provided a good scapegoat. One could blame the parents for inculcating the wrong standards, for failing to back up the teacher, or for getting in her way. The parent who did not conform to her expectations was necessary to the teacher. Certainly, although she knew (on one level) that no parent was going to think the way she did, she could (on another level) demand that it happen, could express surprise and outrage that it did not happen, and could blame the parent's failure for the inadequacies of the pupil. All the communication in the world, all the attempts to bridge the gap with informal visits and casual contacts, would probably not change the basic difference in outlook that was built into the roles. Change would not come because this difference was functional not only for the teacher and for the parent, but also, as Waller noted so perceptively, for the child trying to grow up and away from both home and school.[35] The pressures on the child were not the same and, therefore, to that degree they were less overwhelming.

6 POWER AND CONTROL: THE AUTHORITY VACUUM

Challenged by the parent, struggling to teach the pupil, the Adams teacher looked for guidance, direction, and control to those positions in the organization that were designated as having legitimate authority over her. These were four: Superintendent of Schools, Mr. Mongoose; the school board; the elementary supervisor, Mrs. Milton; and the principal, Mr. Hanson. The important question to be asked about the relation of the Adams teacher to the administration is not: "How well does the authority structure operate?"[1] but: "What is the authority structure? Is anyone in charge?" From the teacher's point of view the situation was characterized by the apparent unwillingness of any official in the formal structure to exercise authority. No member of the administration was anxious to give orders, to specify demands, to set limits. In such an authority vacuum, the older Adams teacher in particular was unsettled and disturbed. Her responses were ambivalent and confused. Occasionally she gloried in her freedom, comparing her present status favorably to the degree of control she had experienced during her early teaching years or to the restrictive control reported by teachers in nearby towns. Usually, however, she was bewildered. She kept looking for situations in which the formal authority was so legitimated and clear that compliance became a social duty, even a moral obligation.[2] The newer teacher, although she had no previous standards developed from earlier school experiences, was equally confused and bewildered by a situation for which her familiarity with other organizations had in no way prepared her. She posed to the older teachers questions they could not answer about who was responsible for decisions, what the administration was supposed to do.

From my vantage point as teacher I cannot explain just why this authority vacuum developed, but a few elements seem relevant. In part, some confusion about the locus of authority is characteristic in a school like Adams which because of its small size had a double formal authority structure, descending in one line from the State Board of Education and in the other from the Adams School Board (a bipartisan locally elected group of laymen). The superintendent and the elementary supervisor were employees of the State Board; the principal was an employee of the local school board. The teacher was directly subject to orders from the principal and the elementary supervisor. The teacher did not have any way of knowing how the spheres of authority and competence were formally distributed within the structure. What powers, for instance, did the superintendent have over the principal? How was control supposed to be apportioned between the elementary supervisor and the principal? Was the superintendent supposed to give her direction or did he delegate all his authority to the supervisor and to the principal?

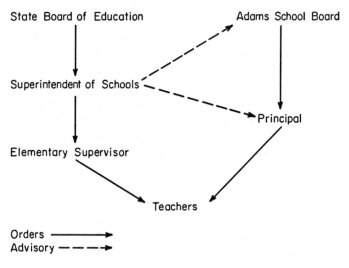

3. Adams Authority Structure

The double structure (see Figure 3) is not in itself sufficient to explain the absence of control over teachers in Adams at the time of this study. Until the late 1950s the superintendent, Mr. Murdstick, appointed by and responsible to the State Board of Education, was the only significant authority figure in the Adams School. He worked closely with the local school board, hiring teachers, setting up the salary schedules, controlling and restricting the ordering of books and supplies, and determining school policy and rules. He also visited classrooms, supervised curriculum and teachers, and administered discipline. Mrs. Milton, the state-appointed elementary supervisor, worked closely with him. She had more frequent and intimate contact with both teachers and pupils. She conducted the school in-service program for the teachers, helped them plan the curriculum, supervised pupil promotion, and gave advice on teaching methods and pupil problems. The boundary between her sphere of authority and that of Mr. Murdstick was clear and unproblematical. Mrs. Preston, the sixth grade teacher during these years, was teaching principal of the elementary school, a position that involved responsibility for communication and coordination of activities, but one that did not carry with it authority over the other teachers. Mr. Hanson as high school principal had only occasional contact with or figurehead responsibility over the elementary teachers (mostly as Mr. Murdstick's representative).

When Mr. Mongoose was appointed to replace Mr. Murdstick, and Mr. Hanson became principal of both the high school and the elementary school, the situation rather radically changed. Mrs. Preston was no longer elementary principal. Mr. Mongoose took little part in the activities of the school, appearing infrequently, not directly involved in teacher hiring or supervision, not concerned with supplies, books, classroom management, or salary schedules. Mrs. Milton also seemed to change at this time, as if in response to a change in job definition. She withdrew much of her involvement and interest, came to the school less often, and frequently acted as if she were unsure of the boundary between her authority and that of Mr. Hanson. One incident reveals the confusion. In previous years, final decision on pupil retention had been made by Mrs. Milton after consultation with the classroom teacher. Mr. Hanson had approved the recommendation (a mere formality), and the teacher had informed the parent. In the study year, neither Mrs. Milton nor Mr. Hanson made the decisions. Each left them to the other. Their suggestions were so tentative that the final decisions to retain certain pupils were made by the teachers themselves. They did not inform either Mrs. Milton or Mr. Hanson, and neither inquired as to their decisions, their reasons, or their justifications.

With these changes in the way in which authority was apportioned, the teacher found no one really taking charge and giving orders. Naturally, she was bewildered. Also, she was dissatisfied because she was in an exposed position. She now felt herself open to the demands and expectations of all those who were concerned about what she did with the child, in particular, the parents.

THE SUPERINTENDENT OF SCHOOLS: A REMOTE FIGURE

The teacher held expectations for each of the positions above her and then attempted to deal with the shattering of these expectations. Those she directed at Mr. Mongoose derived from the past, from the way in which the role of superintendent had been played by his predecessor, Mr. Murdstick. Consequently, these particular expectations were held only by the teacher who had taught at Adams for a few years.

The Adams teacher had sometimes vocally resented Mr. Murdstick's interference in classroom management and his rigid standards for teachers, including the rules he made concerning proper dress, voice, and manner. However, he had had definite expectations of the teacher which she had understood and which she had accepted as legitimate and binding. But Mr. Mongoose was so different. He seemed to have little interest in meeting or knowing her, and even less in controlling her.

Whatever resentment the older teacher had felt over Mr. Murdstick's dominance was forgotten in her resentment over Mr. Mongoose's failure to fill the position in the old way, to play the appropriate part. Actions of Mr. Murdstick once criticized by a teacher as "interference" were recalled nostalgically as signs of the time when the superintendent had set standards: "Remember he told Mr. Scranton never to teach without his coat on no matter how hot a day it was." "Remember how he told you how important it is to get order right at the beginning of the year." "Remember how he knew all the children's names and used to quiz them when he visited."

Mr. Mongoose was doubly resented, both for what he did not do, and occasionally for what he did. Although the teacher received no personal guidance from Mr. Mongoose, she was still aware of his existence as a result of occasional directives in which he seemed to be working against her interests. It was he who announced that there would be no more half-days of school before holidays; he who ruled that teachers might not close the attendance registers before the last day of school; he who sent a formidable document to the staff outlining the teacher's responsibility relating to student accidents.

The teacher was in no position to know whether the change in the behavior of the superintendent resulted from a change in the job specifications from above (State Department of Education) or from a change in the person holding the status. Regardless of the reasons for the change, she did not like it. Anything Mr. Mongoose attempted to do was resented by the Adams teacher. He was the usurper in a position that had been defined in very personal terms by a very strong leader.[3] But even more than this, since Mr. Mongoose seemed to have chosen not to define himself in any relation to the teacher, she blamed him for failing her and turned elsewhere for guidance. The newer teacher, with no experience of Mr. Murdstick, had no expectations of Mr. Mongoose as an authority figure. She looked for guidance to positions closer at hand.[4]

ADAMS SCHOOL BOARD: ULTIMATE AUTHORITY

The Adams teacher had only indirect relationship with the school board, and this relationship remained quite constant over the years. The expectations she held of the board and the expectations the board apparently held of her were limited and congruent.

The members of the Adams School Board, three Democrats and three Republicans, usually came from different sections of the town and represented diverse occupational and economic

positions. Some, but not all, were of higher social status and had
more wealth than the Adams teachers. A simple class distinction
between board members and teachers did not exist. Some board
members were considered by the teacher to have lower social
status and certainly less education than she did. Particular scorn
was directed by the Old Guard teacher toward a few board
members from the Hill who sent their own children to private
schools while they themselves were responsible for the education
of the local children.

Teachers and board members had some personal informal ties.
They knew one another through political party affiliation,
neighborhood contacts, and through having children in the
elementary school. These informal contacts, casual friendships,
and even occasional antipathies in no way seemed to influence
the response of the teacher toward the school board viewed as a
status position above her in the formal structure. As a locus of
authority the board had to be viewed with deference and respect.
The board as a unit was dissociated in the teacher's mind from
the board as a collection of individuals who could be and were
gossiped about by the Old Guard teachers.

Respect for the board meant that the elementary teacher
rejected the use of aggressive action for salary increases as
recommended by some of the younger male high school teachers.
To urge aggressive action was impolite: "They are so rude and
unmannerly, just not well brought up." And when the board, as it
rarely did, commanded, a teacher obeyed. After Mrs. Calhoun
was personally asked to attend a board dinner for the teachers
she commented, "I couldn't ignore that even though I have a
class that night. It was like a command from the throne."

Despite her respect and deference the Adams teacher had few
expectations of direct board control over her. Insulated from the
board by the position of the principal, she pretended not to know
that the board did have the ultimate authority to make the
decisions on the curriculum, on the selections of textbooks, on
standards for teachers. Since the board rarely exercised its
authority in these areas, she was resentful when it did. On one
occasion the board invited both high school and elementary
teachers to explain their academic programs at a series of board
meetings. The teachers resented the request and its implications
of surveillance. Mrs. Crane said crossly, "If they want to know

the curriculum let them read *The Curriculum Guide.* Why should I go there and talk to them? It's not their business. They won't understand what it's all about."

Occasional board "interference" in pupil placement and teacher allocation was also resisted. When in one such instance Mr. Hanson made no secret of his disagreement with board action, the teachers quite freely and vocally expressed their own resentment.

Although this relationship between teachers and school board was clearly structured as indirect and the board as noncontrolling, the Adams teacher did occasionally seek support and direction from the school board. Mrs. Preston frequently told the other upstairs teachers that she was going to go to the board to get support on discipline problems, since "we receive no help from Mr. Hanson." On one occasion the elementary teachers banded together and requested Mr. Hanson to ask the school board for permission to use corporal punishment. However, the teachers never learned how the board reacted to this request or even whether Mr. Hanson transmitted it.

THE ELEMENTARY SUPERVISOR: IDEAL IMAGE AND REALITY

Neither the superintendent nor the school board played a significant controlling part in the teacher's role-set. But with her direct superiors, Mrs. Milton and Mr. Hanson, the situation was different. Each teacher had clear expectations for these positions and suffered severe frustration of these expectations.

An Old Guard teacher considered the elementary supervisor to be the only administrative official qualified in any degree to "interfere" with purely educational matters, because she had specialized training in curriculum, methods of instruction, and classroom management. It was therefore legitimate, although annoying, for the supervisor to visit the classroom, to watch the teacher teach, to discuss the learning problems of the pupils with her, to help her select textbooks, and to help her make decisions on promotions.

The expectations and anticipations of Mrs. Milton, the supervisor, held by the Adams teacher were highly influenced by the teacher's degree of experience. The new teacher might desire and need guidance and direction from outside more than the experienced teacher did. However, she had fewer expectations of receiving these from Mrs. Milton than did the experienced teacher, since she lacked previous experience with supervisors. So, the ambivalent responses of the Old Guard teachers to Mrs. Milton were dominant at Adams.

Mrs. Milton had been elementary supervisor in Adams and five surrounding towns for over fifteen years. She had taught second grade one year herself, and then became a supervisor. She was in her sixties, a soft-spoken, well-dressed, attractive woman. Her surface relationship with the Adams teachers was friendly and casual, full of small talk about family and home.

She usually visited the school each week. She never lost her temper, never gave an order, never did more than make tentative suggestions to a teacher. She accompanied her occasional mild criticisms with a deprecatory laugh or an apology. Even in the classroom she attempted to be unobtrusive. She did sometimes express veiled criticism: "I think they might have been a little quieter." "It's too bad you don't have children's work up on the bulletin board, although those are nice pictures."

Even while making her expectations clear to the teacher she was fussy rather than domineering, laissez faire in manner rather than authoritarian. The Adams teacher responded to this kind of supervision with ambivalence. On the one hand, she resented the lack of help given: "The new teachers find it very peculiar that no one at all has been around to observe. They have no one to tell them anything. We are used to it, but they don't know what to do." "How can a new teacher get along in this school? We need a homework policy. Why doesn't she help? Mrs. Milton doesn't do anything."

It was the failure of Mrs. Milton to help, to give practical advice, or to make suggestions that rankled with these teachers: "I asked her what to do about the child who cries all day long. She said, 'Send her to the nurse.' Hah! That's a lot of help." "She's no help at all with the parents either."

On the other hand, the teacher equally or more vehemently resented Mrs. Milton's visits, her supervision (casual as it was), and her direction.

Mr. Scranton warned the new teachers early in the fall, "The authorities are here. You had better be careful. She always visits the new teachers every time she comes."

Miss Tuttle complained, "Doesn't she ever go upstairs to visit? Why does she always come on Fridays?"

As soon as she arrived, a teacher would suggest hopefully that she might possibly leave before lunch. Jocular suggestions would be exchanged for getting rid of her: "I will get out a *Weekly Reader.* She hates them." "I will give a test. That will chase her away." "You can keep her out if you open the windows since she doesn't like cold weather." "Get them all to talk at once. She hates disorder."

Part of this response was the teacher's anxiety about being evaluated. When Mrs. Crane told us that Mrs. Milton had to make a full report on every classroom visit, we were impressed, a bit pleased, and yet frightened. Naturally, her visits meant that we had to work that much harder: "I was planning to give them a study period, but now I will have to teach them something."

The teachers teased Mrs. Crane (with some envy) about her special math lessons that she saved for Mrs. Milton's visits. Even Mrs. Preston gave up a precious noon hour to preparing a lesson on atoms since Mrs. Milton planned to visit her science class.

But more than anxiety underlay the resentment. Every teacher hated to give up her freedom from observation and her autonomy.[5] Although she recognized that Mrs. Milton had the right to visit and advise, she objected to her advice because of the inevitable difference between her perspective as teacher and the perspective of Mrs. Milton as supervisor. She was convinced that no administrator, even one specially trained, could understand what went on in the classroom, could understand her problems or her needs.[6] She succinctly summed it up by saying that Mrs. Milton had "forgotten what it is to be in a classroom."

Each teacher considered Mrs. Milton's attitudes to be a result of lack of classroom experience. She had been out of teaching too long, and all this "theoretical" knowledge about teaching was useless: "Why does she object to workbooks? I don't have time to make up all those exercises." "So they shouldn't read aloud. How can I tell if they know the words if they don't read aloud?" "Why is she so bothered about noise? She wants everything in order and on schedule and then she wants us to do special projects which make for noise."

One teacher shot back at Mrs. Milton, but not until she was out of earshot, "I don't care if the text *isn't* original. I just want enough exercises to keep them busy."

Miss Tuttle remarked that Mrs. Milton was always explaining something to her class that she had already told them many times. She commented, "This is humiliating."

Thus, the resistance to the invasion of the exclusive territory and domain of the teacher caused some of the resentment. But this was not all. For the Old Guard teacher was also annoyed about the kind of supervision that Mrs. Milton gave. This annoyance was a product of the ideal supervisor image against which this teacher measured Mrs. Milton and with which she sometimes tried to identify her. This ideal image was a construct, put together from the memories of the supervisor Mrs. Milton used to be before she began to retreat from real participation, from the memories of supervisors the teacher had known in her early teaching days, and from stories about supervisors in other towns.

No one knew why Mrs. Milton had changed, and there was much speculation among the teachers about her illness, her age, her family problems, but all remarked on her lack of interest: "She hasn't seemed to care for two or three years." "She hasn't once looked at my plan book and she used to every year." "I never made a daily schedule this year. She didn't ask for one last year or this. She used to every year."

On the verbal level, at least, this change in Mrs. Milton was not appreciated: "Miss Elmer in Cliffton is so helpful. She really works with the teachers and the children and the families. She is a helpful supervisor." "Miss Whitton was really helpful. The children loved her. She even took a reading group for me one day."

The teacher recalled her early supervisors as rigid, domineering, and yet helpful. Mrs. Gregory once happily reminisced to me: "Your plans were checked; you were observed; and he wrote comments in a notebook. We had one teacher who was always getting called down for not following plans, but she learned. It was wonderful for a new teacher."

The Adams teacher's ambivalence about Mrs. Milton: "She leaves us alone. We are lucky"; but: "She never helps or supervises," extended to this "ideal supervisor image." Although the teacher praised the discipline of her early teaching days, she praised it primarily because the discipline was over. Any hint of domineering or authoritarian behavior in Mrs. Milton was not praised.

Significantly, though, the teacher often treated Mrs. Milton as if she really was this tough, dominant, vitally-interested supervisor. Mild-mannered, soft-spoken, diffident Mrs. Milton was described by one teacher as an "ogre." Mrs. Preston told us that Mrs. Milton had "bawled out" Mrs. Wilson. Mr. Scranton reported that Mrs. Milton was "very angry" at Miss Tuttle for the noise in her room.

"When she couldn't find anything else to criticize she told me my brooch was on crooked."

Each Adams teacher acted as if Mrs. Milton's disapproval was so threatening that it must be avoided at all costs. None ever expressed to Mrs. Milton her disagreement with Mrs. Milton's mildly expressed views. The teacher might ignore the recommendations since she believed Mrs. Milton did not know what was going on, but she was apologetic, secretive, and timid about such resistance. And even when she expressed most vocal annoyance to the other teachers, her actions contradicted her. Criticized for a teacher-prepared bulletin board, Mrs. Preston complained, "It is good for the children to see a nice bulletin board sometime even if they don't make it themselves." But she took it down and allowed some of her pupils half a school day to create a new one: "Dreadfully messy, isn't it?"

A suggestion was interpreted as an order, a negative comment as a complete rejection, a bit of faint praise as the highest accolade, a lukewarm response as the most vital interest.

What the teacher seemed to be doing here was criticizing Mrs. Milton both for deviating from the ideal role-expectation and for embodying this role-expectation (an embodiment projected onto Mrs. Milton by the teacher herself). The teacher rejected her both for failing to carry out the ideal role and for carrying it out. The desire to be controlled and the desire to be free clearly ran into one another here.

THE PRINCIPAL: THE BOSS

With no separate elementary principal in the Adams School, Mr. Hanson was the only school official with rights and duties formally designated for this position. Every teacher, experienced and inexperienced, turned her expectations for control, protection, and support toward him.[7] Her past teaching and learning experiences, her teacher training, and the cultural stereotypes associated with the status of principal created in her expectations that he would direct and that she would willingly obey him. "The boss" should be in charge. "That is what he gets paid for," as Mrs. Crane put it. The "ideal administrator" whom I asked the teachers to describe in their interviews was interpreted by all teachers to mean the principal. He was the one who should give orders, should help with discipline and student problems, should understand elementary education, should see that activities were coordinated, the one who should stand between teacher and school board, between teacher and parents, and the one who should be strong enough to keep the teacher from being pushed around by anyone else. "The job is to stay behind the teacher at all times unless proved the teacher is wrong."

The Adams teacher, of course, was in no position to know how Mr. Hanson pictured his role-obligations. But she did know that either he saw his role very differently from the way she did, or he was prevented from successfully carrying it out. Her frustration at the discrepancy underlay all of the relations between the teacher and Mr. Hanson during these years.

Mr. Hanson was a local boy who made good. He grew up in Adams Hollow, a member of the small Swedish farming community. He stayed in Adams until he went to college. After teaching for a few years in another state, he returned to Adams to teach science. He soon received a small administrative post and then moved rapidly up to become first high school principal and then principal of the whole school. Some of his subordinates had been his own teachers in school; others of the Old Guard had known him as a child and young man ("I pushed him in a baby carriage"). His interests at Adams, even after his advancement, were in the science program and the physical education department. Pushed into control of the elementary school because of administrative reshuffling, he made no pretense of having had any training or background in elementary education.

The teachers liked Mr. Hanson as a person: "He is such a nice man, such a kind person." And they respected him as a science teacher. They also found him to be nervous, self-effacing, forgetful, and mild-mannered.[8]

Like Mr. Mongoose, Mr. Hanson suffered from the handicap of following the strong and forceful Mr. Murdstick who had imbued the position of boss with deep personal influence.[9] Mr. Hanson's method of handling the change differed somewhat from that of Mr. Mongoose; rather than completely self-efface himself, he chose to be accepted through his deference to the opinions and greater knowledge of others.[10] So, with the schedule set, the curriculum established, and Mrs. Milton at her post when he assumed command he sat back and waited. Although he held monthly faculty meetings, he obviously expected Mrs. Milton to run them. But she progressively retreated from decision-making obligations, turning most of them back to him. He found himself called upon to make decisions on all matters of curriculum, discipline, books, and promotions. He had to accept his official responsibility for all these matters, but in action he continued to defer to the teachers, in particular the Old Guard teachers: "Of course, I don't know anything about elementary school, so you will have to tell me what you need. You have had many years of experience and don't need me to tell you how to do things. It would be silly for me to come and supervise you."

During the first year the teachers were flattered by this catering to their knowledge and experience and pleased that their freedom and autonomy were assured by Mr. Hanson's disinclination to disturb the even tenor of their ways.[11] After the first year, however, the relationship of Mr. Hanson to his teachers became more and more difficult. First of all, he did change slightly. He took charge more often, by necessity, but with obvious reluctance. And frequently when he did so the teachers would reject his competence, even quoting against him his own words about his ignorance. During a faculty discussion about whether to order social studies books for the primary teachers, his tentative suggestion that they should teach without textbooks was overridden by the teachers. When he made pronouncements about science, however, even though the teachers resented his lack of understanding of the difference between elementary teaching and high school teaching, they accepted his views, partly because of the firmness with which he expressed them.

As time passed Mr. Hanson became more outspoken and willing to direct the newer teachers, addressing them by their first names and even denying them certain privileges. However, he continually preserved his humility and deference to the older teachers, addressing them by their married names and rarely denying a request (even when it was not expressed as a request). Mrs. Preston commented: "When I took the day off for Harry's wedding, I didn't ask him. I told him and he knew better than to argue with me about it."

But, despite these slight changes, the teachers more and more saw him as uninterested and vacillating, and the initial enjoyment of freedom gave way to complaints over his lack of control: "Is he a man or a mouse?" "He gets out of work by saying about any problem, 'Put up with it or I, uh,' and then nothing."

What were the expectations the teacher had of Mr. Hanson? She wanted him to care, which meant to show his concern for her problems, to take her work seriously, and to give help when possible. When plans were taking shape to build a new elementary school separate from the high school, many of the teachers looked forward to the chance to have their own principal: "There we could have a principal who would care." When the plans fell through, Mrs. Crane said sadly, "We will have to go another whole year without knowing what to do."

Mrs. Preston returned one day from the high school office grumbling, "Every other principal at least *speaks* to his teachers."

The failure to care sometimes was seen as a personal affront. In January and again in June, Mr. Hanson gave a party for the high school teachers. Each elementary teacher felt neglected and, although she joked, it hurt: "You weren't there, really? You mean you weren't invited? When he was just principal for the high school maybe it made sense for him to have those private parties but now it doesn't. It certainly wasn't very nice of him."

Unhappiness about his lack of awareness of her as a person was mild compared to the elementary teacher's strong feeling that he did not really respect her as a teacher. His unguarded remark one day that he liked to hire young, new, enthusiastic teachers with or without experience was interpreted by Mrs. Preston to mean: "They would be glad to see us go. We cost too much. Experience isn't important. Why should they care as long as they can get it cheaply?"

The lack of respect for her work and lack of interest in the elementary school were pointed up by Mr. Hanson's failure to visit the elementary school or to seem to know what was going on in it:

"You will be interested to know the boss is here today."

"Oh, really. I don't think I know him."

"You know, the little bald headed eagle."

Unable to find him in the elementary school, the teacher sought him out in his office, only to find that he seemed indifferent to her problems. "What can I do?" or "Do what you want" were frequent responses, each of which exasperated the teacher. As Mrs. Crane said, "He doesn't know anything at all. He might as well be in Timbuktu." The teacher even began to believe that he was not just indifferent, but that he belittled the problems she had. Her sensitive feelings were stung by his laughter. When the Anderson children played hookey for a whole week and Mrs. Preston went for help, she returned crushed: "He said, 'What difference does it make?' and then laughed."

Requests by teachers were often forgotten or bypassed. Mrs. Gregory once remarked, "Oh, he just conveniently forgot it. He always does that when he doesn't want to deal with something. He did that with separate tables for teachers. He said he would look into it and that was the last ever heard about it." Such incidents were frequent enough to cause some cynicism about going to Mr. Hanson for anything. Many of these incidents resulted from the poor communication channels in the Adams school. Burdened with full-time high school obligations, his office in the high school building, Mr. Hanson rarely had time to visit the elementary school, to talk to the teachers, to find out what was going on. He had few useful channels for acquiring information or for giving directives. The only link between him and the elementary teachers was Mrs. Preston who no longer had official standing as principal in the elementary school. No formal system was ever worked out for transmitting information or directives in either direction. Everything moved by word of mouth, and often information did not reach those for whom it was intended. To the elementary teacher this signified a deliberate indifference: "Suppose we all stayed home, who would know it?" He constantly "forgot" to inform the primary teachers of the dates on which they were supposed to send out report cards, to let the teachers know of important meetings they should attend, even once to attend a meeting he called himself. Book fairs, science exhibits, lectures to which teachers knew they were invited were never mentioned by him: "What happened to our invitation?" Frustration over this lack of interest was more than once summed up in the disgusted comment: "We don't have any principal here or any administration."

The elementary teacher was convinced that Mr. Hanson was not interested in the elementary school because he was only interested in the high school. His perspective was that of a high school teacher: "He thinks we don't count, aren't important. Everything is high school, high school."[12] He had not even made the effort to acquire the knowledge of elementary education which the teacher believed a principal should have. In two faculty meetings the teachers discussed educational matters. The first time, at his request, they talked about the teaching of penmanship; the second time, at the request of one of the new teachers, they talked about how to mark the report cards. In neither discussion did Mr. Hanson participate through guidance at the beginning or opinions at the conclusion. So no teacher knew which policy he preferred or what standards he expected her to follow.

This picture of Mr. Hanson as indifferent, ignorant, uninformed about his staff and its work, holding few expectations for his teachers and setting few guidelines, resulted in the proliferation of rumor in the school. The story ran through the school that Mr. Hanson was going to hire a former teacher to teach upstairs, a teacher whom all the other teachers strongly and obviously disliked. That he would make such an unpopular choice convinced the teachers that either he did not know their feelings or, that if he did, he did not care. The teacher was not hired, but whether because I went to warn him of the hostility or because the rumor was false, no one knew. The rumor had done its work in straining teacher morale. Rumors proliferated that the school day was to be lengthened, that class size was to be doubled, that one teacher was in Mr. Hanson's bad graces, that he was favoring another teacher. No direct information was ever offered to check these rumors.

The teacher's response to the lack of communication and the indifference was frequently to attempt to force information and problems to Mr. Hanson's attention. As she did with Mrs. Milton, she invented in Mr. Hanson a concern that he never showed. Every year, the teachers took him more and more problems, even problems she knew perfectly well that he could not solve. He was repeatedly asked what to do about the sixth

grade girl who was so dirty that she smelled up every classroom.
He had no answer as each teacher knew: "I'm glad I'm not in his
place." And each was wickedly delighted when the poor girl
fainted one day and Mr. Hanson had to take her home,
supporting her down the stairs and into his car. "Now he'll know
what it's like to have Mary near you."

Whenever a teacher was particularly frustrated about
something else, she would manage to bring a conversation with
him around to the overcrowding in the third grade classroom,
although she knew that it was not his problem to solve: "And he
always says, 'Poor Polly,' and never does anything about it."

The teachers were most punctilious about carrying out their
formal obligations to Mr. Hanson. Each one would ask his
permission if she wished to leave school before three-thirty. He
never seemed to hear the request, which he granted automatically.
On one occasion, when three of us left early without asking
permission, "sneaking" noisily out of the building, we met Mr.
Hanson in the parking lot. "We got caught that time," said Mr.
Scranton apprehensively, even though we were all aware that Mr.
Hanson seemed quite unaware of our misdemeanor.

At noon the teachers frequently joked nervously about what
"Mr. Hanson will think" of their drinking coffee in the teachers'
room rather than being on duty on the playground. Mrs. Preston
rushed into the teachers' room one noon: "I must go outdoors at
once. The boss is there, angry as can be because no teacher is
out. He is right down at the corner yelling at the children." We
were all impressed, disturbed, upset. But I discovered that Mr.
Hanson was actually calmly eating his lunch in the cafeteria, not
roaring around on the playground. Mrs. Preston's powers of
imputing authority exceeded that of any of the other teachers, but
they all did it with Mr. Hanson as they did with Mrs. Milton.

The teachers worked extremely hard to get their monthly
reports done "early" so that Mr. Hanson would not be annoyed
with them. Mrs. Gregory warned Miss Tuttle each month that
Mr. Hanson would be really angry with her if her report was not
ready by three o'clock. He never showed any anger, however,
when she just as regularly failed to have it done. Every time the
upstairs teachers changed their schedules they would go to Mr.
Hanson for approval, "because it is his duty to make the
decisions, but he will say anything we want to do is all right."

One important aspect of "caring" by Mr. Hanson was that he should protect and support the teacher against the pressures of parents and pupils. And here she felt Mr. Hanson really let her down: "Principals elsewhere back their teachers."[13] As I noted earlier, the teacher did not know how much Mr. Hanson actually interposed himself between her and the parents, but what she saw was that she was exposed, that he seemed to cater to the upper-class parents, and that he resisted any attempt to push him into the middle. He once refused to move an upper-class child into the B division of the sixth grade even though all the teachers asked him to. Instead he suggested that the child be kept in the A division "to help her social adjustment" and be given special help by the teachers. This merely confirmed the conviction already held by the teachers that he would do anything to help himself up the social ladder in Adams. Under pressure from a Hill parent who disliked the "social climate" in the B division, he tried to convince the upstairs teachers that a child be moved from the B to the A group. Failing this, his suggestion that the child be moved and then failed, which would cause less trouble with the parent, led to much critical comment by the teachers about his being two-faced.

The teachers particularly resented Mr. Hanson's obvious attempts to avoid confrontation with the parents. He always recommended that special meetings with parents be held in the classroom rather than in his office and that Mrs. Preston be the spokesman. As Mrs. Preston griped, "I'm not the principal. Why can't *he* take responsibility?" But he did not. And the teachers learned that if there was a classroom problem, he preferred for the teacher to call the parent. When a child was not to be promoted, the teacher knew she had to write the letter to the parent.

Failure to protect her against the parents rankled and so did failure to support her in dealing with the pupils.[14] It was this failure to live up to her ideal role-expectation for which the Adams teacher most blamed Mr. Hanson. Principals in other schools were commended: "Mr. Pringle has real discipline. You can send a troublemaker to him and there will be no more trouble." That the principal should be the "boss" was central to her expectations. Again, although Mr. Hanson often failed her here, she sometimes pretended that he would play this role: "If

Bob or Richard acts up I will take them to him. He certainly can't expect me to put up with it again this year. It is too much. I am not going to have it." Whenever a teacher complained to another about noise or defiance or disobedience from particular pupils, she was told, "Take him to the office," or "Let Mr. Hanson handle it."

And when she followed this advice, sent a pupil to the office, asked Mr. Hanson to do something about the troublemakers, her expectations were frustrated. And she would complain, "What good does it do to send them over? Nothing will be done. We can't expect it with our principal."

As Mr. Hanson calmly said one day in the faculty meeting, "There is little I can do if you send them over to me. I can talk to them, but that is about all. It is embarrassing to me to have the problem children in the office and there is no other place I can put them."

Each teacher knew that a pupil sent to the office was usually allowed to sit on the bench in the waiting room and watch all the exciting high school traffic go by. This seemed to be the extent of the punishment: "I sent two of them to the office and they came back grinning all over." "They like to go to the office, you know. It's no punishment for them."

On the rare occasion when Mr. Hanson did use authority and forcefulness with pupils and parents, the incident was told and retold by a teacher to an audience that remained skeptical. Such an occasion was unusual: "He picked Richard up and shook him, actually shook him."

"Oh come on, his arms would get tired out just picking him up."

Discipline problems multiplied during the school year, and the teachers became more and more disturbed. Finally Mr. Scranton suggested at a faculty meeting that Mr. Hanson ask the school board for permission to let the teachers use corporal punishment. This unprecedented request was supported by all the teachers except for Miss Tuttle, who "loved" all the children. Both Mr. Hanson and Mrs. Milton seemed extremely surprised and even shocked at the suggestion. The near unanimity of the teachers might indicate in-group loyalty to Mr. Scranton rather than a desire to use corporal punishment, but, in the discussion that followed, even the Old Guard teachers revealed their concern about the effectiveness of their classroom control and the need for formal backing for their authority. As Mrs. Crane said, "It is hard work never to smile, never to let down, never to have fun with them since they always take advantage. One can't be friends with the children any more. We have to preserve control."

Mr. Hanson did promise to do something about the situation, to visit the classrooms and to transmit the request to the school board. Nothing further was then heard: "I notice how he comes over and observes. Ha!" "Bet he never told the school board at all." No apparent change in the handling of discipline problems occurred during the year.

Another expectation held by the teacher for Mr. Hanson was that he should represent the ideal role-model of the "educator." This was not a clear-cut expectation since it was blurred by some awareness that as an administrator Mr. Hanson would not look at things exactly as a teacher did. Nevertheless, she expected him to represent her in public as a teacher and as a professional. Somehow, he must, as the top official within the structure become the embodiment of the norms and standards of teachers. So he was expected to represent to outsiders the teacher's educational goals, to understand how the teacher looked at things, and to be more professional, more correct than she. Only Mr. Hanson was criticized by the teachers for not being "professional." They never made such accusations against one another. The teacher did not herself have to care about whether there was a new high school library or even whether more money was put into education, but she expected Mr. Hanson to care about these matters publicly. When Mr. Hanson attacked a plan for an elementary school library as unnecessary, the teachers were angry: "Whatever other people do, your principal should come out for education."

When Mr. Hanson occasionally acted as "administrator" against the teacher's desires, she resented this strongly. He occasionally insisted on rigid adherence to rules.[15] He refused to allow Miss Tuttle a day off to visit another school and the teachers all agreed that this was unjust, even though he was following school policy. That the points of view of an administrator and a teacher were different was often ignored in the teachers' annoyance at Mr. Hanson's "pettiness." Mrs. Gregory could not understand why Mr. Hanson was angry when she made a private arrangement for obtaining a substitute without informing him "so I wouldn't have to bother him. Why does he have to be told?" Poor communication added to the teachers' failure to understand Mr. Hanson's job: "He'll be over with our checks. That's the only time we ever see him. Doesn't he have anything else to do?"

In November the deep rift between the teacher's expectations for Mr. Hanson and his behavior as well as the steady deterioration of discipline in the school led to a rare breakdown in organizational solidarity. Usually the teacher stood with those inside, even administrators, against anyone outside the organization. But at the time of the fall parent-teacher conferences some of the upstairs teachers, disturbed by disciplinary problems, feeling isolated and unsupported by Mr. Hanson and Mrs. Milton, complained about the situation to some of the parents. They talked about how hard it was to teach so many children who did not want to learn, did not listen and did not behave. "Eighty percent of our time is spent on police work," Mrs. Crane reported she told a number of parents. To complain about the children was not unusual, but it was unusual publicly to throw the responsibility for the problem on the administration.

When Mr. Hanson heard what had happened, he was (according to Mrs. Preston) deeply disturbed by what he felt was teacher disloyalty, and he called a meeting of the four upstairs teachers. Before the meeting the teachers showed some bravado and some guilt about tattling: "If he ever listened we would go to him. How many times have we sent Richard over and what has he ever done? What help has he given?"

At the meeting Mr. Hanson behaved in his usual friendly and modest way, although he did say that he thought it was very bad for the teachers' problems to be revealed to the parents. The teachers asked whether he might occasionally visit the elementary classrooms. He retreated at once, "You don't need supervision. Some of you have taught longer than I. You know your business."

Bolder now, Mrs. Preston said, "We want backing for our discipline, not supervision."

But he resisted, "All I can do is bawl them out and they will turn right around and do it again."

Although he kept insisting that he would not "interfere in any way," he finally agreed to try to help. Tension subsided and the more usual topic of discussion took over — criticism of parents.

For a short period of time Mr. Hanson visited classrooms and talked to the teachers about their problems. However, the brief transformation did not last, and the earlier state of affairs soon returned.

When sometime later a teacher suggested taking to the PTA a plan for setting up a special class for slow learners in order to get their support since Mr. Hanson seemed to oppose the idea, Mrs. Crane quickly said, "We got bawled out before for going over his head. You better go to him first."

To which Mr. Scranton responded, "Why don't we bring it up to him at the teachers' meeting, but not me, you?"

No one did and no one tried again during the year to force Mr. Hanson into conformity with the ideal expectation for a strong principal standing behind his teachers.

Most of the teacher's expectations for Mr. Hanson revolved around a desire for control and direction which he did not give her. However, we must not forget that the Adams teacher was also concerned about her autonomy. She was as ambivalent about Mr. Hanson in this regard as she was about all superior positions. But her concern with autonomy was less evident than her desire for control, because he interfered with her freedom so little. The ambivalence revealed itself clearly in an incident in the spring. The upstairs teachers agreed that a pupil who had done almost no work during the year and had made almost no gain on the achievement tests should not be promoted to seventh grade, in part as a warning to the other pupils. However, they were reluctant to take this step since he was a troublemaker and it would be annoying to have him in the building another year. So, in sardonic mood, they sent me over to ask Mr. Hanson to make the decision. He asked me what the teachers recommended. I told him that they reluctantly thought retention was a good idea. "Retain him then," he said without interest. I returned to my colleagues who complained bitterly about his words, remarking that, since Mr. Hanson knew nothing about the situation and did not know the boy, he should refrain from making snap judgments. The teachers then talked themselves around to the conviction that Mr. Hanson had no right to make this decision. This was their territory. Shortly thereafter it was easy to persuade Mr. Hanson, who seemed completely indifferent, to reverse his decision. His second statement supporting promotion was then used by the teachers "against our better judgment" as the reason for the promotion.

This series of events was not unusual at Adams. Taking place over time it did not appear to be such bald manipulation in action as it must in the telling. Out of the desire for control, and yet the insistence on autonomy, came this invented authority when authority was absent.

CONTROL, AUTONOMY, AND EVASION

The extent of the authority vacuum in the Adams School is certainly not typical of most elementary schools nor is it within the experience of most elementary teachers. However, the response of the teachers to it and the ways in which they handled it do seem to represent common expectations for positions of authority. Contradictory pressures can be reduced if a person can use the "differences in the power of those involved"[16] by seeking support from the legitimate source of power. If the authority figures abdicate their authority, the teacher is unprotected. Therefore, she seeks to find other sources of support in the rule book or from colleagues, or through inventing authority even where it does not actually exist: "I have to do it this way since these are the rules. This is what the boss requires me to do. It's not my fault."[17] However, as soon as the external pressure or the threat of external pressure was withdrawn, the Adams teacher concentrated on preserving her autonomy, her insulation from observability, her uninvaded territory. Since no administrator could possibly understand what it meant to teach, no administrator should interfere with her teaching. We have seen how this shifting back and forth between the desire for control and the desire for autonomy influenced the Adams teacher in her relations with Mrs. Milton and Mr. Hanson. Ambivalence about her autonomy resulted in part from the teacher's awareness that if the administrators knew more about what went on they could be of more help to her.[18] So the teacher did try to keep Mr. Hanson informed when she behaved in nonroutinized ways. Even when she felt it was unnecessary, she let him know if she engaged in new or deviant action.[19]

With so few directives and commands to follow, the Adams teacher primarily acted on the basis of past experience and habit, while still pushing in all "legitimate" directions for more guidance. She complained a great deal and much of the time showed dissatisfaction with her work and with her unimportance to those above her. She believed that the administration did not care about her dissatisfactions since it made so few efforts to change the conditions about which she complained. As Mr. Hanson remarked in what seemed genuine puzzlement, "Your school runs itself. You don't need any help."

With no specific direction from agents in authority the Adams teacher often displayed strict conformity to the norms and rules of the school system. She imputed to them a rigidity and formality they did not in actuality possess, partly to reduce her sense of exposure and defenselessness. The Old Guard teacher took the lead here, resisting the "dangerous tendency" toward novelty and innovation that, like the measles, occasionally swept over the newer, less-experienced teacher.

Just as direct defiance of the rules by the pupils was almost unknown at Adams, so indirect or direct evasion of the rules by the teacher was rare. "Institutionalized evasions of institutional rules" usually occur in an organization when deviance has become functional for a group within the organization and often become a prelude to structural change in the organization. Merton and others have discussed in some detail the conditions under which these evasions are likely to emerge and to continue.[20]

At Adams, institutionalized evasions were uncommon since most of these conditions did not obtain. Common norms and rules had been traditionalized over the years and they made sense to the Old Guard teacher, fitting as they did with her background, training, and experience. Usually, change was so slow that little happened to necessitate change in these norms. A new teacher who might want to change the norms and evade the rules usually did not receive support from others. Turnover of new teachers was too rapid, and there were too few new teachers at any one time. When one teacher acted individually it was usually easy for the Old Guard to check her. In addition, many of the norms were so general that they could be interpreted as the teachers saw fit. Most of what the teachers did could not be defined as evasion. With few directions or commands there were few patterned evasions. The only condition conducive to the development of evasion was a lack of observability since the

Adams teacher was well screened from surveillance by the administration and outsiders.

What few evasions occurred emerged when a changed situation could not be handled through the existing rules and the administration was either unaware of the discrepancy or, having no solution for it, preferred to shut its eyes. One such evasion related to the playground duties of the teacher. Legally and officially each teacher was responsible for her pupils not only in the classroom, but also on the playground throughout the morning and noon recesses. In actual fact, at morning recess she supervised them only by glancing occasionally at them through a window in the cafeteria while drinking her coffee and chatting. At noon recess there was at least a ten-minute interval when all the teachers ignored the schedule of playground supervision. Between the time the children poured out on the playground and the time the teacher joined them, she finished her lunch, used the bathroom facilities, and then believed it was her right to have a smoke, a chat, or a cup of coffee. This discrepancy between rule and performance was never directly mentioned by the teachers except in an occasional defensive remark: "I must hurry out. There's no time to do anything around this place. How can we be through eating in five minutes when we don't get served until after the children?" Some of the defensiveness showed through in criticisms by teachers of one another for "not going out until it is time to bring the children back in."

This evasion emerged because of changes that had occurred over time. The overcrowding in the lunchroom and the tightness of the scheduling of classes in the departmental arrangement had not been accompanied by any comparable change in the rules for supervising the pupils. Also, the teachers had begun during this year a great deal more informal, coordinated teacher activity that led to a group coffee break in the morning and to social visiting in the teachers' room at noon. This evasion then strengthened the informal group and had group support even if it was not talked about. The lack of surveillance over the teachers' recess activities made it easy to evade the rules.

Another institutionalized evasion that I observed was the refusal by the upstairs teachers to allow pupils with unfinished academic work to attend physical education classes. This was a direct violation of the state law which specified that all pupils must attend such classes each week. The teachers made no bones about discussing their evasion, justifying their behavior by calling upon its academic necessity. However, they did not reveal it to the physical education instructors nor to the administration.

The conditions giving rise to this evasion were similar to those for the other. The teachers had difficulty in ensuring pupil conformity to their academic demands without supervisory backing. They were supported in their common values through frequent interaction and the similar experiences they all had as upstairs teachers. And they were free from surveillance in carrying out this evasion. In both situations, privacy, informal group support, and a social situation incompatible with the existing rules led to the evasion.

It is important to note here that evasion of a specific rule did not necessarily result from dissatisfaction with that particular rule. No teacher said that she thought children should play without supervision or that physical education was unimportant. Rather, the evasion indicated that some other norm was more important to the teacher and that this norm was incompatible with practice of the rule. Evasions are often indirect and cannot always be understood by examining the rule deviated from.

I would predict that more institutionalized evasions will occur at Adams under certain kinds of conditions: if the newer teachers begin to outnumber the Old Guard and gradually form a coherent informal group; if the administration, without increasing communication up the line, increases the directives and commands it sends down the line; if the administration defines the existing rules and requirements for action more specifically and demands greater conformity to them; or if a change occurs in the social situations that face the teachers with no corresponding adaptation of rules and norms (such as a rapid increase in school population).

Because patterned evasions deny the validity of the accepted norms of the organization, public exposure of them requires their elimination and punishment of the offenders.[21] The year following the study, Mr. Mindon, a new teacher, reported the evasion of playground duty directly to Mr. Hanson. Mr. Hanson then issued a directive specifying the times at which each teacher had to be on the playground for noon duty. Although this public exposure eliminated part of the evasion, some of it remained. Mr. Hanson in his specification of time left a few minutes free when the children were still unsupervised on the playground, and this was now legitimate unstolen time, given to the teacher by administrative fiat. It is interesting to speculate whether this free time resulted from Mr. Hanson's ignorance of the lunch schedule or whether he left this loophole in a calculated fashion to avoid trouble.[22]

Mrs. Wilson, the year after the study, destroyed the second evasion by threatening to expose the practice to Mr. Hanson. Her argument was simply, "It is wrong." The practice was then drastically cut back, and where it was continued there was much more secrecy. It was hidden even from other teachers, like those as nosy as Mrs. Wilson: "It isn't her business anyway. She is a primary teacher." In addition, other excuses were substituted for keeping pupils from physical education that were less "illegitimate."

The core of the relationship between the Adams elementary teacher and the administration was the frustration of what the teachers believed were legitimate expectations. She handled this frustration in different ways with the different officials, through jocularity, through displacement, through invention, through complaining. She pushed for control and less often for autonomy and freedom from control. The demand for autonomy expressed itself most completely when outside pressure was at a minimum. And even when expressed, the desire for autonomy did not mean for the Adams teacher innovation, rebellion against tradition, or "progressivism" in teaching. The value strand that was most dominant at Adams was conformity and obedience to command and to tradition. Her expectation for control was not so much a fear of anarchy as a desire for a sign that she was not alone, not going to be pushed in all directions by contradictory expectations from outsiders, a desire for a sign that someone cared enough to support her.[23]

7 PERIPHERAL RELATIONSHIPS

With the relationship to the pupil the core of the teacher's role-set, her colleagues, the parents, and the administration (particularly the principal) were the most significant others with whose expectations she had to deal and toward whom she herself had definite expectations. But there were other members of her role-set. (See Figure 4.) Some who had direct contact with the children, the health staff and the kitchen staff, were important to

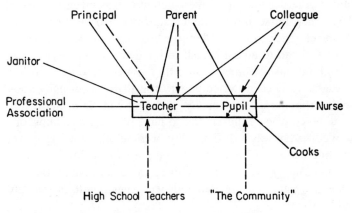

Role-relationship ⟶

Expectations for teacher-pupil relationship ⇢

4. The Teacher's Role-Set

her because their spheres of influence and control had to be demarcated from hers. Other nonteaching personnel, the custodial staff, had contact with the teacher herself but were in no important way involved with the pupils. Other people outside of the elementary school, high school teachers and "the community," had only peripheral relations with the teacher, but she imputed to them expectations which she then had to incorporate into her own self-image. Finally, the teacher had a tie to the local and state professional associations, a tie that meant that she must respond to her picture of what these organizations expected of her, and in turn, that she had some expectations of the profession as her guide and supporter.[1]

HEALTH STAFF, KITCHEN STAFF, AND CUSTODIAL STAFF

The Adams Elementary School was formally responsible not only for educating the pupil, but also for providing him with health services and feeding him. Provision was made for periodic physical examinations, for the full-time services of a school nurse, and for dental care. Time and space were allocated for the school lunch program, and no child was allowed to leave the school grounds during the noon hour. Although dental visits and the hot lunches were paid for by the parents, making participation voluntary, the scheduling of these activities was given priority.

The school nurse and the dental staff planned their program without reference to the academic schedule so the teacher had no control and had to adjust herself to the demands of these nonteaching staff members rather than ask them to defer to her. No Adams teacher protested either officially or informally about these interferences. Occasionally she might complain that it was hard to teach when children had to have physical checkups, or that Wednesday was a difficult day because the dental visits kept disrupting her class. Mrs. Garten told me that the kindergarteners were emotionally disturbed by visiting the dental clinic. But no teacher suggested that the demands were illegitimate or that she should resist them.

The teacher did have some discretion about visits to the nurse. Physical illness was a legitimate reason for such requests, but the child was only allowed to go to the nurse when the teacher permitted it, not at his own discretion. Whether or not a child was to be sent home was up to the nurse. Although the nurse and the teacher did not always agree as to the seriousness of the ailment, the teacher almost never challenged the nurse's right to make the decision. On the other hand, the nurse never interfered with the scholastic activities of the pupils. Her only authority over them concerned their physical well-being.

Despite the fact that the teacher and the nurse were dealing with the same third party, the child, and that the activities of the health staff curtailed the prerogatives of the teacher and her authority over the child, there was no conflict and no hostility. The amity resulted from three factors. The arrangement was clearly and formally defined and legitimated by the social structure of the school. Also, although there was a limitation on the scope of the teacher's authority, her academic function was not infringed upon. She was only limited in her extended responsibility for the child in his total school life. Finally, all the members of the health staff were trained personnel, respected as equals by the teachers. The teachers and the nurse mutually exchanged small gifts at Christmas; they called each other by their first names; and there were friendly, relaxed, even though infrequent, informal contacts.

The relationship of the teachers with the kitchen staff was more ambiguous. The kitchen staff's tie to the child was parallel to that of the teacher. Formally established, the lunch program did not ordinarily produce tension and hostility. The cooks had no authority over the pupils or over the teachers, but they did have certain rights they jealously protected. They could exert a subtle control over the children through the size of the portions of food, through the limitations on second helpings, through the denial of ketchup. The teacher accepted this control and ignored complaints from pupils about being discriminated against. I only took action once in response to a complaint about the food, and then the complaint came from a parent not a child. Also, I mentioned the complaint to a colleague rather than to the cook, although it reached the cook's ears within an hour.

The kitchen staff's only formal authority was over the kind and amount of food to be served and the times at which this was done. This authority was exercised over the teacher even more than over the pupils. The frequent use of the cafeteria by the high school as a study hall, a classroom, a recreation room, and an assembly hall deeply disturbed the cooks. They complained to the elementary teachers that they had to keep the doors in the kitchen shut in order not to bother the classes, that the lunchroom tables were scratched and marred with ink and crayon, that books and papers were scattered everywhere, that there was no time to prepare the tables for lunch. The one area of the school over which they formerly had had complete say had recently been invaded as high school enrollment had increased. Resenting the invasion of their territory and the limitation on their control, they shared with the elementary teachers a common hostility to the high school. As a result, the cooks were more insistent than ever on preserving what little power they had left. That the elementary classes sometimes were late to lunch was a slight: "It ruins our schedule, you know." The chief cook even complained to Mr. Hanson that Mrs. Merrick "always" brought her class in late, "and their mashed potatoes get cold."

The Old Guard teachers accepted as legitimate the demand for punctuality and they attempted to respect it. They even tried to force Mrs. Merrick into conformity through the usual hints and indirection and therefore had very little success. The teachers did complain to one another about the small size of servings and the refusal to give second helpings, but they did nothing to change the situation. Their resentment about "unfair treatment" was heightened by the fact that it was levied against them as well as against the children. Not only was the pupil given a smaller portion of food than he believed sufficient, but so was the teacher. She ate what her pupils ate. Although she paid more for her lunch, the size of her portion depended on the grade level she taught. When fried chicken was served, the second grade teacher got a small chicken leg, the fifth grade teacher a thigh, and only the high school teachers and high school students got breast meat and two helpings. Often the cooks prepared for the high school students and teachers special dishes, desserts, or biscuits, not served to the elementary pupils and their teachers.

The elementary teacher saw this treatment as blatant inequity: "What are they saving it for? She acts as if she were paying for all the food herself." It seemed part and parcel of the discrimination the teacher always felt subjected to in the lunchroom. The high school teachers had a separate table and were served by the cooks. The elementary teacher had to eat with her class and even stand in line with the children to be served.

A complicated process of prestige jockeying was operating

here. The cooks recognized their status inferiority to the high school staff. Since the elementary teacher also believed she was discriminated against by the high school teachers, on the level of informal banter the cooks were leagued with the elementary teachers against the high school. However, on a more serious level, the elementary teacher considered herself occupationally superior to the cooks. Training and salary gave her a position above the kitchen staff. She did not wish to be treated as equal to them and thus as inferior to the high school teachers. The teachers gave Christmas gifts to the cooks, but did not receive them. Mrs. Hamble was a close acquaintance of Mrs. Preston outside of school. They shopped together, attended church together, visited one another at home. However, Mrs. Preston treated Mrs. Hamble with cool formality at school.

The elementary teacher was thus pushed in two directions at once, to line up with the cooks against the "snobbish" high school teachers, and to stand above and apart from the cooks in order to preserve her equal status with the high school teachers. The cooks in turn attempted to reduce the status difference between themselves and the elementary teacher in order to retaliate for the snubs received from the high school teachers. In this status struggle the pupil who was refused the second helping was merely a pawn, not a participant.

Whenever an elementary teacher did request more food, a cup of coffee, or some special consideration, she was quickly and graciously accommodated. Nevertheless, she continued her complaints which she rarely focused directly on the kitchen staff since she believed they were unwitting dupes of the high school clique. When Mr. Hanson offered to explore ways to improve the lunchroom situation and meet the teachers' objections to eating with the children, the elementary teachers ignored his offer and went on complaining as if he had not spoken. It would thus seem that complaining was functional for the teacher. It defined the common enemy, enhanced in-group unity, and provided an outlet for inferiority feelings. All of these functions were more important to her than would have been a bigger piece of chicken.[2]

The teachers thus were more ambivalent about the kitchen staff than about the health staff, at least partly because of displacement of hostility from another source and the jockeying for prestige in an unclear status situation. The expectations held by the kitchen staff for the pupils and indirectly for the teachers only slightly influenced the teacher's activity as a teacher, but they did impinge on her picture of her own importance and worth.

The janitors had no defined relationship with the pupils,[3] but they had some influence on the teacher's self-image. Although no teacher had formal authority over a janitor (she was supposed to transmit all requests through the administration), she did frequently request that he unplug a sink, take the basketballs off the roof, replace a light bulb, or oil the pupils' desks. She even sometimes requested a pupil to ask a janitor to do something, but the request was always made in her name. She learned never to give orders to a janitor, and if a pupil became peremptory in making the request the janitor usually balked. Elmer Wingdale complained one day to some of the Old Guard teachers about Mrs. Merrick giving him orders, "She's not my boss. Who does she think she is?" Conflict did sometimes arise because the teacher was never officially informed about her lack of authority over the custodial staff. She discovered this gradually through observation and occasional hostile encounters. As long as she was polite, did not complain outside, and put her wishes as requests, she found that the janitors were willing to mail packages, change a tire on her car, and even carry boxes of books for her.

No janitor accepted orders from a pupil, but neither did a janitor give orders to a pupil. However, this restriction on giving orders to pupils did not prevent the janitors from threatening reprisals against the boys who messed up the bathroom or broke windows. The ultimate authority of any adult over all children in the schools is revealed here, rather than any specific authority of position.

Elmer Wingdale, as brother to a selectman, old resident, and participant in informal social activities with members of the Old Guard and the younger male high school teachers, seemed to be equivalent in social status to the elementary school teachers, despite his occupation. Before school each day he, Mrs. Gregory, Mrs. Preston, and Mrs. Crane chatted informally about local town matters and acquaintances they had in common. School matters were never discussed. But despite the seeming congruence of status between Elmer and the teachers, each teacher in the school still jealously preserved the in-school status differential. She gave unreciprocated Christmas gifts to him as well as to the other janitors. Pupils as well as teachers called all the janitors by their first names. The elementary teacher was convinced that her education, her salary, and her job title placed her above any janitor and no amount of informal and casual friendliness (One must never act "snooty") or joint participation in school picnics and basketball games could erase this differential. However, the differential was threatened by a lack of clarity about what was her job and what his. The teacher believed that the janitor responsible for the elementary school did not do enough work. There was too much dirt, too much disorder, too many things that she had to do to keep a "nice room." It was surprising how much of the informal talk among teachers was concerned with invidious comments about janitorial service.

Typical complaints were heard: "I don't think he has been in that cloakroom once this year." "My room is dirtier than when I left." "Look at the stairs. I think the dirt has been there for a week." "What are we supposed to do? Everything! He never dusts or washes boards as the custodians in other schools do."

A teacher was uncertain of the justice of her complaints since she herself was unclear about the limits of her job. She did believe that if she was supposed to do housework as well as teach her superior status was threatened. Unless she could delegate the dirty work down to the custodian she lost dignity.[4] She felt guilty about her messy, dirty room, but also resentful.

Only once that I know of was this private in-school disagreement publicly aired. Mrs. Preston, angered that her room was not cleaned before the science fair because it was full of equipment, made the children clean it, saying, "Now they can go home and tell their parents *they* had to clean the room. Then we'll see." As far as I ever heard, nothing happened; there was no outrage from home.

Since the role of the elementary teacher was so unclearly specified, she often found herself on the brink of the positions she defined as below hers. The high school teacher, she believed, was far more secure in his status and the acceptance of his status by others. She was not at all sure whether she had the right to refuse to do certain jobs, and to make matters worse she believed that she would not be recognized for her skill as a teacher if she was always doing menial chores.

HIGH SCHOOL TEACHERS

It should be clear from the above that the high school teachers represented one of the most disturbing role-partners the elementary teacher had. In an independent elementary school, high school teachers like college teachers or elementary teachers elsewhere may constitute a reference group for the teacher, a group with which she compares herself.[5] This was true at Adams, but in addition, in this school system where the high school was adjacent to the elementary school and there was some contact between the teachers in the two schools, the high school teachers played a significant part in the role-set of the elementary teacher. Since they seemed to hold strong negative stereotypes about the upstairs teacher's relationship with the pupil and about her teaching, she found herself having to respond to these stereotypes, even if only defensively.

The Adams elementary teacher did not consider the high school teacher as her colleague since she had no formal relationship with him (except in the Teachers' Association). Also, with separate class buildings, separate faculty meetings, and only briefly-overlapping lunch hours, there was a minimum opportunity for informal social contact. Although the teachers occasionally met at morning coffee or after school, these casual contacts did not change the designation of the high school teachers as part of *they* for the elementary teachers. The *we* and the *they* changed depending on the pressures on the teachers,[6] but the *we* almost never included the high school teachers even though community, professional, and legal definitions lumped all the teachers in the school together.

The use of the term *they* was a powerful unifier for the teachers' group because it was so indefinite and could hold within it whatever groups or individuals one wished to exclude from the inner circle. Thus, at varying times for the elementary teacher, it meant the school board, the newly rich in town, the high school teachers, the administration, or the community as a whole: "They never do anything right over there." "They took over the PTA so that all the local people dropped out." "You might expect they would goof it up. They always do." "They decided to move the first grade and then did nothing all spring to get the library started."

Even the usual identification of the parent as the "enemy" was sometimes countered by a tendency to identify the *we* as the Hollow community of good, clean, respectable folk against the *they* of the upper-class Hill people, the private schools and their lackeys, the high school administration and teachers. It was obvious to the Old Guard teacher that the high school favored the Hill children, "giving in" or "kowtowing" to anyone with power and privilege.

It was the Old Guard teacher who particularly resented the social snobbery of the Hill, the privileged position of the high school teacher in town and with the Hill families, and the combination of youth and advantage. But since the definition of *they* was left unspecified, the newer teacher, less personally hostile, could join with the Old Guard against *they*.

One of the strongest defensive resentments was felt by the upstairs teachers against the junior high school teachers who seemed dissatisfied with the "product" the elementary teachers turned out. Whenever a junior high school teacher criticized a seventh grader for poor spelling or for being unable to read, the fifth and sixth grade teachers interpreted this as criticism of them. When there was criticism the teacher did her best to throw the blame on someone else: "The administration makes us send the children over. They assume we send them to seventh grade knowing everything."

This defensive hostility was accompanied by the conviction that the high school teachers did not appreciate what the elementary teacher did. So with both humility and a sense of superiority the elementary teacher scanned the high school honor roll, making comments and appropriate gestures of shock and disbelief: "What kind of standards must they have over there? We mark much harder than they do, I guess." "How did *she* get on the honor roll? When I had her she couldn't learn at all. I even thought of retaining her. But now she's over *there*."

The reason I stress the attitudes of the upstairs teachers here is that the primary teacher was protected from the high school teachers by the presence of the upper grade elementary teachers. The primary teacher did not seem to be aware of the "impossible" expectations emanating from the high school. Nevertheless, she too had the conviction that the high school teacher was contemptuous of her work, thought she did not know very much, and believed that she did not work very hard: "They think we have it easy." Any casual encounter with a high school teacher served to confirm this conviction in the mind of the elementary teacher. The most frequent remark at morning recess from any high school teacher was likely to be similar to "Well, what are you having? A picnic? Add a couple and the whole elementary faculty would be here. Doesn't anyone in your school have to work?"

The most serious problem with this negative stereotype was that the elementary teacher, having little contact with the high school, had no clear way to challenge the imputation of lack of knowledge, dedication, or diligence. This left her only one response, counterattack. Mrs. Preston would complain to the high school teachers or to Mr. Hanson that the high school pupils were always bothering the elementary pupils on the playground or in the boys' room. Mrs. Merrick stormed out of her room any time high school students walked through the elementary school halls: "How can we work with so much noise?" But, since the high school teachers seemed unmoved, in no way chagrined or deflated by her accusations, the teacher's anxiety and hostility were increased.

The high school teacher had no defined and direct relationship with the elementary teacher. He showed her no expectations, idealistic or realistic, about how she should behave toward the pupil. He merely seemed to hold a negative stereotype of her and to preserve his superior status through clinging to this picture of her as inferior. Since the stereotype was useful to him, the elementary teacher saw no way to change it, even as she resented it. Her inability to change the stereotype was compounded by the fact that she shared it. She had a double image of herself, as inferior to the high school teacher and as deserving equal status with him. She was both anxiously hostile and inordinately sensitive about his most casual remark. She believed that the high school teacher had higher status and prestige in the community than she and that both the town and the administration gave their support to the high school and the high school teachers. When a high school teacher wanted new textbooks, he got them. When a high school class wished to use the gymnasium, the sixth grade had to stop practicing for graduation. The PTA raised money for a high school scholarship. The high school athletic program took a large part of the school budget. In addition, the high school teacher had special privileges. He had a free period once a day. He did not make out his own report cards, mimeograph his stencils, or do bus and playground duty. Instead, he could concentrate on his skilled professional work. It was the elementary teacher who had to do routine, unskilled, and menial tasks. This was the way the elementary teacher viewed the high school teacher, although the high school teachers themselves complained about the number of routine menial tasks they had to do which lowered their professional standing.

THE COMMUNITY

The Adams teacher was less upset and hostile about stereotypes held by members of the "community" than about those emanating from the high school teachers, because she felt very little pressure from outside. She did not have to counter patriotic organizations, citizens' committees, or organized parents attempting to interfere with curriculum, censor textbooks, or control her out-of-school behavior.[7] The Adams teacher, in fact, was more likely to comment on lack of interest and concern than on interference. She talked of the "good old days" when the citizens took a benevolent interest in the schools. Mrs. Preston and Mrs. Gregory often reminisced about the days when the Hollow and the school were a unit, when there was "local" pride and involvement. Since those good days the Hill had been "taken over" by outsiders with money who ran the town and ignored the school. However, even while regretting the good old days, the teachers reveled in their independence. As Mrs. Crane put it, "It's better to be us than the teachers in Woodcock where the parents and the townspeople interfere all the time. They try to run everything. It is always one committee or another studying the school, visiting, poking around. It would be awful."

Although the teacher experienced no group pressure, she did believe that the community members constantly talked about her in critical ways: "It is a good thing we can't hear what they say about us or we would all have to leave." It was easy for Mrs. Preston to put us all on the defensive by a remark such as, "People over town think we let the children have too much outdoor play." None of us ever asked who had been critical. Instead, we tried to justify our own program to each other.

When a casual criticism was reported: "What do you teachers do over there? Can't you avoid accidents on the playground?" much self-searching would go on among the teachers, including both self-criticism and self-affirmation. The annoyance about Mrs. Wilson's gossiping around town was increased because of the fear that "they might believe her."

On a superficial level, social contacts between the Adams teacher and the townsperson were stereotyped, friendly, even jocular. Humorous references to "the little monsters" greeted the teacher downtown. She was inevitably bombarded at the start of vacation: "How pleased you must be to have a vacation, but their parents aren't so happy." "Now you can loaf. Wish I had that kind of job." The remarks tended to be patronizing rather than deferential.[8] The shopkeepers were comradely, accepting the teacher as someone similar to themselves, enviable for her short hours and long vacations, but of no higher status than they.

Any Adams teacher would testify that the citizens of Adams held stereotypes of her similar to those described by Waller, the hostile caricature and the idealization.[9] However, she did not interpret these stereotypes as demands on her or as interference, primarily because she held similar stereotypes about herself.[10]

The teacher thus did not respond to the community stereotypes in the same hostile defensive way that she responded to those of the high school teacher. She tended to respond with self-justification and some effort at conciliation. It was only when community members invaded her territory that she expressed hostility toward them.

When a citizens' committee of PTA members was formed to encourage the establishment of a school library, the Old Guard teachers opposed the move. Two of them placed on the committee resisted all pressures for the library, commenting back to the rest of us that the local committee members were snoopy and arrogant and "act as if they know everything." It was clear to me from conversations with these teachers that they did not really object to a library, but they did object to untrained laymen pretending knowledge about school affairs and interfering. When the librarian who was appointed turned out to be an upper-middle-class Hill resident, the appointment was strongly resented: "She doesn't know anything. What are they thinking of, hiring her? She is just a lot of talk."

The argument against her, that she was untrained, was not mentioned when one of the teachers in the school, also untrained, applied for the job. The resentment was really against the outsider.

Any substitute teacher in the school who was not an ex-teacher was patronized. Local women with "little or no training" were condescended to even though with occasional sympathy: "Poor Estelle. She is too nice. She lets them get away with everything."

The resistance to the outsider invading her territory was in part a desire to protect her activities from observation and critical scrutiny.[11] When it was suggested to Mrs. Garten that she ask the school board to get her some volunteer community helpers for the kindergarten she was very ambivalent: "You have to be very careful. Be sure you get someone good who would not talk over town about the school. Many who help don't understand our ways and do more harm than good with their talk." The other teachers responded in a similar way to suggestions for hiring volunteers to help in the cafeteria or to grade papers.

But there was ambivalence. The teacher knew she needed "help," someone on her side, a chance for coalition against the pressures from other role-set members. Frustrated by slow learners, disciplinary problems, lack of support from the administration, a teacher would often suggest inviting citizens into the school to "see what it is like." The substitute from the Hill might be snubbed and condescended to, but she was also useful: "Now they will know what we have to put up with. She will see that it is not so easy teaching all these dopes." How, though, was one both to protect oneself from unfriendly, critical, and illegitimate observation and also to derive support and backing from the community? In all situations I was able to follow through, the motive for protection and insulation proved the stronger. The desire for those outside to "find out" was temporary, a verbal exaggeration to show the other teachers that one was very upset. Ordinarily the teacher preferred to be insulated and unsupported than to endanger her autonomy.

THE PROFESSION
The Adams teacher had an ambiguous relationship with the professional teachers' associations to which she belonged. She did not turn to them for support and protection against demands from her role-partners, nor did she look to them for guiding expectations and demands. However, she did join the organizations each year in ritual fashion. The pressures on her from the associations to have a professional attitude, to work with them through lobbying, to seek further training and higher standards of certification, to separate herself from laymen because she was professional,[12] these pressures were not significant in the role-image of the Adams elementary teacher.[13]

Although five Adams elementary teachers joined the National Education Association the year of the study (a rather higher percentage than usual), this organization had little meaning to them. Membership was not considered to entail other obligations. Literature from the NEA was consistently unread. The teachers did not discuss articles on education or bills before Congress. A booklet issued by the NEA, "Who's a Good Teacher?" led to lots of joking about the cost, but no one read it. No teacher expressed any desire to stand with or against the NEA in its policy disputes with the government. Opinions became heated only in connection with the teachers' strike of the American Federation of Teachers in New York. The Adams teacher was strongly opposed to teachers striking and to any suggestion that a teachers' organization was a "labor union." This was the only time I heard an Adams teacher use the term *professional*, except when Mr. Hanson was criticized for not being professional. To strike was not professional. Beyond this, the teacher had no idea why she should join the NEA or what it could do for her or she for it. When Miss Tuttle asked the other teachers why they thought she should join, everyone looked vague and one answered, "Well, they will give you a plaque or something."

There was more identification with the State Education Association to which all the elementary teachers belonged. Membership in the State Association had been traditional as long as any Adams teacher could remember. "It was your duty," said Mrs. Preston. As Mrs. Gregory said, "You have to expect to belong to the organization in any occupation. It is part of the job, and we are lucky it isn't more expensive than it is." Failure to join was interpreted as disloyalty to the school rather than to the profession. But, again, no Adams teacher had much picture of what the State Association could do for her or what she should do for it. One teacher justified joining it, "You can't keep all the money you get. Give it to the Association." The State Association poured out research documents, a magazine, lobbied in the state legislature, sought attendance at institutes, financial support for the building program, and local implementation of state programs. In return, it was ready to respond to local requests for help in salary disputes with local school boards, providing speakers, research data, legal, advisory, and financial support. But no Adams teacher paid very much attention to all this. None thought of the Association as a pressure group or a union. If she talked about the State Association at all it was to describe it as working with the administration and the community for the benefit of all and its projects were of no particular interest to her. Attendance at the state conventions, which had been a matter of course for the older teachers in earlier years, was minimal: "What is there for us to get out of these meetings?" Few teachers attended county or state meetings. No Adams teacher had been a representative at the legislative assembly of the State Association for many years. The teachers did contribute to a fund being raised to build a new state headquarters "because we should," and each elementary teacher was most self-righteous about this, castigating the high school teachers for lack of interest and dereliction of duty. Condemnation of the high school teachers, "They have no school spirit," often seemed more important than concern about the State Association.

Just as the teacher felt no particular obligations toward the State Association, so she had no particular expectations of it. Although she might desire improved salaries and was willing to work for them through the local association, it seemed improper to call upon the State Association for help in negotiations. That was only for "those urban schools."

The local Adams Teachers Association had more importance for the teacher. It held meetings; it raised money for a college scholarship; it had picnics and farewell parties; it presented gifts to departing teachers. However, meetings were sparsely attended unless salary schedules were discussed. Attempts to increase interest through discussion of subjects supposedly of interest to the teachers, town-school relations, curriculum, or ethics, failed dismally. When the president was a high school teacher, the elementary teachers did not attend; when the president was an elementary teacher, the high school teachers did not attend.

Every teacher reiterated in her interview that it was important for the teachers to belong to the organization and support it. A few teachers tentatively suggested that it might help the teachers achieve some of their goals, but no Old Guard teacher had any such expectation. To belong was a teacher's duty. One did not belong because of anything the organization could do for her.

The scholarship drive did activate the association, but with difficulty. At first it was impossible to achieve agreement on any project for raising money. The Old Guard wanted something dignified, such as a book sale, and the new high school teachers something exciting, such as a faculty show. Since I, an elementary teacher, was president, the high school teachers were not very interested anyway. "They only come if we are working on salaries," said Mrs. Gregory. Finally, it was decided to hold a car wash. But, because the suggestion came from a high school teacher and was also undignified, no Old Guard teacher liked the idea. However, no Old Guard teacher expressed her dissatisfaction until the meeting was over: "There is no point in expressing your opinion around here. It just gets you in trouble. You might just as well keep your mouth shut."

The car wash was held in an atmosphere of hostility and anger, but no amount of annoyance destroyed the ritual sense of duty. The Old Guard teachers turned out in force for the car wash and worked harder than anyone else to make it a success: "So no one could say I didn't put in full time, didn't do what I was expected to."

With the success of this endeavor, tempers were cooled for a short time. The Old Guard teachers were no happier with the organization. Mrs. Crane suggested to Mrs. Preston, "I'm not going to work next year. Let's elect high school officials and let them run their own group. We've never had anything in common with them." But duty prevailed, and everyone continued to belong and do what was expected.

Part of the tension in the organization resulted from the fact that a number of years earlier the high school teachers had attempted to push through a salary differential between high school and elementary teachers. The elementary teacher was convinced that she was being patronized, talked down to, and snubbed by the high school teachers. The puzzlement expressed by one high school teacher, "And we try to be friendly all the time. We try to be nice," carried no weight. The elementary teacher also felt no sense of common identity with other teachers as professionals against the community or the parents or other outsiders.

The absence of any professional identification revealed itself in other ways. No Adams teacher wished to take courses, and she took only those that were required or that seemed directly relevant to her immediate teaching: "There's no point in taking a course on the history of math. What use would that be in the fifth grade?"

The Old Guard teacher was convinced that her training in normal school was far superior to the training being given in the teachers' college and completely beyond anything the "special" teacher could have absorbed in her summer course. So she resented pressures from professionals in state and federal positions to increase certification requirements. She also resented the salary increases given to teachers who took extra courses: "I think it's unfair for her to get more money than I do. Just because she's taken some course, she is supposed to be better qualified. I have had far more years of experience."

Not courses or credits but experience was the touchstone of a good teacher. No new teacher could be a very good teacher: "Wait until she learns, gets some experience." The administration, the school board, or some nameless enemy (they) did not believe in experience: "They want to get rid of us and hire a lot of young teachers who don't know anything but have fancy degrees."

The teachers greeted Mrs. Milton's efforts to conduct in-service seminars to improve teaching efficiency with indifference or cynicism. Trying to learn new ways to teach "was such a waste of time." Similarly the outside specialist was viewed skeptically. How could he say anything to her? "He has never taught. How can he know?" She was a bit less skeptical of the professor from teachers' college than she was of the lay expert, the liberal arts professor, or the academic. As one said, "No teacher ever does what she really thinks best. We do the best we can in the circumstances. What you think is a good idea from the outside turns out to be impossible in the classroom."

"Those experts. Have they ever worked with kids, tried any of these things? I wonder. They always know all the answers."

This reaction, exactly the same as that expressed to Mrs. Milton's classroom suggestions, "If she were in my place she would think differently," is a product of a faith in experience. Teaching was best done by the older, wiser, more experienced woman who could call upon her "folk wisdom."

Not every Adams elementary teacher stressed this point of view with the same conviction, nor did every teacher deny completely the importance of support from the profession. But the dominance of the Old Guard in the elementary school hindered the emergence of any other philosophy. There were some signs of change coming. Some of the newer teachers began to become excited about new ways of teaching and to attend conferences from which they returned fired with enthusiasm for what the profession was doing. The cynicism of their compatriots, "Won't they ever learn that nothing new works? There is no new way to teach reading that is better. There is no short cut," did not prevent some of the new ideas from being tried. Departmentalization cut into the older loyalties and bridged some of the gap between elementary and high school. With the development of an academic specialty the teacher began to want to take courses, to get a higher degree, to use training rather than experience as a protection and a support.

The tension at Adams between teachers and community was not that noted by Robin Williams resulting from the influx of "the urban college-trained professional-minded teacher" into the "stable rural small town schools."[14] At Adams the teachers were mostly old residents, hired fresh from normal school, not urbanites with a professional outlook. Only the high school had had any significant influx of young, urban, professionally minded teachers. Also, Adams was not a stable, rural, isolated town. At least part of its population (Hill-based) was more professionally oriented than any of the Old Guard teachers and was thus resented by them. The Old Guard teacher turned for identification, not to the Hill, but to her part of town which was quite stable, slow-changing, and traditional.

To understand the antiprofessional bias of these Old Guard teachers involves some understanding of their place in the community. The position of the husband was the family touchstone.[15] The Old Guard teacher's husband worked "in television," "for Mr. Eggleston," or he "did social work." He was almost never a professional. Mrs. Gregory could be a teacher and her husband a janitor if she did not overplay the professional aspects of her work and make it out as more significant than his. Training was underplayed and experience emphasized. If the wife's occupation had greater prestige than that of the husband, the family unit was threatened. When I was teaching and my husband writing at home, the Old Guard teachers waged a strenuous campaign to find him work. They were delighted when he got a job. It was not necessary that he make more money than I, but he had to be gainfully employed.

The training of the teachers put them slightly above their

neighbors. However, the teacher had chosen one of the three acceptable female positions for those in her class: teaching, nursing, secretarial work. If she did not emphasize what differentiated her from her neighbors, she was comfortably accepted by her peers. How then preserve authority and legitimate her work? She used tradition and her years of experience with children.

It should now be clear why the Adams teacher had so much trouble preserving her status differential from the kitchen and custodial staff. Her training did make her superior to them; she was not a cook or a janitor, but she could not afford to be too "snooty" or too insistent on the privileges of her rank. So she feigned an easy democratic equality. Everyone, teacher and nonteacher alike, attended the faculty picnics. But the teacher still suffered in her attempt to preserve the distinction and the prestige she could not publicly insist on.

In such an atmosphere, age had precedence over youth, tradition over innovation. The profession was no bulwark since it might introduce expectations more threatening than the expectations from parents or pupils. In time, as staff changes and the Old Guard loses its dominance it seems likely that this resistance to professionalism and dependence on experience will become progressively reduced.

Analysis of the less significant aspects of the teacher's role-set in this chapter has told us less about new expectations to which the teacher had to respond than about the problems of determining the boundaries for spheres of control, of consolidating her prestige position relative to other positions, and of legitimating her authority over the pupil.

The important aspects of the teacher's role-set have now been described as well as the ways in which the teacher tried to handle the conflicting pressures in order to succeed as a teacher. That she was beset by anxiety, tension, and strong feelings of inadequacy should be clear. Some of these derived from inevitable conflicts, others from the particular characteristics of the Adams School. We must now look more closely at the ways in which she handled the tensions and anxieties.

8 LOW TEACHER MORALE: ITS IMPLICATIONS

The morning at Adams invariably started with the following exchange between two teachers:

"Good morning."

"What's good about it?"

How this question was asked varied. It could be jocular, cross, casual, aggressive, or aggrieved. But it was always asked, and it set the tone for the day. Enthusiasm was suspect. It disturbed stability and raised questions. Part of the socialization of the new teacher by the Old Guard involved toning down enthusiasm, through teasing, through indifference, through sarcasm. The new teacher, bubbling with some ambitious idea, was greeted with, "It won't work," in a resigned tone tinged with cynicism. Miss Tuttle was suspect not only because she had a noisy classroom, but even more because she did not seem to mind. She seemed happy; she was excited about teaching. She had too few complaints. She was "too self-independent," as Mrs. Crane put it.

To complain too much or to boast too much were both taboo at Adams. Once someone boasted too loudly or complained too bitterly, others began to look. Parents might expect one teacher to succeed as another had. The inevitable teaching failures might be considered the teacher's fault. So the proper stance in such an undefined and yet rigid situation was a slightly sour expression. If you did not expect too much, you would not be disappointed.

To boast was to blow your own horn at the expense of the other teachers. To complain was to expose vulnerability and insecurity. Serious complaining became a demand for a kind of support and closeness that other teachers were unwilling to give. Or it revealed, just as boasting did, a higher level of expectations than was considered appropriate by the other teachers. It encouraged competition and prestige jockeying, creating doubts in the minds of the other teachers about their own standards and their ritual acceptance of the inevitability of what was.

The atmosphere was not a happy one. At Adams morale was low and job satisfaction limited. The cynicism might be faint, but the sourness was evident, and at various times during the year it deepened for most of the teachers to overt dissatisfaction.

Job satisfaction in our society is a product both of objective recognition and of internal confidence.[1] In what ways were these missing for the Adams teacher? External reward and objective recognition were important to the Adams teacher,[2] but she believed that she received little of them. Her salary was adequate, but its size in no way reflected any special competence or achievement. Minimal supervision meant that she was not rated, praised, or advanced because of the way she taught. Even one's colleagues knew little about one's competence as a teacher. One could do a very poor or a very good job as a teacher for a very long time without anyone knowing about it. Naturally, rare crumbs of praise from parents, from Mrs. Milton, or even from a pupil were treasured by the Adams teacher.

Although in a larger school system possibilities for some upward mobility might be found, there were none at Adams unless one wished to leave teaching. It is an interesting anomaly that the teacher, expected to encourage the pupils to mobility, to prepare for the next grade, herself remained at the same level, unable to advance. The only possibility of advancement for an Adams teacher was to become an administrator or to become active within the professional association. The antiprofessional attitude of the Adams teacher made the latter an uncommon avenue, and for most Adams elementary teachers a move into administration seemed remote and unrealistic.

What of internal satisfactions? The Adams teacher, as I have indicated, was very service-minded. She had high ideals; she wanted to do a good job, to succeed in teaching the children (although what this meant to her varied from teacher to teacher) more than she wanted to move up the social ladder or make money. But many stumbling blocks stood in the way of her

achieving satisfaction in her work. The standards for measuring
success were ambiguous: what weight should be given to
achievement test scores; what weight to enthusiasm, interest,
vitality, and curiosity, the less objectively measurable results?
Was it more important to have a room of lively, if noisy and
enthusiastic, children than one in which the assignments were
always neatly completed and correct? Had you succeeded if the
majority accomplished what was expected by Mrs. Milton, but
some seemed to make no gains? What would constitute success
with a class of slow learners? Was it enough that they made a
little progress, that they derived a little satisfaction, or that you
merely created a nonfrustrating atmosphere? For the teacher to
measure her success through the available "objective" criteria,
achievement test scores, was to confront her with the inevitable
failures, the recalcitrance of the human beings she was trying to
teach, or to raise upsetting questions about the relation of these
test scores to learning, to changing, to education. The teachers at
the Adams School in this undefined and threatening situation
relied for job satisfaction primarily on their conviction that at
least they were using the appropriate means, they were working
hard, they were carrying through what they had learned were the
proper procedures.

The teacher at Adams was dissatisfied both because of the
elusive character of her goals, the fact that they were
unmeasurable and often unachievable, and because of the
discrepancy between her goals or standards and what she was
able to achieve.[3] The discrepancy between goals and their
achievement was increased for her because of the pressures
exerted on her by others in her role-set, whose expectations,
values, and goals were often contradictory to hers. They
interfered with her efforts. That her expectations differed from
those of the parent, for example, was not in itself the reason for
anxiety and hostility, but the anxiety and hostility emerged from
the failure of the administration to protect the Adams teacher
from these alien expectations. To cope with pressures from
parents the teacher looked for direction, guidance, and control
from above, a buffer between herself and the outside. Then she
could at least justify herself and her pursuits by relying on this
"authority." When this authority functioned ineffectively, leaving
her exposed, she had to fall back on other kinds of protection:
ritualism, traditionalism, and defensive cynicism.

The dissatisfaction of the Adams teacher was frequently expressed in her posing of alternatives, references to the possibilities of resigning, leaving the job, abandoning the status. Sometimes the teacher threatened to give up teaching altogether; sometimes she merely suggested leaving Adams and trying again in another community.

I noticed over time the interesting phenomenon that the Old Guard teachers suggested the most extreme alternatives, often citing the advantages of taking on an entirely different kind of job: "It would be nice to have a job with *no* people around, particularly *no* children." "Why can't we find a job where we don't have to kill ourselves? Teaching isn't much fun any more. I don't expect to last the year." "It isn't good to have your job your whole life. Other jobs aren't like this. I would like to wash dishes." "I like everything about teaching except the kids."

Some of the suggested alternatives of the Old Guard teachers included: running or working in a brothel; working in a laundromat, grocery store, diaper service, liquor store; being a waitress or a secretary; working in a library; managing a fruit stand.

For the most part these were not intended as realistic alternatives; the complaining and the dissatisfaction were real, the alternatives were window dressing. The Old Guard teacher had no real alternatives. She had not been trained for any job but teaching. The work she suggested as an alternative would pay her less and give her even less status than teaching did. She would have to give up her salary, her retirement benefits, her tenure, at an age when she believed she must provide for her old age. None of these older teachers could afford to stop work; none could afford to give up the investment of time, courses, and money for just a "job."[4]

The newer and younger teacher was often less dissatisfied with teaching as such, but she was more convinced that the problem lay in teaching at Adams. Therefore, her alternative suggestions of going to Waterwich or other near-by towns were less drastic but more realistic. She voiced her complaints in much more specific terms than did the members of the Old Guard. She complained of class size, slow children, lack of guidance, and not nearly so often of a loss of faith in the possibility of teaching. And these alternatives were frequently followed up. The Old Guard members complained more bitterly, but most of them stayed at Adams. The few that did leave went to another school despite the wistful suggestion of the brothel or the laundromat. Serious dissatisfaction then was expressed by a not seriously suggested major alternative while lesser dissatisfaction was expressed by a seriously suggested minor alternative.

Some hint of the kinds of dissatisfactions and frustrations of the Adams teachers can be obtained from looking at the groups with which they compared their lot and their responses to these comparisons.[5]

In the interviews I asked the teachers what grade they would most like to teach. All but one of the teachers (Mr. Scranton, who at that time was so annoyed with teaching that he said it made no difference at all, they were all bad) averred themselves happy with the grade they were teaching. I made no other formal attempt to have the teachers compare their position to other positions. My information on comparisons derives from the spontaneous comments of the teachers. It is thus in no way inclusive. We cannot know how the Adams teacher might have compared herself to some other position if she had been asked about it. But we do know which other positions were expressed reference points for her.

The only comparison that indicated satisfaction rather than dissatisfaction with her lot (and this comparison was rarely made) was that with another elementary teacher at the Adams school. Each teacher seemed glad to be where she was. She did not wish to move up or down even when she was dissatisfied with the role-expectations she had to meet from which another teacher might be immune: "I couldn't teach downstairs. I don't have the patience. I'm no good at all that art work and stuff for the bulletin boards. It's a good thing we don't have to do that." "It must be wearing to teach kindergarten. How can she do it?" "I wouldn't teach first grade for anything. That is the hardest job there is." "I would be afraid to teach upstairs. You have to know so much. I haven't the training for fifth grade. It is more fun at our level."

Comparison rarely took the form of identification with the values of another group in order to move into that group.[6] This kind of comparison usually operates in a system of relatively high social mobility which the school at Adams was not. Since there was no mobility within the teaching group, the only source of mobility for an ambitious teacher was a move into administration. Any teacher who did reveal a sense of identification with the administration was clearly oriented toward moving into an administrative post. This identification had a side effect. Such a teacher was also socially isolated from the informal teachers' group, but whether the isolation preceded or followed the external identification is hard to determine. To identify with the norms of the administration was to some degree to deny the norms and values of the informal groupings of teachers. Such teachers then were the ones who "spilled the beans," who exposed the "institutionalized evasions" of the in-group, ostensibly in the interests of better teaching or of the children, but, from the point of view of the other teachers, really to curry favor with the out-group.

Most comparing comments by Adams teachers expressed the teacher's dissatisfactions with her own lot. The comments were not supportive; they served to symbolize unhappiness. Also, most comparing comments revealed the perspective of the Adams teacher. They tended to be realistic, comparisons with positions that the teacher could imagine herself in rather than positions that seemed completely alien to her.

Nonservice positions, those which eliminated emotional involvement and personal contact with people, were the ones most often mentioned. Since in her interview no teacher mentioned as a source of dissatisfaction the emotional or personal aspects of her work, listing instead such items as record keeping, correcting papers, or getting the pupils washed for lunch, it seems strange that in casual conversation the teacher frequently wistfully imagined the pleasures of working in a remote office or laboratory, in some impersonal, adult environment, isolated from human problems. Which was the more genuine response I cannot say. The way in which the interview question was worded possibly precluded mention of anything as drastic as getting rid of the children.

I never heard the Adams teacher compare herself either favorably or unfavorably with nonworking housewives. Theoretically such a position was available to her and the lack of mention may seem surprising. However, in actuality, the Adams teacher did not consider that she had this choice. Most Adams teachers were not working as teachers because of boredom at home, but rather out of economic necessity. Although the teacher condemned other teachers for working who should have been at home caring for their small children: "You should not work before your children are in school. There should be someone to come home to," and although she complained that she did not have time both to teach and to keep house, she found it unrealistic to think of herself as not working. Her perception of necessity prevented comparison in this direction.

She was able to compare herself, sometimes unfavorably, to a cook or secretary in other organizations, but she did not make any comparisons, favorable or unfavorable, with cooks or secretaries at Adams. The subtle status difference labeled this kind of position as inferior to hers within the school and therefore cut it off for her as a reference point.

As I noted above, an administrative or specialist's post was sometimes mentioned as a possible alternative. As Mr. Scranton said, "I wouldn't want to be a principal with all that paper work and schedule making, but I would like a job in classroom supervision, curriculum, sort of like Mrs. Milton."

Although a teacher might remark that the supervisor "has it easy" and that her job was a lark compared to that of the classroom teacher, she usually added a comment indicating her rejection of this alternative. To become a supervisor was to "give in." It was to acknowledge failure as a teacher: "Oh, yes, there's a lot of work in Mrs. Milton's job, but not like the job of working or trying to work with thirty of them roaming around the room."

For a brief period during the year there seemed to be a real possibility that one of the Adams teachers might be made elementary school principal. During this period there began to be some talk about this position as a realistic job alternative. The teachers often mentioned the advantages of money and freedom, but surprisingly enough, not power, that were to be found in a principal's job. Any teacher who wished to emphasize that she was overworked would refer to Mr. Hanson's job: "I wish all I had to do was sit in an office and make out schedules and talk to people on the phone."

One position to which the elementary teacher frequently compared her lot to her own disadvantage was that of the high school teacher. Again, this comparison was not with the thought of becoming one, but rather to symbolize her own miseries. This was particularly true for the intermediate teacher since the primary teacher was less aware of and less in contact with the high school teacher than she. Also, the primary teacher's job was so different from that of the high school teacher that to call them both teaching is to blunt the significance this difference had for the teacher. This remoteness did not prevent the primary teacher from joining the other elementary teachers in their expressed convictions that everything in the Adams school was designed to help the high school and that the elementary teacher was the proverbial poor relation.

What is important about the comparison of her lot with that of the high school teacher is that the elementary teacher seemed to be saying one thing and meaning another.[7] What she said was that she was clearly deprived because the two positions should be equivalent. The pay scale was the same, the job definition the same, and the educational requirements the same. Since there were radical inequities in treatment — since the high school teacher had free class periods, few nonacademic responsibilities, lunchroom privileges, access to supply, book, and equipment money, as well as greater prestige and even parties at Mr. Hanson's house — she was being unfairly treated.

But, as was noted in Chapter 7, any efforts by Mr. Hanson to remove the differentials were ignored and even deliberately prevented by the elementary teacher. She did not seem to want the symbols of her sense of deprivation to be removed. As a last resort, she would even pretend deafness in the face of suggestions for buying an elementary movie projector or for setting up an elementary lunch table for the teachers. The complaints of the Old Guard elementary teacher covered up the conviction, rarely directly expressed, that the status differential was fundamentally just. The intermediate teacher believed against her own interests that the high school teacher did deserve the greater prestige because he knew more, was more intelligent, and was better educated. "Mr. Holly feels too superior to any of us elementary school teachers. What could he find to talk to any of us about? None of us is intellectual enough for him." This was a threatening admission to the intermediate teacher's self-image relative to the primary teacher. To admit this openly was to threaten to destroy the grounds of her superiority (as emphasizing the *what* rather than the *how* of teaching) over her primary colleague. So, such a remark was rare. Rather, Mr. Holly was criticized for stealing cigarettes or for being rude. Complaints about unfair differentials, about high school teachers' laziness, about the injustice of her inferior lot (external and nonemotion laden items) served to relieve tension, concealed the roots of her resentment, and helped her to stand as one with all the other elementary teachers regardless of grade level.

As became clear in Chapter 2 this was not an easy tightrope to walk. The intermediate teacher was claiming a status advantage over the primary teacher on the basis of her knowledge and academic competence, but then she had to deny the importance of this standard as the basis for comparison with the high school teacher. Rather, she claimed equality with the high school teacher on the ground that she knew the whole child; she was concerned with the *how* of teaching, the same standard she rejected when it referred to the primary teacher: "The high school teachers think we don't work. They think they are so much better. Of course, they do have more training. They have to know more about their own subject. But they don't have to teach everything. They don't have to know children well. That's why our job is so much harder. They couldn't do it. They think we just loaf around."

It is, therefore, not too surprising that the intermediate teacher preferred to conduct her argument with the high school teacher over inequities of supplies and lunchroom facilities rather than over the touchy matter of deserved and undeserved privilege.

The Adams teacher rarely compared herself with teachers in other schools. Lack of observability and thus lack of a realistic basis for comparison curtailed the comparisons made. Distance itself was of less importance than the nature of the other community. A rich and well-favored town, close at hand, would not be discussed, while a community, further away, but similar to Adams in social structure might well be.

Comparative comment made up only a small part of the Adams teacher's conversation. Jocular griping, banter, and exaggerated horror stories of teaching, parents, or stupid pupils dominated discussions in the teachers' room. The teacher might be frustrated and unhappy, but her occupational and cultural horizons shut her off from much serious consideration of the possibility of occupational change.

Since, for most of the Adams teachers, changing jobs or abandoning teaching were not ways to reduce her dissatisfactions, we must examine how she did cope with them. She turned to her informal groups for support as a teacher and in particular as a primary or intermediate teacher. She sought insulation from observability, at least in her actual teaching. She pushed constantly against the administration, seeking to endow it with the legitimate authority it refused to claim. This led her to other contradictions. She was seeking to use the administrators as bulwarks against the demands of others while at the same time she resisted the demands of the administrators on her. She tried to form coalitions with some members of her role-set against the more importunate members and to deny and fight their coalitions against herself. She tried to expose the demands of one group in order to show others how they prevented her from doing her job. All the elementary teachers at Adams handled their problems at different times in all of these ways.

One can suggest five adaptations to frustration that are possible in situations such as those facing the Adams teachers. The first would be to abandon the status. No Adams teacher did this. The second would be to cut down or change the goals she sought, thus adjusting them to a level where they were achieved, or where at least they became unspecific enough so that they might appear to be achieved.[8] That no Adams teacher did this was not because it was unrealistic. But the social conditions necessary for this adaptation were missing at Adams. The service ideal and the conviction of the importance of teaching and what teaching meant were so well internalized in these teachers that much more control by legitimate authority figures would be needed to support a teacher if she were to challenge her own standards. A third possibility would be ritualism. This was a prevalent mode of adaptation at Adams. Its prevalence helps to explain why the Adams teacher failed to interest herself in new teaching methods, to attend conferences, or to become absorbed in educational literature. However, when failure showed through the ritualistic cover to an extent which she could not ignore, then the Adams teacher tended to choose one of the other two adaptations. She would turn the failure outward and blame someone else. She would blame the children for being lazy, indifferent, sick, or poorly motivated. She would blame the parents for hostility or failure to cooperate with her. She would blame the administration for not backing her up. Turning failure away from herself, she did not have to feel inadequate since something was standing in her way.

Or the teacher would turn the failure inward, blame herself when the pupil did not learn and probe her own methods to find out where she had gone wrong: "I can't teach anything. What do we do wrong over here? It is my fault they did so badly on their social studies."

The same teacher might use one or the other of these models at different times or even at the same time: "If they don't try and make no effort, how can one know if one is doing a good teaching job? Maybe it's my fault, the way I teach. I don't know."

To attempt to classify teachers in terms of which of these two final adaptations each regularly chose would be to look at appearance rather than reality. The mask each teacher wore usually covered with a joke, a laugh, or banter, the misery she might feel, the introspective doubts. It was only rarely, in a pair relationship, that a teacher would express her deeper frustrations and dissatisfactions. Turning failure outward was the more usual way to handle frustration before the larger group.

To a degree, personality factors influenced which of these adaptations a teacher was more likely to adopt. For one teacher, self-blame about failure was a normal response, while, for another, failure was always someone else's fault. However, even the most apparently extroverted teacher, Mr. Scranton, when under pressure to succeed as a disciplinarian and when not permitted by his colleagues to lower the standards of performance he found himself unable to achieve, turned his frustrations inward and developed symptoms of emotional disturbance:

"I don't give a damn about my job. I don't care if I never have anything to do with American education again. I'm not made to be a teacher. I should try to do something else. . . . All my days are bad days."

After he left Adams to teach in another town, he quickly reverted to his more usual tone of slightly sour complaint and irritated dissatisfaction, bothered but not self-destroyed, extroverted again.

That the teachers in Adams were frustrated, often unhappy, and suffered from role-set conflict is clear from this study. This role-set conflict had serious effects on the teachers themselves and on their effectiveness in educating the pupils. The organization of the school, providing as it did minimal control from above and minimal protection for the teacher from conflicting pressures, as well as the minimal dependence of the teacher on the profession generated a high level of anxiety and tension particularly for a teacher with any tendency toward self-doubt. An increase in administrative control or a growing reliance of the teacher upon her professional identification would probably help a great deal to support the teacher and reduce some of her conflicts.

Some of the changes that have taken place in the Adams School since the completion of the study bear this out. In particular, the appointment of an elementary principal (a man and an outsider), the increase in the number of teachers who are not Old Guard or local residents, and the stabilization of the departmental program have all helped to make the teachers somewhat less unhappy in their teaching and less insecure about what they are doing. The potential conflict between the teacher's desire for professional autonomy and the requirements for employee obedience to administrative commands in a bureaucratic organization, seen by most authorities as a crucial source of tension for the teacher,[9] is a future possibility at Adams. In the future, conflict between more professional teachers and the majority of traditional Adams residents may very well develop. None of this has as yet emerged. Changes so far have been slow.

It should be clear from this study that much of the teacher's internal conflict is built into the role-set; that the conflicting expectations of different interested parties are not easily changed or made congruent either through organizational changes or improved communication. Melioration does not imply utopia.

How do the conflicts, pressures, and frustrations confronting the teachers affect the pupils, their learning, and the whole teaching enterprise? We can, of course, minimize the problem if we compare the Adams school with an urban ghetto school where the conditions are much more serious than at Adams. Adams was still pretty well isolated from the major dislocations of modern urban America. Most of the pupils did progress, even if limpingly through the grades. Most of them accepted the norms and standards of the school. They attempted to fit in and to be obedient and hardworking. But the Adams School illustrated in microcosm and admittedly in mild form many of the failures so endemic in American education today. One would have to stretch the truth to say the education was a meaningful, important, challenging, and vital experience for most Adams children, or that this school did not operate like most American schools to weed out of the educational mainstream the ones who did not fit, the ones whose attitudes, values, economic and cultural backgrounds in some ways ill-prepared them for the contemporary American school.

Many of these results are the product of the particular orientation and structure of the traditional American school, with its emphasis not only on restricted content but also on a particular kind of orderly, disciplined, and ritualistic way of imparting information. The "innovative teacher," the one who wishes to organize her classroom differently, to teach what is not in the curriculum, the one who believes that discipline may be less important than excitement, is at a real disadvantage and is given little opportunity to try out her ideas. Significant change in the organization, focus, methods, and even goals of the school would necessitate help, encouragement, and specific direction from the administrative hierarchy, from those above the teacher in the system. Furthermore, any radical transformation would require change both in the attitudes of administrators and teachers, which throws the problem back to the teachers' colleges, and in the dominant values of the society in which these schools operate.[10] I am not suggesting that there have not been and are not now revolutionary innovations in methods of teaching and learning being tried in some schools. But I do suggest that these tend to be rare, that they probably require a particularly fortunate combination of either enlightened or indifferent (but willing to pay) citizens, an imaginative, brave, and somewhat iconoclastic administration, and a teaching staff dominated at least to some degree by a group willing to try new things, to break out of the old patterns. There are no easy answers here. Teachers' colleges do not create the values dominant in American education, although they may perpetuate some of them beyond their viability in the present society. The school, to some degree, does represent what our society wants and demands. To channel some on and some out is inherent in the system and a school that relied not at all on competitive advantage (or the "cooling-out function" discussed by Burton Clark)[11] would be extremely vulnerable to community pressures, parental objections, and the limitation of funds. Even if radical changes do take place in the teachers' colleges and in the training of teachers and administrators, the effect these changes may have on the schools is unclear. Those who go into teaching and those who progress up the ranks to become administrators bring to the process their own values, attitudes, and backgrounds that radically restrict the possible success of new ways.

None of this means that real innovation has not occurred. The transformation of the English primary schools as well as successful educational experiments both in the United States and Canada attest to this.[12] However, radical critics of the education system, among them Edgar Friedenberg and Paul Goodman, believe that the problems are much too fundamental to be solved by internal tinkerings with the structure. The most thought provoking of these critics, Ivan Illich, suggests that compulsory schooling itself must be eliminated. In the monopolistic educational system now spreading over the underdeveloped as well as the developed world, "the pupil is thereby 'schooled' to confuse teaching with learning, grade advancement with education, a diploma with competence, and fluency with the ability to say something new. . . . Everywhere not only education but society as a whole needs 'de-schooling'."[13] For Illich the school has an antieducational effect on society and must be demonopolized.[14] His criticisms, if not his solutions, are persuasive and receive discouraging support from the recent studies that have detailed the actual process of "education" as it takes place not only in urban ghetto schools but in middle-class schools as well.[15]

Whether a revolutionary plan to demonopolize the school system, or more moderate plans to provide parents with choice among schools and educational programs through some system of educational entitlements become realities in time,[16] the likelihood of radical change in the school experiences of children in communities such as Adams seems remote for the near future. New ways will be tried, traditional emphases little by little eroded, but for some time the Adams children will experience schooling in much the same fashion as Adams children before them have experienced it. However, at least one positive result might emerge from attempting to decrease the tension and anxiety faced by the Adams teachers as a result of their exposure to role-set conflicts and lack of direction and control. While any system can and does "limp along with a measure of ineffectiveness and inefficiency"[17] even if there is dissatisfaction and contradiction, we can suggest that unhappy, frustrated teachers probably help to produce unhappy, frustrated, and nonlearning pupils. True, a school's effectiveness can not be measured as easily as can the output of a more rationalized system. The tangible product, a pupil with a certain score on a certain standardized test, is as we have indicated only a partially satisfactory measure of whether he has become educated, whether he has learned, whether he has been turned into what we want him to become in our society. As long as the goals of our educational system are unclearly defined, often internally inconsistent, as well as inconsistent with dominant and often themselves inconsistent values in our larger society, it is going to be hard to measure the influence of teacher morale and job satisfaction on producing positive or deleterious effects. But to want children to be productive, to grow, to be creative and imaginative, to enjoy learning and working may be American values as important as the requirement that they succeed, whatever that means. The American school seems to be almost systematically making the former impossible, making of the school experience something deadening, restricting, and limiting rather than growing. Therefore, any efforts to increase flexibility, to cut down the miseries, frustrations and internal conflicts for the teachers are worthwhile if only to encourage some change in the school's atmosphere, its feeling tone.

When I was most discouraged in contemplating what my colleagues and I were doing and failing to do as teachers for the children of Adams, I would recall what one teacher said: "It is wonderful when everyone is working toward the same goal. You feel the group working in the same direction, everyone participating, they learning, and you learning, too. It doesn't happen every day, but it can, and it is exciting. It makes all the unpleasant parts of the job less important. Then it is worth it, being a teacher."

NOTES
BIBLIOGRAPHY
INDEX

NOTES

INTRODUCTION

1. Morris S. Schwartz and Charlotte G. Schwartz, "Problems in Participant Observation," *American Journal of Sociology* 60 (January 1955), 344, 347. See also George J. McCall and J. L. Simmons, eds., *Issues in Participant Observation* (Don Mills, Ontario: Addison-Wesley Publishing Co., 1969).

2. See Schwartz and Schwartz, "Participant Observation," pp. 348–350, for discussion of the problems created by strong affective involvement.

3. On this point, see Howard S. Becker and Blanche Geer, "Participant Observation: The Analysis of Qualitative Field Data," in *Human Organization Research,* ed. Richard N. Adams and Jack J. Preiss (Homewood, Ill.: The Dorsey Press, Inc., 1960), pp. 279, 281.

4. Subjective or perceived role conflict on the part of the actor is termed "ambivalence" by Melvin Seeman, "Role Conflict and Ambivalence in Leadership," *American Sociological Review* 18 (August 1953), 373. See also Frederick W. Terrien, "The Occupational Roles of Teachers," *Journal of Educational Sociology* 29 (1955–1956), 14–20, and Jacob W. Getzels and Egon G. Guba, "The Structure of Roles and Role Conflict in the Teaching Situation," *Journal of Educational Sociology* 29 (1955–1956), 30–40, for clear distinctions between subjective and objective perception of role conflict.

5. See, for example, Ronald Lippitt and David H. Jenkins, *Interpersonal Perceptions of Teachers, Students and Parents: An Action Research Project for the In-Service Training of Teachers* (Washington,

D.C.: Division of Adult Education Service, National Education Association, 1951), who probed the mutual expectations of teachers, parents, and students. Also, Robert Bush, *The Teacher-Pupil Relationship* (New York: Prentice-Hall, Inc., 1954), and Lloyd A. Cook and Elaine F. Cook, "Community Expectations for the Teacher," in *Education in Society, Readings,* ed. Bernard N. Meltzer, Harry R. Doby, and Philip M. Smith (New York: Thomas Y. Crowell Co., 1958).

6. Robert K. Merton, "The Role-Set; Problems in Sociological Theory," *British Journal of Sociology* 8 (June 1957).

7. Neal Gross, Ward S. Mason, and Alexander W. McEachern, *Explorations in Role Analysis: Studies of the School Superintendency Role* (New York: John Wiley and Sons, Inc., 1958).

8. Robert K. Merton, *Social Theory and Social Structure* (Glencoe: The Free Press, 1957), p. 369.

9. Gross, Mason, and McEachern, *Explorations,* pp. 29, 39–43.

10. Following Merton, role-set conflict is more critical for the Adams teacher than status-set conflict. Merton, *Social Theory,* pp. 369–370. Gross distinguishes these as intrarole and interrole conflict. Gross, Mason, and McEachern, *Explorations,* pp. 248–249.

11. See Wilbur Brookover, "Research on Teacher and Administrator Roles," *Journal of Educational Sociology* 29 (September 1955), 10, for criticism of sociologists for ignoring the changing of role-expectations in different situations.

12. The fluidity between ideal and real expectations is implicitly discussed by Howard S. Becker, "Social Class Variations in the Teacher Pupil Relationship," *Journal of Educational Sociology* 25 (April 1952), 451–465, and by Miriam Wagenschein, "Reality Shock: A Study of Beginning Elementary School Teachers" (unpublished Master's dissertation, University of Chicago, September 1950).

13. Theodore M. Newcomb, *Social Psychology* (New York: The Dryden Press, 1950), pp. 213–214.

14. That is, "anticipations" that do not shift in response to changing situations. See Gross, Mason, and McEachern, *Explorations,* pp. 58–59.

15. Willard Waller, *The Sociology of Teaching,* (New York: John Wiley and Sons, Inc., 1932), pp. 58–59.

16. See Gross, Mason, and McEachern, *Explorations,* pp. 50–51.

17. See, in particular, the extensive research by Bruce Biddle and his associates. J. P. Twyman and Bruce J. Biddle, "Role Conflict for Public School Teachers," *Journal of Psychology* 55 (1963), 183–198, and Bruce J. Biddle et al., "Shared Inaccuracies in the Role of Teacher," in Bruce J. Biddle and Edwin J. Thomas, *Role Theory: Concepts and Research* (New York: John Wiley and Sons, Inc., 1966), pp. 302–310. Recent research is cited in Alan Edward Guskin and Samuel Louis Guskin, *A Social Psychology of Education* (Don Mills, Ontario: Addison-Wesley Publishing Co., 1970), chap. i, "The Role Perspective." Provocative studies using

direct classroom observation provide new insights into the teacher's role and its internal conflicts. See, for example, Louis M. Smith and William Geoffrey, *The Complexities of an Urban Classroom: An Analysis toward a General Theory of Teaching* (New York: Holt, Rinehart and Winston, Inc., 1968); Patricia Minuchin et al., *The Psychological Impact of School Experience, A Comparative Study of Nine-Year Old Children in Contrasting Schools* (New York: Basic Books, Inc., 1969); Arno A. Bellak et al., *The Language of the Classroom* (New York: Teachers College Press, 1966).

1. ADAMS: HILL AND HOLLOW, TOWN AND SCHOOL

1. Compare Arthur Vidich and Joseph Bensman, *Small Town in Mass Society: Class, Power and Religion in a Rural Community* (New York: Anchor Books, Doubleday and Co., Inc., 1960), p. 184.

2. All of the fathers of STP teachers were professionals; all of the fathers of teachers' college teachers were blue-collar workers or farmers.

3. Margaret Mead, *The School in American Culture* (Cambridge: Harvard University Press, 1951), pp. 5–6, shows how labels reveal stereotypes. So we speak of fat teachers, old teachers, young teachers, Negro teachers, men teachers. All of these are exceptions to the accepted stereotype of the female teacher in her mid-thirties or forties.

4. On this point, see Neal Gross, "The Sociology of Education," in *Sociology Today, Problems and Prospects,* ed. Robert K. Merton, Leonard Broom, and Leonard Cottrell, Jr. (New York: Basic Books, Inc., 1959), pp. 136–137. Matthew Miles, "Some Properties of Schools as Social Systems," in *Change in School Systems,* ed. G. Watson (Washington, D.C.: National Training Laboratories, National Education Association, 1967), p. 9, notes that such isolation creates problems in judging role-performance. Also, lack of communication among teachers may help to explain the lack of knowledge they have about each other's problems, methods, and progress. See in this regard, David W. Johnson, *The Social Psychology of Education* (New York: Holt, Rinehart and Winston, Inc., 1970), p. 50.

5. Compare Rose Coser, *Life in the Ward* (East Lansing: Michigan State University Press, 1962), pp. 4–5.

6. Waller, *Teaching,* p. 10.

7. See Waller, *Teaching,* pp. 189–211.

2. THE TEACHER'S SELF-IMAGE

1. See Peter Berger, *Invitation to Sociology, A Humanistic Perspective* (New York: Anchor Books, Doubleday and Co. Inc., 1963), pp. 95–98.

2. Frederick W. Terrien, "Occupational Roles," p. 20.

3. Sam D. Sieber, "Organizational Influences on Innovative Roles," in *Knowledge Production and Utilization in Educational Administration,* ed.

Terry L. Eidell and Joanne M. Kitchel (Eugene, Oreg.: Center for the Advanced Study of Educational Administration, 1968), p. 134. The principle of organizational efficiency dictates that cohorts be processed, not individuals.

4. Everett C. Hughes, *Men and Their Work* (Glencoe: The Free Press, 1958), p. 51.

5. See Merton, *Social Theory*, pp. 320–321, 351, for an analysis of observability as it is related to the structure of a social organization.

6. C. Wayne Gordon, "The Role of the Teacher in the Social Structure of the High School," *Journal of Educational Sociology* 29 (1955–1956), 29.

7. Wagenschein, "Reality Shock," pp. 59–60.

8. Erving Goffman, *The Presentation of Self in Everyday Life* (New York: Anchor Books, Doubleday and Co., 1959), pp. 30–31.

9. Eleanor Burke Leacock, *Teaching and Learning in City Schools* (New York: Basic Books, Inc., 1969), p. 87. "Classroom management becomes, not a means to an end, but an end in itself."

10. Sarane Boocock, "Towards a Sociology of Learning: A Selective Review of Existing Research," *Sociology of Education* 39, no. 1 (Winter 1966), 40, reviewing the research on learning, says we "cannot yet say just what it is that the effective teacher is or does."

11. Other research demonstrates this tendency: Sieber, "Organizational Influences," p. 133; Smith and Geoffrey, *Urban Classroom*, pp. 232–233; Philip W. Jackson, *Life in Classrooms* (New York: Holt, Rinehart and Winston, Inc., 1968), pp. 162–163.

12. See Hughes, *Men and Their Work*, pp. 75–76.

13. Compare Wagenschein, "Reality Shock," p. 53.

14. A clear example of the behavior of the marginal man. See Merton, *Social Theory*, pp. 265–271, for expansion of the original idea expressed by E. V. Stonequist.

15. See George C. Homans, *Social Behavior: Its Elementary Forms* (New York: Harcourt, Brace and World, Inc., 1961), pp. 72–78 and chap. xii, "Justice," pp. 232–264.

16. Goffman was one of the first sociologists to probe the fascinating question of territoriality. See also Stanford M. Lyman and Marvin B. Scott, *The Sociology of the Absurd* (New York: Appleton-Century-Crofts, 1970), chap. iv, "Territoriality: A Neglected Sociological Dimension."

17. Recent studies that focus on the self-expectations of teachers include John M. Foskett, *The Normative World of the Elementary School Teacher* (Eugene, Oreg.: The Center for the Advanced Study of Educational Administration, 1967), and the Biddle studies cited in the Introduction. My study differs little from these in the description of the important norms, but it does differ in the method used to uncover them. The norms I explicate in this chapter revealed themselves in observation and conversation over time, not in response to questions posed in formal or informal interviews.

3. COLLEAGUES AND PEERS

1. George Homans, *The Human Group* (New York: Harcourt, Brace and Company, 1950), p. 116.

2. Contrast the views of Dan Lortie and Philip Jackson on the relative importance of pupils and colleagues for the teacher as cited in Emil Haller, "Pupil Influence in Teacher Socialization: A Socio-Linguistic Study," *Sociology of Education* 40, no. 4 (Fall 1967), 317–318.

3. See Goffman, *Presentation of Self,* chap. iii, "Regions and Region Behavior." For the teacher the "backstage region" is defined more by time than by location. When the job is over, the appropriate role-behavior may be dropped, even though the actor can still be observed.

4. See Merton, *Social Theory,* p. 377, and Gross, Mason, and McEachern, *Explorations,* pp. 55–56, concerning the importance of colleagues for "articulating the role-set." See also Leacock, *Teaching and Learning,* and Smith and Geoffrey, *Urban Classroom,* p. 242.

5. Wagenschein, "Reality Shock," pp. 64–65, and Howard S. Becker, "The Teacher in the Authority System of the Public School," *Journal of Educational Sociology* 27 (November 1953), 139, stress the teachers' picture of the colleague group as a defensive, protective organization. For relevant comment on the function of conflict with an outside enemy in strengthening cohesion and in-group loyalty, see Lewis Coser, *The Functions of Social Conflict* (Glencoe: The Free Press, 1956), pp. 33–38, Merton, *Social Theory,* pp. 297–299, and Goffman, *Presentation of Self,* pp. 88–92.

6. Peter Blau, *The Dynamics of Bureaucracy* (Chicago: University of Chicago Press, 1963), p. 271, notes that informal contact among colleagues relieves tensions arising from the officials' relations with public clients.

7. Homans, *The Human Group,* pp. 153–154.

8. Merton, *Social Theory,* p. 265. " . . . poised on the edge of several groups but fully accepted by none of them."

9. Ibid., p. 286.

10. To be the "instrumental-adaptive" leader. Robert Bales, "The Equilibrium Problem in Small Groups," in *Working Papers in the Theory of Action,* ed. Talcott Parsons, Robert Bales, and Edward Shils (Glencoe: The Free Press, 1953), p. 147.

11. Henry W. Riecken and George C. Homans, "Psychological Aspects of Social Structure," *Handbook of Social Psychology,* vol. II, ed. Gardner Lindzey (Reading, Massachusetts: Addison-Wesley Publishing Co., 1954), p. 823.

12. While both formal training and informal anticipatory socialization help prepare a prospective occupant for his new status (Merton, *Social Theory,* p.385), it is clear that this is not enough as Wagenschein, "Reality Shock," and Estelle Fuchs, *Teachers Talk: Views from Inside City Schools* (New York: Anchor Books, Doubleday and Co., Inc., 1969),

eloquently testify. See Seymour Sarason, Kenneth Davidson, and Burton Blatt, *The Preparation of Teachers* (New York: John Wiley and Sons, Inc., 1962).

13. See Goffman, *Presentation of Self,* p. 72, and Hughes, *Men and Their Work,* p. 106.

14. Important research on the relation between occupational choice and personality in teaching is summarized in Jacob W. Getzels and Philip W. Jackson, "The Teacher's Personality and Characteristics," *Handbook of Research on Teaching,* ed. N. L. Gage (Chicago: Rand McNally, 1963), pp. 506–582. Tentatively one might suggest that the incorporation of the self-image and the process of socialization into the role might be less difficult and seem less artificial for some personality types than for others.

15. Sieber, "Organizational Influences," pp. 128–130, and Hughes, *Men and Their Work,* p. 95.

16. "When a group of professors get together, each one of them listens only to what he says, and then sits still and thinks of what he is going to say next. Nobody listens to what the other fellow has to say." Waller, *Teaching,* p. 431.

17. I moved from doctrinal conformity to attitudinal conformity. Robert Merton, "Social Conformity, Deviation and Opportunity Structures: A Comment on the Contribution of Dubin and Cloward," *American Sociological Review* 24 (April 1959), 180. This has been described by Goffman, *Presentation of Self,* chap. i, "Performances," Berger, *Invitation to Sociology,* pp. 96–98, and Mary Jean Huntington, "The Development of a Professional Self-Image," in *The Student-Physician: Introductory Studies in the Sociology of Medical Education,* ed. Robert Merton, Patricia Kendall, and George Reader (Cambridge: Harvard University Press, 1957), and has been characterized by Tom Burns, "Friends, Enemies and the Polite Fiction," *American Sociological Review* 18 (December 1953), 660, as the transition from purely stereotyped to spontaneous behavior as one becomes part of one's role.

18. Compare Blau, *Bureaucracy,* p. 106.

19. Ibid., pp. 107–108, 271.

20. See Coser, *Life In the Ward,* p. 85, for discussion of the importance of jocular griping among nurses.

21. Coser, *Life in the Ward,* pp. 85–86, and Blau, *Bureaucracy,* p. 110. See also Goffman, *Presentation of Self,* pp. 83–84.

22. The joke is "the short cut to consensus." Banter produces consensus while avoiding true intimacy or destroying protective social distance. Burns, "Friends, Enemies," p. 657.

23. Coser, *Life in the Ward,* p. 86.

24. Renée Fox, *Experiment Perilous* (Glencoe: The Free Press, 1959), pp. 175–177.

25. Coser, *Life in the Ward,* p. 88.

4. THE PUPIL AND THE CLASS

1. Waller, *Teaching*, p. 196.
2. The perceptive insights of Willard Waller pertaining to the teacher-pupil relationship have recently begun to be subjected to detailed analysis. See, in particular, Smith and Geoffrey, *Urban Classroom,* Jackson, *Classrooms,* and Robert A. Stebbins, "The Meaning of Disorderly Behavior: Teacher Definitions of a Classroom Situation" (paper presented at CCRE meetings, Ottawa, March 1970). Johnson, *Social Psychology,* provides brief summaries of other significant research.
3. Rose Coser, "Insulation From Observability and Types of Social Conformity," *American Sociological Review* 26 (February 1961), 34.
4. For corroboration of this dual emphasis, see Lippitt and Jenkins, *Interpersonal Perceptions,* pp. 54–57, and Talcott Parsons, "The School Class as a Social System: Some of Its Functions in American Society," in *Education, Economy and Society: A Reader In the Sociology of Education,* ed. A. H. Halsey, Jean Floud, and C. Arnold Anderson (New York: Free Press of Glencoe, 1961). Also compare Jerome Beker, James B. Victor, and Linda Seidel, "School Days," in *Among the People: Encounters With the Poor,* ed. Irwin Deutscher and Elizabeth J. Thompson (New York: Basic Books, Inc., 1968), p. 202.
5. Henry W. Simon, *Preface To Teaching* (New York: Oxford University Press, 1938), p. 69: "Teachers have a moral obligation to be interesting."
6. These particular assumptions among teachers, not thought out or consciously pursued, reflect the dominant cultural emphasis of the society. See Jules Henry, "American Schoolrooms: Learning the Nightmare," *Columbia University Forum* 6, no. 2 (Spring 1963), 24–30. That such assumptions are completely inadequate in dealing with many children has been demonstrated. See, for example, Allison Davis, *Social-Class Influences Upon Learning* (Cambridge: Harvard University Press, 1950), and "Status Systems and the Socialization of the Child," *American Sociological Review* 6 (June 1941), 345–354, as well as Frank Riessman, *The Culturally Deprived Child* (New York: Harper and Bros., 1962). But that the teacher is constrained by the structure of the school from recognizing the inadequacy is also clear. See Leacock, *Teaching and Learning,* p. 202.
7. Compare Arthur J. Hoehn, "A Study of Social Status Differentiation in the Classroom Behavior of Nineteen Third Grade Teachers," in *Readings in the Social Psychology of Education,* ed. W. W. Charters, Jr. and N. L. Gage (Boston: Allyn and Bacon, Inc., 1963), pp. 186–189, on the varying treatment of pupils relating to sex and social class.
8. Merton, *Social Theory,* chap. xi. Compare Leacock, *Teaching and Learning,* pp. 181–182, who shows that the teachers' anticipations for the working-class children are different from those they hold for the middle-

class children, expecting "deviance to be unruliness with regard to behavior and apathy with regard to curriculum."

9. See Jules Henry for detailed analysis of ways teachers control classroom transactions. "Culture, Education and Communication Theory," in *Education and Anthropology*, ed. George Spindler (Stanford: Stanford University Press, 1955), pp. 188–207, and Jules Henry, "Classroom Responses of the Middle-Class Child," in *Education in Society*, ed. Meltzer, Doby, and Smith, pp. 407–411.

10. Henry, "Classroom Responses," p. 407, and "Attitude Organization in Elementary School Classrooms," in *Readings*, ed. Charters and Gage, p. 263.

11. Waller, *Teaching*, p. 389. "One has become a school teacher when he has learned to fear the loss of his dignity."

12. As Jackson, *Classrooms*, pp. 19–22, shows, evaluation and sanctioning by teachers of nonacademic behavior in the classroom is as much or more pervasive than evaluation of the achievement of academic objectives.

13. Contrast T. J. Johnson, K. Feigenbaum, and M. Weiby, "Some Determinants and Consequences of the Teacher's Perceptions of Causation," *Journal of Educational Psychology* 55 (1964), 237–246.

14. The higher the grade level of the teacher the more she preferred to teach the average child. The interview data further indicate that the teacher's response to intelligence was influenced as much by her educational background as by the grade level she taught. Contrast Becker, "Social Class Variations," pp. 454–456. The fear that the Adams teacher had of the bright child may more accurately be seen as a response to the creative child — the one who seemed to use his ability in a nondocile way. See, in this regard, Jacob W. Getzels and Philip W. Jackson, *Creativity and Intelligence: Explorations with Gifted Students* (New York: John Wiley and Sons, Inc., 1962), pp. 30–36.

15. While in actuality these characteristics cannot be so simply dichotomized, the typology outlined here serves to emphasize the extent to which teachers stereotype. This stereotyping becomes more rigid as the pupil progresses from grade to grade and becomes an important influence on the new teacher's judgment of the pupil. For the effects of stereotyping on pupil achievement, see Robert Rosenthal and Lenore Jacobson, *Pygmalion in the Classroom* (New York: Holt, Rinehart and Winston, 1968). The stereotypes are transmitted directly in a small school and indirectly in larger schools through comments on student record forms. See the study by Eigel Pedersen and Mona Farrell, "Background and Personal Factors Associated with IQ Change in an Inner-City Population" (paper presented at the CSAA meetings, Winnipeg, June 1970), on the influence of written teacher comments on IQ change.

16. See Kenneth Clark, *Dark Ghetto* (New York: Harper and Row,

1965), pp. 120–121, on the decline in achievement between third and sixth grade.

17. See, in this context, Kai Erikson, "The Sociology of Deviance," in *Social Problems: Persistent Challenges,* ed. Edward C. McDonagh and Jon E. Simpson (New York: Holt, Rinehart and Winston, Inc., 1965), pp. 457–464, and Lewis Coser, "Functions of Deviant Behavior," in *Social Problems,* ed. McDonagh and Simpson, pp. 500–509.

18. Comparable to Merton's distinction between retreatism and rebellion (*Social Theory,* pp. 140, 155–157), and between aberrant and nonconformist deviance. Robert K. Merton and Robert A. Nisbet, *Contemporary Social Problems* (New York: Harcourt, Brace and World, Inc., 1966), p. 810.

19. Boocock, "Sociology of Learning," p. 35.

20. See, for example, Myron Lieberman, *Education as a Profession* (New York: Prentice-Hall, Inc., 1956), and Burton R. Clark, *Educating the Expert Society* (San Francisco: Chandler Publishing Company, 1962), pp. 164–171. But as Neal Gross, "Critique of 'Social Class Structure and American Education,' " and W. W. Charters, Jr., "Social Class Analysis and the Control of Public Education," *Harvard Educational Review* 23 (Fall 1953), 298–338, 268–283, both warn, one must not assume a direct connection between social class origins and values. It is fallacious to assume that one necessarily internalizes the values of the social class position from which one started.

21. For similar emphases on the importance of the middle-class value domination by the school itself and the lesser significance of the teacher's class origin or personality, see Riessman, *Culturally Deprived Child,* p. 23, William Wattenberg et al., "Social Origins of Teachers and American Education," in *The Teacher's Role in American Society,* ed. Lindley J. Stiles (New York: Harper and Bros., 1957), p. 69, and Leacock, *Teaching and Learning,* p. 23.

22. Discrimination against lower-class children in our schools is not a new revelation. See, for example, W. Lloyd Warner, Robert J. Havighurst, and Martin Loeb, *Who Shall Be Educated?* (New York: Harper and Bros., 1944), and A. B. Hollingshead, *Elmtown's Youth* (New York: John Wiley and Sons, Inc., 1949).

23. An illustration of the potential conflict between the universalistic role of the teacher and the need for particularistic personal relations between teacher and pupil to motivate learning, first described by Waller, *Teaching,* and since developed by numerous investigators. See, for example, Sieber, "Organizational Influences," p. 130, and M. D. Shipman, *The Sociology of the School* (London: Longman's, Green and Co., Ltd, 1968), pp. 121–135. Pupil manipulation of the teacher becomes clearest in high school. See Waller, *Teaching,* C. Wayne Gordon, *The Social System of the High School, A Study in the Sociology of the Adolescent* (Glencoe: The Free Press, 1957), and James S. Coleman, *The*

Adolescent Society: The Social Life of the Teenager and Its Impact on Education (New York: The Free Press of Glencoe, 1961).

24. Compare to the ambivalent authority relationship between officers and men in the army. Samuel A. Stouffer et al., "Barriers to Understanding between Officers and Enlisted Men," in *Reader in Bureaucracy,* ed. Robert Merton et al. (Glencoe: The Free Press, 1952), p. 268.

25. Waller, *Teaching,* pp. 196, 390.

26. See Henry, "Classroom Responses," p. 411, Lippitt and Jenkins, *Interpersonal Perceptions,* p. 78, and David Riesman, *Constraint and Variety in American Education* (Lincoln: University of Nebraska Press, 1956), pp. 126–128. Riesman suggests that children learn in their "child-centered homes to exploit the adults' need for affection and approval."

27. An example of one form of the "tertius gaudens." Georg Simmel, *The Sociology of Georg Simmel,* trans. and ed. Kurt Wolff (Glencoe: The Free Press, 1950), p. 232.

28. As Simmel, *Sociology,* p. 160, says, "The favorable position of the tertius disappears quite generally the moment the two others become a unit."

29. Compare Orville Brim, *Sociology and the Field of Education* (New York: Russell Sage Foundation, 1958), p. 49. See N. L. Gage, Philip J. Runkel, and B. B. Chatterjee, "Changing Teacher Behavior through Feedback from Pupils: An Application of Equilibrium Theory," in *Readings,* ed. Charters and Gage, pp. 173–181, on how changing behavior to conform to pupil expectations cuts down internal strain for teachers.

30. See discussion by Jean Piaget, *The Moral Judgment of the Child* (Glencoe: The Free Press, 1948), pp. 293, 316, on equity. Piaget notes, p. 316, "a development of equalitarianism in the direction of relativity." The Adams fifth and sixth graders had not arrived at relativity; equity to them meant *equal* treatment for all. Through grade placement they were considered as equivalent to one another in requirements and assignments. They thus believed that they should be treated equivalently. These pupils carefully distinguished their rights from those of pupils above and below them, thus demonstrating a clear acceptance of Homans's elementary proposition about equity. *Social Behavior,* chap. xii, "Justice."

31. Maybe an illustration of Homans's Proposition 5: "The more to a man's disadvantage the rule of distributive justice fails of realization, the more likely he is to display the emotional behavior we call anger." Homans, *Social Behavior,* p. 75.

32. Piaget, *Moral Judgment,* p. 250, states, "Collective responsibility seems to us to be missing from the moral make-up of the child." My data allow no such sweeping conclusion, but it was true at Adams that

little sense of collective responsibility existed despite pupil consciousness of class unity.

33. An important norm among teachers, See Becker, "Teacher in Authority System," p. 139.

34. On the power of the group, see Waller, *Teaching*, pp. 297, 304, as well as Mary A. Bany and Lois V. Johnson, *Classroom Group Behavior* (New York: The Macmillan Co., 1964), and William Clark Trow et al., "Psychology of Group Behavior," in *Educational Psychology*, ed. Arthur Coladarci (New York: The Dryden Press, 1955), pp. 229–245.

35. Waller, *Teaching*, p. 297.

36. See Harry L. Gracey, "Learning the Student Role: Kindergarten as Academic Boot Camp," in *Readings in Introductory Sociology*, ed. Dennis H. Wrong and Harry L. Gracey (New York: The Macmillan Co., 1967), pp. 288–299.

37. Fritz Redl and William W. Wattenberg, *Mental Hygiene in Teaching* (New York: Harcourt, Brace and Co., 1951), p. 213, point to the distinctive personality of each school class.

38. Waller, *Teaching*, pp. 162–163, 185.

39. Ibid., p. 297. The specific procedures through which the experienced teacher imposes her definition of the situation are depicted in Smith and Geoffrey, *Urban Classroom*.

40. I use the term *identification* to describe a relationship that involves direct interaction but ambivalence because of difference in position. While somewhat impersonal it is also affectual, encompassing the superior's conviction that what happens to the subordinate is also happening to him. Concerned with the subordinates' interests the superior has a sense of responsibility for them. The term here does not indicate identification with a reference group, as in Merton, *Social Theory*, pp. 356–358. Nor is it used as assimilation of feelings (emotional absorption), as in Gardner Murphy, Lois Murphy, and Theodore M. Newcomb, *Experimental Social Psychology* (New York: Harper and Bros., 1937), pp. 188–189, 208, 210, and Talcott Parsons and Edward Shils, eds., *Towards a General Theory of Action* (Cambridge: Harvard University Press, 1951), p. 308.

41. See the discussion of similar kinds of relationships in Homans, *Human Group*,, pp. 244–247.

42. Ferenc Merei, "Group Leadership and Institutionalization," *Human Relations* 2 (1949), 33–34, shows how it is often the marginal group member who seeks contact with the new leader.

43. See Goffman, *Presentation of Self*, p. 201.

44. Waller, *Teaching*, p. 59.

45. Haller, "Pupil Influence," pp. 325–328, finds that teachers' mode of speech changes to adapt to the grade at which they teach.

46. Waller, *Teaching*, p. 252. This need for love and affection may be

a function of the personality needs that Egon Guba, Philip W. Jackson, and Charles E. Bidwell, "Occupational Choice and the Teaching Career," in *Readings*, ed. Charters and Gage, pp. 271–278, find most characteristic, particularly of long-term teachers.

47. Peter Blau and Richard Scott, *Formal Organizations* (San Francisco: Chandler Publishing Company, 1962), p. 142. See Charles E. Bidwell, "The School as a Formal Organization," in *Handbook of Organizations*, ed. James G. March (Chicago: Rand McNally and Co., 1965), pp. 978–984, 990, for a summary of studies dealing with this double aspect.

5. NATURAL ENEMIES: TEACHERS AND PARENTS

1. Waller, *Teaching*, p. 68.
2. Parsons, "School Class," pp. 443–444.
3. Jules Henry, "American Schoolrooms," p. 30.
4. As noted by Parsons, "School Class." See also Robert Dreeben, *On What Is Learned In School* (Reading, Massachusetts: Addison-Wesley Publishing Co., 1968).
5. Waller, *Teaching*, p. 248.
6. For extended discussion, see Lieberman, *Education as a Profession*, in particular, chap. viii, "Teachers and their Characteristics," pp. 214–256. Also, Ronald Corwin, *A Sociology of Education* (New York: Appleton-Century-Crofts, 1965), pp. 235–237. See George Baron and Asher Tropp, "Teachers in England and America," in *Education, Economy*, ed. Halsey, Floud, and Anderson, p. 549, for explanation of the higher prestige of British teachers.
7. Waller, *Teaching*, pp. 58–62.
8. David Riesman, *Constraint and Variety*, p. 113.
9. Howard S. Becker, "Schools and Systems of Stratification," in *Education, Economy*, ed. Halsey, Floud, and Anderson, and Wagenschein, "Reality Schock," pp. 63–64.
10. The most frequent objection by teachers to parent-teacher conferences. Compare the English situation cited by M. D. Shipman, *The School*, p. 127, where one-half of the manual worker parents and one-third of the nonmanual worker parents never visited their children's primary school.
11. In the fifth and sixth grade homerooms: A groups — 91 percent attendance; B groups — 47 percent attendance. As academic placement and social class were closely related at Adams, the lower attendance of B group parents might reflect the unwillingness of the lower-class parents to subject themselves to an ego-threatening conference with the teachers.
12. In the Lippitt and Jenkins study, *Interpersonal Perceptions*, pp. 41–42, 85 percent of the teachers stated they wanted the parents to visit the school.

13. Waller, *Teaching*, p. 59.

14. Compare Waller, *Teaching*, p. 74, on dominant parental concern with the nonacademic.

15. Contrast similar demand of parents for particularistic treatment in other schools where the emphasis is reversed — parents demanding more pressure on the child; teachers focusing on the whole class rather than on each pupil. Compare this with the study by Sam Sieber and David E. Wilder, "Teaching Styles: Parental Preferences and Professional Role Definitions," *Sociology of Education* 40, no. 4 (Fall 1967), 302–315.

16. See Foskett, *Normative World*, pp. 85–86, on teachers' inaccurate perceptions of parental expectations.

17. See Lippitt and Jenkins, *Interpersonal Perceptions*, p. 45.

18. Waller, *Teaching*, p. 77, notes that when a school official publicly repudiates his teachers, teacher loyalty is radically reduced.

19. See Joseph A. Kahl, "Educational and Occupational Aspirations of 'Common Man' Boys," *Harvard Educational Review* 23 (Summer 1953), 189, 201. The teacher's stimulation of aspirations makes no significant impact on the attitudes of "common-man" boys.

20. See Hughes, *Men and Their Work*, pp. 81–82, on the use of technical language to give a profession the license "to talk in shocking terms about its clients and their problems." Haller suggests that teachers lack a specialized terminology ("Pupil Influence," pp. 143–144). However, for the less-educated parent, the teacher's talk (even if not technical) may be misunderstood and misinterpreted.

21. The relation between social class and education is not perfect. Hostility to private school teachers was directed less to their social class position than to their occupation. As teachers, they were privy to secrets and thus dangerous.

22. One mechanism for "articulating the role-set." Merton, *Social Theory*, p. 377.

23. See, for example, Becker, "Teacher in Authority System," p. 139, Hughes, *Men and Their Work*, pp. 76–77, and Goffman, *Presentation of Self*, p. 82.

24. See L. Coser, *Social Conflict*, pp. 69–72, discussing Simmel's views on renegadism.

25. Contrast Merton, *Social Theory*, p. 378. The Old Guard teachers at Adams can be considered "locals" rather than "cosmopolitans." (See Alvin W. Gouldner, "Cosmopolitans and Locals: Towards an Analysis of Latent Social Roles," *Administrative Science Quarterly* 2 (1957–1958), 281–306, 444–480.) External professional identification was not central to their self-image. (See note 13, Chapter 7.)

26. In this connection, see Hughes, *Men and Their Work*, in particular chap. vi, "Licence and Mandate," and chap. vii, "Mistakes at Work." Also Corwin, *Education*, p. 235.

27. Lippitt and Jenkins, *Interpersonal Perceptions,* pp. 22, 42, 45.

28. Robert S. Lynd and Helen M. Lynd, *Middletown in Transition* (New York: Harcourt, Brace and Co., 1937), p. 233. "If parents trained in another era are at sea as regards the present elaborate high school curriculum, they still think they know what an elementary education should be and feel that they can insist upon 'essentials' there."

29. See Merton, *Social Theory,* p. 375, and Wilbert Moore and Melvin W. Tumin, "Some Social Functions of Ignorance," *American Sociological Review* 14 (December 1949), 787–795.

30. See, in this regard, Goffman, *Presentation of Self,* chap. iii, "Regions and Region Behavior."

31. See, for example, Jean Grambs, "The Roles of the Teacher," in *Teacher's Role,* ed. Stiles, p. 87, and Lippitt and Jenkins, *Interpersonal Perceptions,* p. 18.

32. Biddle and his colleagues suggest that shared inaccuracies may serve certain important functions which help to explain why they are perpetuated. "Shared Inaccuracies," pp. 309–310.

33. Kenneth Burke, *Permanence and Change* (New York: New Republic, 1935), p. 70. "A way of seeing is also a way of not seeing."

34. Contradictory demands do not necessarily cause internal conflict. A role-occupant can shift back and forth and reinterpret the expectations. Robert J. Havighurst and Bernice L. Neugarten, *Society and Education* (Boston: Allyn and Bacon, Inc., 1957), p. 389. In this context, see also Jackson Toby, "Some Variables in Role-Conflict Analysis," *Social Forces* 30 (1952), 323–327.

35. Waller, *Teaching,* p. 69.

6. POWER AND CONTROL: THE AUTHORITY VACUUM

1. For this approach, see Merton, *Social Theory,* p. 340, Chester I. Barnard, *The Functions of the Executive* (Cambridge: Harvard University Press, 1938), and Homans, *Human Group.*

2. Blau, *Bureaucracy,* p. 228. Following Gross, Mason, and McEachern, *Explorations,* chap. xvii, "A Theory of Role Conflict Resolution," in particular, pp. 289–295, the older Adams teachers had a strongly "moral" orientation, resolving intrarole conflicts in expectations through the search for the demand legitimated by order, rule, or tradition. Partial explanations for this orientation can be found in Francis S. Chase, "Factors Productive of Satisfaction in Teaching" (unpublished Ph.D. dissertation, University of Chicago, 1961), p. 89, and in Guba, Jackson, and Bidwell, "Occupational Choice," pp. 273, 277–278.

3. Merton, *Social Theory,* pp. 348–349.

4. For the Adams teacher to look to the superintendent for control meant that she had had some experience with superintendents as those who control, or that she held some stereotype of superintendents as

controlling. The need for authority alone would not determine the particular direction of her expectations.

5. Chase, "Satisfactions in Teaching," p. 130, found freedom to operate on one's own the factor mentioned most frequently by teachers as contributing to teaching satisfaction. See also Merton, *Social Theory,* pp. 374–375.

6. The difference in perspective and social values of role-partners, particularly those from disparate social statuses, produces instability and conflict in the role-set. Merton, *Social Theory,* pp. 370, 380.

7. He had for her the "authority of position." Barnard, *Executive,* p. 173. See Blau, *Bureaucracy,* p. 224.

8. Mr. Hanson may not have possessed the functionally appropriate personality characteristics necessary for holders of executive positions. Certainly for the Adams teacher Mr. Hanson's personality was a detriment to his effectiveness as a "boss."

9. " ... carryover of old loyalties is one of the most difficult things which the new executive has to face." Waller, *Teaching,* p. 96.

10. Although Blau, *Bureaucracy,* pp. 292–293, suggests that a new superior can extend his influence and authority beyond formal limits by yielding to group pressure and permitting some violation of rules, at Adams, Mr. Hanson continued this pattern for so long that its efficacy became diluted.

11. See Waller on this point, however. *Teaching,* p. 427.

12. Merton, *Social Theory,* p. 198.

13. For similar beliefs see Becker, "Teacher in Authority System," pp. 133–135.

14. As Gordon, "The Role of the Teacher," pp. 44–45, notes perceptively, unless the principal supports the teacher in classroom discipline the teacher is forced to fall back on personalized leadership which is often unsuccessful and at all times hard to sustain. In this context, see also Wagenschein, "Reality Shock," p. 57.

15. The objection related primarily to Mr. Hanson's inconsistency. He only "occasionally" acted in this way, illustrating Blau's contention that resistance often arises to "arbitrary power," authority that rests on the superior's discretion to decide whether or not to issue certain orders. Blau, *Bureaucracy,* p. 220.

16. Merton, *Social Theory,* pp. 372–373.

17. It would be worth investigating similar patterns in other contexts. To resist external pressures, a status occupant might well attribute to the legitimate authority figure demands and expectations that are not actually expressed, resist these demands vocally, and yet carry them out. One possible parallel might be the behavior of the adolescent from the permissive middle-class home who invents and responds to an image of a dominant father as a bulwark against peer demands, while also vocally objecting to this dominance. Another might be the buck passing within formal organizations where demands from subordinates or outsiders are

"reluctantly" rejected because they are said not to conform to the orders from above, even though these orders may never actually have been given.

18. See, in this context, Waller, *Teaching*, p. 424, Merton, *Social Theory*, pp. 341, 376, and Coser, "Insulation from Observability," pp. 34–36.

19. Merton, *Social Theory*, pp. 346–347.

20. Merton, *Social Theory*, pp. 318, 343–344, 356, and Robin M. Williams, Jr., *American Society: A Sociological Investigation* (New York: Alfred A. Knopf, 1951), pp. 354, 356–366, and Samuel Stouffer, "An Analysis of Conflicting Social Norms," *American Sociological Review* 14 (December 1949), 708.

21. Williams, *American Society*, p. 354.

22. Covert acceptance of evasions even by those in positions of authority is widespread. See, for example, Williams, *American Society*, chap. x.

23. A few years later, an elementary principal was appointed. As might have been expected, the teachers' response was ambivalent. They resented the sudden imposition of orders and of directives. They resisted changes in their routines and talked far more of autonomy and freedom than they ever had before. The resentment over control vied with an equal satisfaction in having protection and backing against parents and pupils. While morale seemed to be higher and teacher anxiety less, the expectations and demands of the teachers were the same, operating in a somewhat different ambience than before.

7. PERIPHERAL RELATIONSHIPS

1. A role-set, the "complement of role-relationships," includes role-definers as well as role-relationships and also role-relationships excluding the teacher. As Merton indicates, the relationships among members of the role-set, other than the status occupant, may be very important in influencing what the status occupant can do. Merton, *Social Theory*, pp. 376–377.

2. See F. J. Roethlisberger and W. J. Dickson, *Management and the Worker* (Cambridge: Harvard University Press, 1939), pp. 265–269, on the need for a clear distinction between the manifest and latent content of complaints. This emphasis may, of course, lead to an underestimation of the manifest complaints.

3. See Waller, *Teaching*, p. 80, on the importance of the janitor.

4. Hughes, *Men and Their Work*, p. 52.

5. Ralph Turner, "Role-Taking, Role Standpoint, and Reference Group Behavior," *The American Journal of Sociology* 56 (January 1956), 328.

6. Group boundaries do not remain fixed but "are dynamically changing in response to specifiable situational contexts." Merton, *Social Theory*, p. 286.

7. Contrast Corwin, *Education,* chap. xi, "The School in Its Power Environment," pp. 343–390. Why the Adams School was to a great degree exempt from external pressures I am not able to say, except insofar as it was still, even in the early 1960s, a traditional and somewhat insulated community.

8. See Waller, *Teaching,* chap. x, "Teachers in the Community."

9. Ibid., p. 419.

10. Ibid., p. 420. "From long imprisonment within the stereotype the teacher grows unused to freedom."

11. See Goffman, *Presentation of Self,* chap iii, "Regions and Region Behavior."

12. A. M. Carr-Saunders, *Professions: Their Organization and Place in Society,* The Herbert Spencer Lecture, Oxford, 1928 (London: The Clarendon Press, 1928), p. 5.

13. This kind of response, commented on earlier in this work, may seem unusual since in many occupations the professional association serves to protect status-occupants from pressures by role-partners. See, for example, Merton, *Social Theory,* p. 378. Sieber, "Organizational Influences," noting the "quasi-professional status" of teachers in our society, asserts that the full-fledged professions are the reference group for teachers leading to a sense of status insecurity (p. 129). As "locals," the Adams teachers did not take the full-fledged professions as their reference group although they did seem to suffer from status insecurity. See Bidwell, "Formal Organization," pp. 1007–1008, for characteristics of teachers with low professional commitments. See also James G. Anderson, *Bureaucracy in Education* (Baltimore: The Johns Hopkins Press, 1968).

14. Williams, *American Society,* p. 287.

15. See Talcott Parsons, *Essays in Sociological Theory, Pure and Applied* (Glencoe: The Free Press, 1949), p. 243.

8. LOW TEACHER MORALE: ITS IMPLICATIONS

1. Parsons, *Essays,* p. 196.

2. See Chase, "Satisfaction in Teaching," pp. 9–12.

3. See Merton, "Social Structure and Anomie," in *Social Theory,* pp. 131–160. Guba, Jackson, and Bidwell, "Occupational Choice," p. 278, show that the teachers who most closely fit the typical teacher personality type were also those who were least satisfied and felt least effective. Dissatisfaction and low morale may be partly a function of personality, not just a response to teaching.

4. See discussion of "irrevocable" occupational commitments in Peter Blau, *Exchange and Power in Social Life* (New York: John Wiley and Sons, Inc., 1964), pp. 160–161.

5. Here, I consider those reference groups to which the individual compares himself in making a self-judgment (Merton, *Social Theory,* p.

283), a judgment which requires examination only of the external attributes of the other in order to decide whether "to be satisfied or dissatisfied with his lot." Turner, "Role-Taking," p. 327. These are called equity groups by Theodore D. Kemper, "Reference Groups, Socialization and Achievement," *American Sociological Review* 33, no. 1 (1968), 32–33.

6. A form of anticipatory socialization. Merton, *Social Theory*, p. 265.

7. As Blau points out, one does not resent higher awards going to those whose investments have been greater or those not in an equivalent status position to oneself. Blau, *Exchange and Power*, pp. 157–158.

8. A common adaptation in some schools. See Becker, "Social Class Variations," pp. 456–458. But note the conflict between structural looseness and the bureaucratic pressures to produce a uniform product of a certain quality in Bidwell, "Formal Organization," pp. 974–978. These pressures for minimum achievement and also grade advancement for most children each year lead to serious difficulty. See Smith and Geoffrey, *Urban Classroom,* for detailing of problems facing the teacher in trying to teach material beyond the capacities and unrelated to the background and understanding of pupils. Not only administrators but also pupils resist changing of standards. They know "the way it spozed to be" even if they are unable to do it. James Herndon, *The Way It Spozed to Be* (New York: Simon and Schuster, Inc., 1968).

9. See Bidwell's review of the paucity of research in this area, in "Formal Organization," p. 992. For a recent useful study, see Anderson, *Bureaucracy in Education.*

10. Paul Lauter and Florence Howe, "How the School System is Rigged for Failure," *New York Review of Books* (June 18, 1970), 14–15, believe that the schools rather than failing have actually been "horrifyingly successful" in blocking economic mobility and intensifying class distinctions.

11. Burton Clark, "The 'Cooling-Out Function' in Higher Education," *The American Journal of Sociology* 45 (May 1960), 569–576.

12. Discussion of recent innovations can be found in the articles by Joseph Featherstone in *The New Republic:* "Schools for Children," 157 (August 19, 1967), 17–21; "How Children Learn," 157 (September 2, 1967), 17–21; "Teaching Children to Think," 157 (September 9, 1967), 15–19; "Experiments in Learning," 159 (December 14, 1968), 23–25; "Schools for Learning," 159 (December 21, 1968), 17–20; and "Why So Few Good Schools," 160 (January 4, 1969), 18–21. Two works of relevance here are *Children and Their Primary Schools,* A Report of the Central Advisory Council for Education (England), vol. I, *The Report* (London: Her Majesty's Stationery Office, 1967), and John Blackie, *Inside the Primary School* (London: Her Majesty's Stationery Office, 1967). See also Charles E. Silberman, *Crisis in the Classroom* (New York: Random House, 1970).

13. Ivan Illich, "Why We Must Abolish Schooling," *New York Review of Books* (July 2, 1970), 9.

14. Ibid., pp. 10–11.

15. See, for example, Silberman, *Crisis,* as well as the writings of the major critics (Edgar Friedenberg, John Holt, Paul Goodman, and so on) of our educational system.

16. See, for example, Illich, "Schooling," p. 13, and Peter Schrag, "End of the Impossible Dream," *Saturday Review* 53 (September 19, 1970), 96.

17. Merton, *Social Theory,* p. 497.

BIBLIOGRAPHY

Anderson, James G. *Bureaucracy in Education.* Baltimore, Maryland: The John Hopkins Press, 1968.

Bales, Robert. "The Equilibrium Problem in Small Groups," in *Working Papers in the Theory of Action.* Edited by Talcott Parsons, Robert Bales, and Edward Shils. Glencoe, Illinois: The Free Press, 1953.

Bany, Mary A. and Lois V. Johnson. *Classroom Group Behavior.* New York: The Macmillan Company, 1964.

Barnard, Chester I. *The Functions of the Executive.* Cambridge, Massachusetts: Harvard University Press, 1938.

Baron, George and Asher Tropp. "Teachers in England and America," in *Education, Economy and Society.* Edited by A. H. Halsey, Jean Floud, and C. Arnold Anderson. New York: Free Press of Glencoe, 1961.

Becker, Howard S. "Schools and Systems of Stratification," in *Education, Economy and Society.* Edited by A. H. Halsey, Jean Floud, and C. Arnold Anderson. New York: Free Press of Glencoe, 1961.

————. "Social-Class Variations in the Teacher-Pupil Relationship," *Journal of Educational Sociology* 25:451–465 (April 1952).

————. "The Teacher in the Authority System of the Public School," *Journal of Educational Sociology* 27:128–141 (November 1953).

———— and Blanche Geer. "Participant Observation: The Analysis of Qualitative Field Data," in *Human Organization Research.* Edited by Richard N. Adams and Jack J. Preiss. Homewood, Illinois: The Dorsey Press. Inc., 1960.

Beker, Jerome, James B. Victor, and Linda Seidel. "School Days," in

Among the People: Encounters With the Poor. Edited by Irwin
    Deutscher and Elizabeth J. Thompson. New York: Basic Books,
    Inc., 1968.
Bellak, Arno A., Herbert M. Kliebard, Ronald T. Hyman, and Frank L.
    Smith, Jr. *The Language of the Classroom.* New York: Teachers
    College Press, 1966.
Berger, Peter. *Invitation to Sociology: A Humanistic Perspective.* New
    York: Anchor Books, Doubleday and Company, Inc., 1963.
Biddle, Bruce J., Howard A. Rosencranz, Edward Tomich, and J.
    Paschal Twyman. "Shared Inaccuracies in the Role of the Teacher,"
    in *Role Theory: Concepts and Research.* Edited by Bruce J. Biddle
    and Edwin J. Thomas. New York: John Wiley and Sons, Inc., 1966.
Bidwell, Charles E. "The School as a Formal Organization," in
    Handbook of Organizations. Edited by James G. March. Chicago,
    Illinois: Rand, McNally and Co., 1965.
Blackie, John. *Inside the Primary School.* London: Her Majesty's
    Stationery Office, 1967.
Blau, Peter. *The Dynamics of Bureaucracy: A Study of Interpersonal
    Relations in Two Government Agencies.* Chicago, Illinois: University
    of Chicago Press, 1963.
———. *Exchange and Power in Social Life.* New York: John Wiley and
    Sons, Inc., 1964.
——— and Richard Scott. *Formal Organizations.* San Francisco,
    California: Chandler Publishing Company, 1962.
Boocock, Sarane. "Towards a Sociology of Learning: A Selective Review
    of Existing Research," *Sociology of Education* 39:1–45 (Winter 1966).
Brim, Orville. *Sociology and the Field of Education.* New York: Russell
    Sage Foundation, 1958.
Brookover, Wilbur. "Research on Teacher and Administrator Roles,"
    Journal of Educational Sociology 29:4–14 (September 1955).
Burke, Kenneth. *Permanence and Change.* New York: New Republic, 1935.
Burns, Tom. "Friends, Enemies and the Polite Fictions," *American
    Sociological Review* 18:654–662 (December 1953).
Bush, Robert. *The Teacher-Pupil Relationship.* New York: Prentice-Hall,
    Inc., 1954.
Carr-Saunders, A. M. *Professions: Their Organization and Place in
    Society.* The Herbert Spencer Lecture, Oxford, 1928. London: The
    Clarendon Press, 1928.
Charters, W. W., Jr. "Social Class Analysis and the Control of Public
    Education," *Harvard Educational Review* 23:268–283 (Fall 1953).
——— and N. L. Gage, eds. *Readings in the Social Psychology of
    Education.* Boston, Massachusetts: Allyn and Bacon, Inc., 1963.
Chase, Francis S. "Factors Productive of Satisfaction in Teaching."
    Unpublished Ph.D. dissertation, University of Chicago, 1961.
Children and Their Primary Schools. A Report of the Central Advisory

Council for Education (England). Vol. I, *The Report.* London: Her Majesty's Stationery Office, 1967.

Clark, Burton. "The 'Cooling-Out Function' in Higher Education," *The American Journal of Sociology* 45:569–576 (May 1960).

———. *Educating the Expert Society.* San Francisco, California: Chandler Publishing Company, Inc., 1962.

Clark, Kenneth. *Dark Ghetto.* New York: Harper and Row, 1965.

Coleman, James S. *The Adolescent Society: The Social Life of the Teenager and Its Impact on Education.* New York: The Free Press of Glencoe, 1961.

Cook, Lloyd and Elaine F. Cook. "Community Expectations of the Teacher," in *Education in Society: Readings.* Edited by Bernard N. Meltzer, Harry R. Doby, and Philip M. Smith. New York: Thomas Y. Crowell Co., 1958.

Corwin, Ronald. *A Sociology of Education.* New York: Appleton-Century-Crofts, 1965.

Coser, Lewis. *The Functions of Social Conflict.* Glencoe, Illinois: The Free Press, 1956.

———. "Functions of Deviant Behavior," in *Social Problems: Persistent Challenges.* Edited by Edward C. McDonagh and Jon E. Simpson. New York: Holt, Rinehart and Winston, Inc., 1965.

Coser, Rose. "Insulation from Observability and Types of Social Conformity," *American Sociological Review* 26:28–39 (1961).

———. *Life in the Ward.* East Lansing, Michigan: Michigan State University Press, 1962.

Davis, Allison. "Status Systems and the Socialization of the Child," *American Sociological Review* 6:345–354 (June 1941).

———. *Social-Class Influences on Learning.* Cambridge, Massachusetts: Harvard University Press, 1950.

Dreeben, Robert. *On What Is Learned in Schools.* Reading, Massachusetts: Addison-Wesley Publishing Co., 1968.

Erikson, Kai. "The Sociology of Deviance," in *Social Problems: Persistent Challenges.* Edited by Edward C. McDonagh and Jon E. Simpson. New York: Holt, Rinehart and Winston, Inc., 1965.

Featherstone, Joseph. "Schools for Children," *The New Republic* 157:17–21 (August 19, 1967).

———. "How Children Learn," *The New Republic* 157:17–21 (September 2, 1967).

———. "Teaching Children to Think," *The New Republic* 157:15–19 (September 9, 1967).

———. "Experiments in Learning," *The New Republic* 159:23–25 (December 14, 1968).

———. "Schools for Learning," *The New Republic* 159:17–20 (December 21, 1968).

————. "Why So Few Good Schools," *The New Republic* 160:18–21 (January 4, 1968).

Foskett, John M. *The Normative World of the Elementary School Teacher.* Eugene, Oregon: The Center for the Advanced Study of Educational Administration, 1967.

Fox, Renée. *Experiment Perilous.* Glencoe, Illinois: The Free Press, 1959.

Friedenberg, Edgar Z. *Coming of Age in America.* New York: Random House, 1965.

Fromm, Erich. *The Sane Society.* New York: Holt, Rinehart and Winston, 1955.

Fuchs, Estelle. *Teachers Talk: Views from inside City Schools.* New York: Anchor Books, Doubleday and Co., Inc., 1969.

Gage, N. L., Philip J. Runkel, and B. B. Chatterjee. "Changing Teacher Behavior through Feedback from Pupils: An Application of Equilibrium Theory," in *Readings in the Social Psychology of Education.* Edited by W. W. Charters, Jr. and N. L. Gage. Boston, Massachusetts: Allyn and Bacon, Inc., 1963.

Getzels, Jacob W. and Egon G. Guba. "The Structure of Roles and Role Conflict in the Teaching Situation," *Journal of Educational Sociology* 29:30–40 (1955–1956).

Getzels, Jacob W. and Philip W. Jackson. *Creativity and Intelligence: Explorations with Gifted Students.* New York: John Wiley and Sons, 1962.

————. "The Teacher's Personality and Characteristics," in *Handbook of Research on Teaching.* Edited by N. L. Gage. Chicago, Illinois: Rand McNally, 1963.

Goffman, Erving. *The Presentation of Self in Everyday Life.* New York: Anchor Books, Doubleday and Co., 1959.

Goodman, Paul. *Growing Up Absurd.* New York: Random House, 1950.

————. *Compulsory Mis-education and the Community of Scholars.* New York: Vintage Books, 1962.

Gordon, C. Wayne. "The Role of the Teacher in the Social Structure of the High School," *Journal of Educational Sociology* 29:21–29 (1955–1956).

————. *The Social System of the High School: A Study in the Sociology of the Adolescent.* Glencoe, Illinois: The Free Press, 1957.

Gouldner, Alvin W. "Cosmopolitans and Locals: Towards an Analysis of Latent Social Roles," *Administrative Science Quarterly* 2:281–306, 444–480 (1957–1958).

Gracey, Harry L. "Learning the Student Role: Kindergarten as Academic Boot Camp," in *Readings in Introductory Sociology.* Edited by Dennis Wrong and Harry Gracey. New York: The Macmillan Company, 1967.

Grambs, Jean D. "The Roles of the Teacher," in *The Teacher's Role in*

American Society. Edited by Lindley J. Stiles. New York: Harper and Bros., 1957.

Gross, Neal. "A Critique of 'Social-Class Structure and American Education'," *Harvard Educational Review,* 23:293–338 (Fall 1953).

———. "The Sociology of Education," in *Sociology Today: Problems and Prospects.* Edited by Robert K. Merton, Leonard Broom, and Leonard Cottrell, Jr. New York: Basic Books, Inc., 1959.

———, Ward Mason, and Alexander W. McEachern. *Explorations in Role Analysis: Studies of the School Superintendency Role.* New York: John Wiley and Sons, Inc., 1958.

Guba, Egon, Philip W. Jackson, and Charles E. Bidwell. "Occupational Choice and Teaching Career," in *Readings in the Social Psychology of Education.* Edited by W. W. Charters, Jr. and N. L. Gage. Boston, Massachusetts: Allyn and Bacon, Inc., 1963.

Guskin, Alan Edward and Samuel Louis Guskin. *A Social Psychology of Education.* Don Mills, Ontario: Addison-Wesley Publishing Co., 1970.

Haller, Emil J. "Pupil Influence in Teacher Socialization: A Socio-Linguistic Study," *Sociology of Education* 40:316–333 (Fall 1967).

Halsey, A. H., Jean Floud, and C. Arnold Anderson. *Education, Economy and Society: A Reader in the Sociology of Education.* New York: Free Press of Glencoe, 1961.

Havighurst, Robert J. and Bernice L. Neugarten. *Society and Education* Boston, Massachusetts: Allyn and Bacon, Inc., 1957.

Henry, Jules. "Culture, Education and Communication Theory," in *Education and Anthropology.* Edited by George D. Spindler. Stanford, California: Stanford University Press, 1955.

———. "Classroom Responses of the Middle-Class Child," in *Education in Society: Readings.* Edited by Bernard N. Meltzer, Harry R. Doby, and Philip M. Smith. New York: Thomas Y. Crowell Co., 1958.

———. "American Schoolrooms: Learning the Nightmare," *Columbia University Forum* 6:24–30 (Spring 1963).

———. "Attitude Organization in Elementary School Classrooms," in *Readings in the Social Psychology of Education.* Edited by W. W. Charters, Jr. and N. L. Gage. Boston, Massachusetts: Allyn and Bacon, Inc., 1963.

Herndon, James. *The Way It Spozed To Be.* New York: Simon and Schuster, Inc., 1968.

Hoehn, Arthur J. "A Study of Social Status Differentiation in the Classroom Behavior of Nineteen Third Grade Teachers," in *Readings in the Social Psychology of Education.* Edited by W. W. Charters, Jr. and N. L. Gage. Boston, Massachusetts: Allyn and Bacon, Inc., 1963.

Hollingshead, A. B. *Elmtown's Youth.* New York: John Wiley and Sons, Inc., 1949.

Holt, John. *How Children Fail.* New York: Dell, 1964.

Homans, George C. *The Human Group.* New York: Harcourt, Brace and Company, 1950.

———. *Social Behavior: Its Elementary Forms.* New York: Harcourt, Brace and World, Inc., 1961.

Hughes, Everett C. *Men and Their Work.* Glencoe, Illinois: The Free Press, 1958.

Huntington, Mary Jean. "The Development of a Professional Self-Image," in *The Student-Physician: Introductory Studies in the Sociology of Medical Education.* Edited by Robert Merton, George Reader, and Patricia Kendall. Cambridge, Massachusetts: Harvard University Press, 1957.

Illich, Ivan. "Why We Must Abolish Schooling," *New York Review of Books* (July 2, 1970), 9–15.

Jackson, Philip W. *Life in Classrooms.* New York: Holt, Rinehart and Winston, Inc., 1968.

Johnson, David W. *The Social Psychology of Education.* New York: Holt, Rinehart and Winston, Inc., 1970.

Johnson, T. J., R. Feigenbaum, and M. Weiby. "Some Determinants and Consequences of the Teacher's Perception of Causation," *Journal of Educational Psychology* 55:237–246 (1964).

Kahl, Joseph A. "Educational and Occupational Aspirations of 'Common Man' Boys," *Harvard Educational Review* 23:186–203 (Summer 1953).

Kemper, Theodore D. "Reference Groups, Socialization and Achievement," *American Sociological Review* 33:31–45 (1968).

Kohl, Herbert. *36 Children.* New York: New American Library, Inc., 1967.

Kozol, Jonathan. *Death at an Early Age.* Boston, Massachusetts: Houghton Mifflin Co., 1967.

Laing, Ronald D. *The Politics of Experience.* New York: Random House, Inc., 1967.

Lauter, Paul and Florence Howe. "How the School System is Rigged for Failure," *New York Review of Books* (June 18, 1970), 14–21.

Leacock, Eleanor Burke. *Teaching and Learning in City Schools: A Comparative Study.* New York: Basic Books, Inc., 1969.

Lieberman, Myron. *Education as a Profession.* New York: Prentice-Hall, Inc., 1956.

Lippitt, Ronald and David Jenkins. *Interpersonal Perceptions of Teachers, Students and Parents: An Action Research Project for the In-Service Training of Teachers.* Washington, D.C.: Division of Adult Education Service, National Education Association, 1951.

Lyman, Stanford M. and Marvin B. Scott. *The Sociology of the Absurd.* New York: Appleton-Century-Crofts, 1970.

Lynd, Robert S. and Helen M. Lynd. *Middletown in Transition.* New York: Harcourt, Brace and Co., 1937.

McCall, George J. and J. L. Simmons. *Issues in Participant Observation.*

Don Mills, Ontario: Addison-Wesley Publishing Co., 1969.

Mead, Margaret. *The School in American Culture.* Cambridge, Massachusetts: Harvard University Press, 1951.

Meltzer, Bernard N., Harry R. Doby, and Philip M. Smith. *Education in Society: Readings.* New York: Thomas Y. Crowell Co., 1958.

Merei, Ferenc. "Group Leadership and Institutionalization," *Human Relations* 2:23–39 (1949).

Merton, Robert K. *Social Theory and Social Structure.* Glencoe, Illinois: The Free Press, 1957.

———. "The Role-Set: Problems in Sociological Theory," *British Journal of Sociology* 8:106–120 (June 1957).

———. "Social Conformity, Deviation and Opportunity Structures: A Comment on the Contribution of Dubin and Cloward," *American Sociological Review* 24:177–189 (April 1959).

——— and Robert A. Nisbet. *Contemporary Social Problems.* New York: Harcourt, Brace and World, Inc., 1966.

Miles, Matthew. "Some Properties of Schools as Social Systems," in *Change in School Systems.* Edited by G. Watson. Washington, D.C.: National Training Laboratories, National Education Association, 1967.

Minuchin, Patricia, Barbara Biber, Edna Shapiro, and Herbert Zimiles. *The Psychological Impact of School Experience: A Comparative Study of Nine-Year Old Children in Contrasting Schools.* New York: Basic Books, Inc., 1969.

Moore, Wilbert E. and Melvin W. Tumin. "Some Social Functions of Ignorance," *American Sociological Review* 14:787–795 (December 1949).

Murphy, Gardner, Lois Murphy, and Theodore M. Newcomb. *Experimental Social Psychology.* New York: Harper and Bros., 1937.

Newcomb, Theodore M. *Social Psychology.* New York: The Dryden Press, 1950.

Parsons, Talcott. *Essays in Sociological Theory, Pure and Applied.* Glencoe, Illinois: The Free Press, 1949.

———. "The School Class as a Social System: Some of Its Functions in American Society," in *Education, Economy and Society: A Reader in the Sociology of Education.* Edited by A. H. Halsey, Jean Floud, and C. Arnold Anderson. New York: Free Press of Glencoe, 1961.

——— and Edward Shils, eds. *Towards a General Theory of Action.* Cambridge, Massachusetts: Harvard University Press, 1951.

Pedersen, Eigel and Mona Farrell. "Background and Personal Factors Associated with IQ Change in an Inner-City Population" (ms.). Winnipeg: CSAA Meetings, June 1970.

Piaget, Jean. *The Moral Judgment of the Child.* Glencoe, Illinois: The Free Press, 1948.

Redl, Fritz and William W. Wattenberg. *Mental Hygiene in Teaching.* New York: Harcourt, Brace and Co., 1951.

Riecken, Henry W. and George C. Homans. "Psychological Aspects of Social Structure," in *Handbook of Social Psychology,* vol. II. Edited by Gardner Lindzey. Reading, Massachusetts: Addison-Wesley Publishing Co. Inc., 1954.

Riesman, David. *Constraint and Variety in American Education.* Lincoln, Nebraska: University of Nebraska Press, 1956.

Riessman, Frank. *The Culturally Deprived Child.* New York: Harper and Bros., 1962.

Roethlisberger, F. J. and William J. Dickson. *Management and the Worker.* Cambridge, Massachusetts: Harvard University Press, 1939.

Rosenthal, Robert and Lenore Jacobson. *Pygmalion In the Classroom.* New York: Holt, Rinehart and Winston, Inc., 1968.

Sarason, Seymour, Kenneth Davidson, and Burton Blatt. *The Preparation of Teachers.* New York: John Wiley and Sons, Inc., 1962.

Schrag, Peter, "End of the Impossible Dream," *Saturday Review* 53 (September 19, 1970).

Schwartz, Morris S. and Charlotte G. Schwartz. "Problems in Participant Observation," *American Journal of Sociology* 60:343–354 (January 1955).

Seeman, Melvin. "Role-Conflict and Ambivalence in Leadership," *American Sociological Review* 18:373–380 (August 1953).

Shipman, M. D. *The Sociology of the School.* London: Longman's, Green and Co. Ltd, 1968.

Sieber, Sam D. "Organizational Influences on Innovative Roles," in *Knowledge Production and Utilization in Educational Administration.* Edited by Terry L. Eidell and Joanne M. Kitchel. Eugene, Oregon: Center for the Advanced Study of Educational Administration, 1968.

——— and David E. Wilder. "Teaching Styles: Parental Preferences and Professional Role Definitions," *Sociology of Education* 40:302–315 (Fall 1967).

Silberman, Charles E. *Crisis in the Classroom.* New York: Random House, 1970.

Simmel, Georg. *The Sociology of Georg Simmel,* trans. and ed. Kurt Wolff. Glencoe, Illinois: The Free Press, 1950.

Simon, Henry W. *Preface To Teaching.* New York: Oxford University Press, 1938.

Smith, Louis M. and William Geoffrey. *The Complexities of an Urban Classroom: An Analysis Toward a General Theory of Teaching.* New York: Holt, Rinehart and Winston, Inc., 1968.

Stebbins, Robert A. "The Meaning of Disorderly Behavior: Teacher Definitions of a Classroom Situation" (ms.). Ottawa: CCRE Meetings, March 1970.

Stiles, Lindley J., ed. *The Teacher's Role in American Society.* New York: Harper and Bros., 1957.

Stouffer, Samuel. "An Analysis of Conflicting Social Norms," *American Sociological Review* 14:707–717 (December 1949).

————, Edward Suchman, Leland De Vinney, Shirley Star, and Robin Williams, Jr. "Barriers to Understanding Between Officers and Enlisted Men," in *Reader in Bureaucracy.* Edited by Robert K Merton, Ailsa P. Gray, Barbara Hockey, and Hanan C. Selvin Glencoe, Illinois: The Free Press, 1952.

Terrien, Frederick W. "The Occupational Roles of Teachers," *Journal of Educational Sociology* 29:14–20 (1955–1956).

Toby, Jackson. "Some Variables in Role-Conflict Analysis," *Social Forces* 30:323–327 (1952).

Trow, William C., Alvin E. Zander, William C. Morse, and David H. Jenkins. "Psychology of Group Behavior," in *Educational Psychology:A Book of Readings.* Edited by Arthur Coladarci. New York: The Dryden Press, 1955.

Turner, Ralph. "Role-Taking, Role Standpoint, and Reference-Group Behavior," *American Journal of Sociology* 61:316–328 (January 1956).

Twyman, J. P. and Bruce J. Biddle. "Role Conflict For Public School Teachers," *Journal of Psychology* 55:183–198 (1963).

Vidich, Arthur J. and Joseph Bensman. *Small Town in Mass Society: Class, Power and Religion in a Rural Community.* New York: Anchor Books, Doubleday and Company, Inc., 1960.

Wagenschein, Miriam. "Reality Shock: A Study of Beginning Elementary School Teachers." Unpublished M.A. dissertation, University of Chicago, September 1950.

Waller, Willard. *The Sociology of Teaching.* New York: John Wiley and Sons, Inc., 1932.

Warner, W. Lloyd, Robert J. Havighurst, and Martin W. Loeb. *Who Shall Be Educated?* New York: Harper and Bros., 1944.

Wattenberg, William, J. Wilmer Menge, Roland Faunce, John Sullivan, Ruth Ellsworth, Mildred Peters, Marie Rasey, and Elmer McDaid. "Social Origins of Teachers and American Education," in *The Teacher's Role in American Society.* Edited by Lindley J. Stiles. New York: Harper and Bros., 1957.

Williams, Robin M., Jr. *American Society: A Sociological Interpretation.* New York: Alfred A. Knopf, 1951.

INDEX